LONGMAN LINGUISTICS LIBRARY
Title no 19
PRINCIPLES OF FIRTHIAN LINGUISTICS

LONGMAN LINGUISTICS LIBRARY

General Editors

R. H. Robins, University of London

G. N. Leech, University of Lancaster

Title no:

THE LINGUISTIC SCIENCES AND LANGUAGE TEACHING 1
M. A. K. Halliday, Angus McIntosh and Peter Strevens

GENERAL LINGUISTICS 2
AN INTRODUCTORY SURVEY
R. H. Robins

A SHORT HISTORY OF LINGUISTICS 6
R. H. Robins

ESSAYS ON THE ENGLISH LANGUAGE 8
MEDIEVAL AND MODERN
Randolph Quirk

STUDIES IN ENGLISH ADVERBIAL USAGE 9
Sidney Greenbaum

TOWARDS A SEMANTIC DESCRIPTION OF ENGLISH 10
Geoffrey N. Leech

ELICITATION EXPERIMENTS IN ENGLISH 11
LINGUISTIC STUDIES IN USE AND ATTITUDE
Sidney Greenbaum and Randolph Quirk

PHONETICS IN LINGUISTICS 12
A BOOK OF READINGS
Editors: *W. E. Jones and J. Laver*

STRUCTURAL ASPECTS OF LANGUAGE CHANGE 13
James M. Anderson

PHILOSOPHY AND THE NATURE OF LANGUAGE 14
David E. Cooper

SEMANTICO-SYNTAX 15
Frans Liefrink

FROM SIGNS TO PROPOSITIONS 16
THE CONCEPT OF FORM IN EIGHTEENTH-CENTURY SEMANTIC THEORY
Stephen K. Land

SPATIAL AND TEMPORAL USES OF ENGLISH PREPOSITIONS 17
David C. Bennett

THE ENGLISH VERB 18
F. R. Palmer

PRINCIPLES OF FIRTHIAN LINGUISTICS 19
T. F. Mitchell

PROBLEMS IN FRENCH SYNTAX 20
TRANSFORMATIONAL-GENERATIVE STUDIES
Nicolas Ruwet
Translated by: *Sheila M. Robins*

Principles of Firthian Linguistics

T. F. Mitchell
Professor of Linguistics
University of Leeds

LONGMAN

LONGMAN GROUP LIMITED LONDON
Associated companies, branches and representatives throughout the world

First published 1975
ISBN 0 582 52455 5

Made and printed in Great Britain by
William Clowes & Sons, Limited, London, Beccles and Colchester

Preface

In the English-speaking world of linguists little more than fifteen short years ago, the talk was ever of grammatical models labelled 'Item and Arrangement', 'Item and Process', and 'Word and Paradigm'. Before and since, grammar was and is variously styled 'phonological', 'tagmemic', 'stratificational', 'systemic', or otherwise designated according to the theoretical stance of a particular linguist or group of linguists. Of recent years, notably from the appearance in 1957 of Chomsky's *Syntactic Structures*, it is 'transformational' or 'transformational-generative' grammar (TG for short) that has undoubtedly and deservedly called the tune, although here, too, diversification has set in. These have been times of turmoil in the affairs of men, no less in linguistics than elsewhere. From one's own coign of vantage – and there is much relativity in linguistics, let alone in language itself – one forms the impression that at least some linguists have retired to regroup, as it were, and who is to say what the picture will be a few years hence? At all events, it is not out of place and time to advance the claims to appropriate attention of the 'Firthian' kind of linguistics illustrated in this book. Its insights may seem to merit inclusion in the theoretical and descriptive synthesis that it is hoped the discipline will one day achieve. Perhaps this may come about via the newly emergent 'variationism' in the United States, with which approach Firthianism seems to have much in common. Might the latter thus find the crystallization and formalism that it has hitherto tended to lack?

The book is concerned to exemplify what may perhaps be termed the 'philosophy of language' of J. R. Firth and, although it is not theoretically oriented and illustrations are informally presented – even anecdotally, I dare say – nevertheless concern with aspects of adequacy in the analysis of speech is implicit throughout, as well as the view that abstract argument and discussion of descriptive technique should rest on accurate and detailed knowledge of individual languages in all their variety. Yet the definition of Firthian concepts and terms – 'system' and 'structure', for instance – must be sought elsewhere. That systems were paradigmatic, made up of units or terms having mutual value, that structure comprised elements having places to which systems were referred, that rules were 'statements of structure other than systems' and that, typically of Firth, they were to include the expression 'as a rule', that systems of structures were permissible, all this and much else of the jargon was acceptable enough but decidedly subordinate to the 'business of descriptive linguistics to make statements of meaning at all levels.' The material old and new making up the book has been selected or newly written in order to illustrate Firth's insistence on the primacy of meaning, on the need for a basically inductive approach to language study in response to our present superficiality of acquaintance with the vast majority of languages, and in particular on the syntagmatic aspects of language structure that seemed to him greatly to outweigh the narrow segmentalism representative of the linguistics of his time and indeed of much linguistics today. Since Firth himself followed the then fashion and devoted almost all his efforts to phonology, I have tried to include as much lexical, grammatical, and situational material as phonological. After an introductory statement of what seem to be salient aspects of Firthianism, the main body of the book comprises seven essays: the first ('*Caveat* to the general') stresses a basic inductiveness of approach to the subject matter; this is followed by two essays on phonology, the first on 'prosodics' ('Not of the letter, but of the spirit'), the second also prosodically motivated but perhaps more immediately suggestive of the possibility of rapprochement between Firthianism and TG ('Prominence and syllabication in Arabic'); thereafter follow two papers of mostly lexico-grammatical relevance ('Linguistic "goings-on"' and 'Aspects of gender revisited'), and the book concludes with two sociolinguistic essays ('Covert matters best disclosed' and 'The language of buying and selling in Cyrenaica').

Any satisfactory linguistic theory will have to account for the systematic behaviour of interlocutors in speech; whatever its imperfections, Firthianism tries to do just this. Perhaps in any event it is time for us to get down to cases again, and in the detail that scholarship requires. This book is not concerned to describe easily identifiable forms of language in terms of some known theory. The sorties that it makes into this or that language can be seen as partial contributions to their description but, more generally, they are probably indicative of an underlying wish to return to methodology and to provide checks on the personal idiosyncrasies of the researcher by attempting to observe some aspects of what actually goes on in living language. It is a pity that suitable data was not available from, say, those widespread koineized forms of speech, like educated spoken Arabic, which so well illustrate the variability, albeit accountable variability, to which language is subject in the processes of speech. Moreover, most of the research embodied in the book was carried out years ago and the careful control of data in the manner of its collection and elicitation is no doubt at times all too obviously missing. Perhaps, however, the effort was not wholly wasted, since it is true that, although current sociolinguistic literature contains much that is suggestive, even convincing, nevertheless a fully satisfactory (socio-) linguistic theory has yet to be elaborated. Parts of the book, therefore, may contribute to an area of development and expansion in theory. At all events, if some of the categories recognized below might otherwise go unheeded by the non-Firthian linguist, and if they and their exemplification can be considered to contain any measure of significant interest, then credit is due to my teacher and mentor, who formed me tolerably in his likeness and to whom linguistics in this country, as well as this particular linguist, owes so much.

University of Leeds TFM
February 1975

Acknowledgments

We are grateful to the following for permission to reproduce material in this volume:

Sphere Books Limited and the Editorial Board of *Archivum Linguisticum* for the paper published in Vol II (1971) of the new series of the journal with the title 'Linguistic "goings-on": collocations and other lexical matters arising on the syntagmatic record' and to be published in expanded form in Vol X (ed W. F. Bolton) of the *Sphere Library History of Literature in the English Language.*

The Editorial Board of *Archivum Linguisticum* for what appears in this volume of the article 'Aspects of gender revisited, with special reference to Sindhi and Cairene Arabic', Vol IV (New Series), 1973.

The School of Oriental and African Studies for 'Prominence and syllabication in Arabic', *Bulletin of the School of Oriental and African Studies,* XXIII/2, 1960.

Language in Society for extracts from the editorial introduction by Dell Hymes in the issue 1/1, 1972.

We regret we have been unable to make contact with the editor and publisher of *Hespéris* (now *Hespéris-Tamuda,* University of Rabat) for permission to include 'The language of buying and selling in Cyrenaica', 1957, and would appreciate receiving any information that would enable us to do so.

Contents

Transcriptional Conventions

Brief conventions for reading transcribed material in the book are as follows:

1. Arabic (mostly, Cairene and Cyrenaican)

Consonant-letters

'θ', 'ð' voiceless and voiced dental fricatives; 'ʃ' voiceless palato-alveolar fricative, 'j' voiced palato-alveolar affricate (Egypt) and voiced palato-alveolar fricative (Cyrenaica); 'r' an alveolar flap, 'rr' an alveolar roll; 'x', 'ɣ' voiceless and voiced uvular fricatives; 'ħ', '9' voiceless and voiced pharyngal fricatives; 'q' a voiceless uvular plosive; 'ˈ' a glottal plosive; 'S', 'T', 'Đ', 'D', 'Z', 'emphatic' (often misleadingly termed 'velarized' or 'pharyngalized') consonants, corresponding to non-emphatic 's', 't', 'ð', 'd', 'z' respectively and in the pronunciation of which the tongue is laterally expanded throughout its length and flattened in rear of the tip, while lip-position is neutral; for 's', 't', 'ð', 'd', 'z', the tongue is laterally contracted and the front raised towards the hard palate, and the lips are spread.

Notes

(i) 'y' is pronounced as a half-close to close front vowel, 'w' as a half-close to close back vowel, when preceding a consonant ('y9ɑTi', 'yjalwlan') or when final following a consonant ('sa9y', 'filw').

(ii) It is not, of course, possible here to enter into a detailed discussion of Arabic pronunciation but it should perhaps be mentioned that the domains of the phonological features of 'emphasis' and 'non-emphasis' are never limited to a single consonant segment. The quality of sounds in the vicinity of 'emphatics' and 'non-emphatics' varies considerably, though regularly; a back grade of open vowel, for example, regularly accompanies 'emphatics'. Moreover, differences of *eg* muscular tension in tongue and lips or of tongue flattening and broadening are noticeable between individuals and dialects. 'T', for instance, is rather 'weakly' articulated in Cairo but is very tense in Cyrenaican (Bedouin) Arabic, wherein experimental evidence seems to confirm it as not only 'emphatic' in the above terms but also as an interesting example of a voiceless imploded consonant. 'D' does not occur in Cyrenaican (Bedouin) Arabic.

Vowel-letters

'i' is a half-close front spread vowel, close when final or long; 'u' a half-close back to central vowel, rounded (Egypt), unrounded (Cyrenaica), close rounded when final or long; 'a', 'ɑ' front and back open vowels; 'e' and 'o' (Egypt only), mid- to half-close front and back vowels, spread and rounded respectively; 'ie' (Cyrenaica only) a falling diphthong moving from half-close front to mid-front and occurring only in prominent syllables.

Note

In general, the transcription is the simplest possible consistent with the object of SUGGESTING a suitable pronunciation. No transcription can be completely 'phonetic' and there are good grammatical reasons beyond our present terms of reference for writing 'utTɑbbux' (she cooks), where 't' marks the 3rd person singular feminine of the imperfect tense, when in fact pronunciation would be more accurately indicated by 'uTT-'. Conversely, the transcription glosses over many important facts of grammar and phonology, including, as far as vowels are concerned, the syllabic status of elidable close short vowels versus non-elidable open short vowels, and the need to recognize anaptyctic or prothetic vowels (symbolized 'ə' elsewhere) in dealing with facts of Arabic syllabication and the 'avoidance' of certain consonant sequences. The initial portion of 'utTɑbbux', for example, is better represented phonologically as 'ətT-'. These matters are dealt with in the subsequent essay on prominence and syllabication in Arabic. In those rare cases in the book where it has been felt necessary to refer to more detailed facts of pronunciation a transcription has been given in square brackets and following the conventions of the International Phonetic Association.

Doubled letters

Arabic long vowels are indicated by doubling the vowel-letter. Doubled consonants are pronounced longer than their single counterparts and with greater tenseness of articulation.

Acute accent

Where relevant, the prominent or accented syllable of a word or phrase is indicated by an acute accent placed over the appropriate vowel-letter.

2. Berber (Zuara)

Again, this has not been felt to be the place to give more than the grossest indications of Berber phonetic and phonological features that are, in fact, worthy of the highest specialist interest. The transcription corresponds to that used for Arabic with the addition of 'R' (an emphatic alveolar flap) and one or two other comparatively infrequent emphatic consonants, which are also transcribed with appropriate capital letters. The total inventory is as follows:

Consonants

f; b; m; w; t, d; T, D; s, z; S, Z; r; R; l; n; ʃ, j (fricative); k, g; x, ɣ; q; ħ, 9; h

Vowels

ə; a, ɑ; i; e; u; o

Notes

(i) One of the most striking general characteristics of Berber pronunciation is its long sequences of consonantal articulations.

(ii) The difference between 'emphatic' and 'non-emphatic' articulation is very strongly marked. The domain of 'emphasis' is subject to an interesting form of free positional variation by which *eg* 'tamuRt' (city; Tripoli) may be pronounced either [ta·m̵ɔ·r̵ŧ] or [ŧɑ·m̵ɔ·r̵t]. Emphasis sometimes occurs in forms that do not contain 'T', 'D', 'S', 'Z', or 'R', *eg* 'yəMMɑ́' (he said).

(iii) It has not been possible to confirm or deny my subjective perceptual impression that pharyngal articulation in this dialect is typically made not in the usual way with narrowing between the base of the tongue and the pharynx wall but rather by the approximation of the top (annular) surface of the trachea and the under-surface of the epiglottal fold. My informant accepted the former type of articulation but regularly responded more favourably to the latter.

(iv) Interesting forms of (morphological) gemination in indigenous Berber forms include 'qq' from 'ɣ', 'TT' from 'D', and 'gg' from 'w'.

(v) As far as vowels are concerned, 'ə' is a short vowel behaving very similarly to the anaptyctic vowel of colloquial Arabic (Cyrenaican) and exhibiting similarly wide qualitative variation. 'a', 'ɑ', 'i', and 'u' are pronounced long in certain contexts, *eg* when accented or in pre-pausal closed syllables. The open vowels of the transcription respond to vocalic variation between front and back in co-variation with non-emphasis and emphasis respectively. The two close vowels are markedly opener in emphatic domains, and 'i' is also centralized. Glide vowels, usually central in quality, are very noticeable in the neighbourhood of emphatic consonants.

3. Sindhi

Letter-symbols have been differently used for the reading transcription of Sindhi.

Consonants

Perhaps the most economical method of presenting the conventions to be associated with the consonantal symbols of the transcription is the following 'traditional' table based on the five zones of articulation characteristic of Sindhi and cognate languages:

				Bilabial	Dental	Alveolar (Retroflex)	Palatal	Velar
Plosives	Unaspirated	Voiceless		p	t	ʈ	c	k
		Voiced		b	d	ɖ	j	g
	Aspirated	Voiceless		ph	th	ʈh	ch	kh
		Voiced		bh	dh	ɖh	jh	gh
Nasals	Unaspirated			m	n	ɳ	ɲ	ŋ
	Aspirated			mh	nh	ɳh		
Implosives				b'		ɖ'	j'	g'
'Liquids'	Unaspirated	Lateral				l		
		Flap	Non-retroflex			r		
			Retroflex			ɽ		
	Aspirated	Lateral				lh		
		Flap	Non-retroflex			rh		
			Retroflex			ɽh		
Fricatives & Frictionless continuants	Voiceless				f	s	ʃ	x
	Voiced				v	z	y	ɣ

Note

The status of aspirated nasals and 'liquids' is phonemically problematical but relevant articulatory complexes have been transcribed in similar manner to the aspirated plosives in order to suggest pronunciation more accurately in *eg* 'sumhaɳ' (to sleep), 'paɽhaɳ' (to read, study), 'maaɳhuu' (man), 'g'aalh' (speech, story), etc. 'l' in *eg* 'g'aalhaaiɳ' (to speak; abuse) is 'breathy' and syllable division is 'g'aa-lhaa-', not 'g'aal-haa-'.

Vowels

The following list indicates the most important varieties of vowel sound and *grosso modo* the pronunciation values to be associated with relevant symbols. Long vowels have been shown by doubled letters and vary in length according to context; they are invariably distinguished qualitatively from short counterparts. There are many possibilities of vowel sequence.

i	half-close, front, spread
ii	close, front, spread
ee	mid, front, spread
a	open, central, lips neutral; noticeably fronted when final
aa	open, back, lips neutral
oo	mid, back, rounded
u	half-close, back, rounded; markedly fronted when final
uu	close, back, rounded

Notes

(i) Final '-u', a retracted variety of [ø], is rare in Lāṛī Sindhi, on which our examples are mostly based (see *p* 31, n 3), in contrast with the 'standard' language and – notwithstanding the case functions of final short vowels – is rarely distinguished from '-i'. For example, 'saooʈ' (cousin [male or female]) corresponds to 'saooʈᵘ' (male cousin) and 'saooʈⁱ' in Hyderabad; differentiation only occurs in Lāṛī in the vocative and agentive cases, where 'saooʈᵃ' (male cousin) contrasts with 'saooʈⁱ' (female cousin).
(ii) 'i' is often elided in medial (open) syllables before a consonant, *eg* 'maar(i)boo'.

Breath and Nasality

Not only may plosive, nasal and liquid consonants be aspirated but the whole syllable, word or syllable sequence may be breathy throughout, *eg* 'aahee' (is), 'aahyãa' (am). 'h', therefore, does not have the same linear implications as other symbols. This is also true of the tilde symbolizing nasality. The processes by which, say, a Sindhi spelling 'aa-hi-yãa' corresponds to 'aayhãa' in pronunciation, also operate across word boundaries. Thus, in isolation, the final vocalic phase '-ãah' of 'heeɖ'ãah' (here) is breathy and nasal throughout, but 'ac' (come!) is neither nasal nor breathy; nevertheless the sentence 'heeɖ'ãah + ac' (come here!) has the form 'heeɖ'ahãac' in pronunciation. This is not the place for any attempt at systematic phonological statement but such important aspects of pronunciation must clearly be mentioned. The examples could be multiplied many times over; without concomitant nasality, we find, for example, 'maaɳis' (his mother) + 'huii' (was [fem sing]) pronounced as 'maaɳisuhii', and 'muu + vaʈ + hoaa' as 'muvaʈohaa' (it was with me, I had it).

As to nasality in particular, this has been indicated by placing the tilde above the first vowel letter of a nasalized syllable but the extent of the feature is never less than the whole syllable and may often include more. Moreover, not only the extent but also the form taken by nasality must be considered. Any vowel is strongly nasalized in the environment of a preceding nasal consonant; thus, for example, 'vaɲẽe' (you may go) and 'vaɲee' (he may go) are homophonous, although elsewhere '-ẽe' and '-ee', 2nd and 3rd person affixes, are distinguished by nasality. Similarly, a word like 'naanuu' (grandfather) is 'fully' nasalized throughout. But vowels may also be nasalized 'in their own right', so to speak; thus, not only 'nauu' (new [masc sing]) is fully nasal throughout but so, too, is 'sãvaa' (straight [masc pl]), while 'cavãa' (I say) is so only in its final syllable. The nominal/adjectival suffixes '-uu' and '-aa' in 'nauu' and 'sãvaa' are regularly non-nasal in other environments but the verbal ending '-ãa' is always nasal; it is, therefore, morphological considerations that lead us to write 'nauu', 'sãvaa', and 'cavãa', although the final syllables are equally nasal in all three. As we have seen, nasality and breath are often coterminous; for example, 'mĩih' (rain), 'mĩiha' (rains), 'sũuh' (oath), 'sũuhuu' (knowledgeable [masc sing]), etc are 'fully' nasal and breathy from start to finish. There is also noticeable the 'fluctuation' of 'h' commented on earlier; for instance, 'mẽeh' (she-buffalo) is pronounced 'as expected' before a consonant as in 'mẽeh gaah paii khaaee' (the (she-)buffalo is eating the fodder) but as 'mẽhe' before a vowel as in 'mẽhe acii paii' (the (she-)buffalo is coming). 'h' and '~' would clearly not lend themselves to 'placing' or 'segmentation' in the manner of any recognizable kind of analysis in terms of phonemes or features.

Homorganic nasal

Nasality takes a *consonantal* form in certain contexts, notably when associated with a short vowel preceding a plosive consonant. In these circumstances, a nasal consonant is pronounced homorganically with the following plosive, *eg* 'ãb' [ʌmb] (mango), 'sĩdh' [sɪn̪dh] (Sind), 'bũḍ' [bʊɳɖ] (firewood), 'gãj' [gʌɲɟ] (treasure), 'jãg' [ɟʌŋg] (war). In the case of a long vowel in comparable contexts, as generally also in the case of Urdu, nasality takes the form of a long nasalized vowel before a *voiceless* plosive and of a half-long nasalized vowel + half-long homorganic nasal consonant before a *voiced* plosive, *eg* 'cãaṭh' [cɑ̃ːʈh] (threshold), 'sẽeṭ' [sẽːʈ] (scent, perfume) but 'sẽed' [sẽˑ^{n}d] (friendship), 'bũuḍ' [bũˑ^{ɳ}ɖ] (snout (of boar)), 'sãag' [sɑ̃ˑ^{ŋ}g] (impersonation), etc. Similar features of pronunciation characterize polysyllables, *eg* 'dũboo' (lamb), 'gãdoo' (dirty [masc sing]), 'kũḍa' (corner), 'mũhjoo' (my [masc sing]), 'vĩgoo' (curved [masc sing]), 'kãaba' (loin-cloth), 'kãaca' (pyjama trousers), 'pĩighoo' (cradle), etc.

Note

For practical purposes, the above conventions may also be used in relation to Hindi/Urdu and (rare) Panjabi examples quoted in the book.

Introductory

A noncommittal *Aspects* was perhaps more titularly apt than a variously committed *Principles*, but the temptation proved irresistible to take Firth's own word from his projected but unrealized *Principles of Linguistics* or, as the title appeared in advance in some booksellers' lists, *Principia Linguistica*. Perhaps *Principles* here is best equated with *Principia* or with *Principes* as often used – by de Saussure among others – in French, that is with the non-technical sense of the beginnings, bases, mainsprings, or sources of the linguist's study of language and languages. In this general sense, of course, there is more to linguistic starting-points than, say, the classificatory principles by which we devise and order lexico-grammatical rules within or without a somewhat shadowy framework of linguistic universals, nor is the linguist obliged to take his point of departure in some other discipline away from his own observation of speech events, for example in the propositions of logic or in the perceptual and productive processes that concern the psychologist. The help that can be obtained from other specialists in validating theoretical assumptions underlying descriptive linguistic categories is a matter of relevant disciplinary overlap, but should certainly not entail new forms of linguistic apprenticeship at some remove from the close study of living speech. Firth for one certainly thought he was centrally involved with the development of a theory and technique of description appropriate to the patterned regularity or internal ordering revealed by language/s and expressible as far as he was concerned in terms of paradigmatic and syntagmatic relations (phonological, lexical, syntactic) obtaining between items of texts, but he was also deeply concerned with the full humanness of language, not with the question of our mental 'specification' for language but rather with the uses and concomitant forms to which we adapt this 'gift of tongues'. Above all he was concerned with *meaning* and with the elaboration of a linguistics that responded to the full meaningful variety of language and rested both on the meticulous observation of speech events and on a wide experience of languages. Notwithstanding some stylistic obscurity, considerable inconsistency, and an unfortunate lack of exemplification in his writings, Firth's position on a number of basic issues was quite unequivocal. There were four major points he emphasized.

1 *The paramountcy of meaning, source and object of the linguist's interest in language.* Form and meaning were indivisible save for the secondary purposes of description, and the *context of situation* and in some measure also the concept of *collocation* were attempts, following respectively Malinowski and H. E. Palmer, to escape from the strait-jacket of a narrowly denotational, exclusively word-based semantics and from the view of the latter as separable from other areas of linguistic analysis and statement. Historically, what could have been further from the outright rejection of meaning by structuralists of the time?[1] Firth, moreover, was not content to accept a theory of language based on a single language function (denotation, reference, or however termed) to the exclusion of a pervasive and greatly varied remainder lumped together under such labels as 'stylistic variation'. The dichotomy was unacceptable not only because in the absence of any definition of 'stylistic variation' the entailed 'definition' of denotation (sometimes even called 'meaning proper')[2] must fail, but also because in the last analysis such theories seem to be founded on some not very clear universal categories of experience and on *a priori* definitions of words based on the notion of their supposed 'central cores or features of meaning'. This could represent little advance from a semantic *status quo* and was in practice of no great help to the research worker, who was trying to come to terms with meaningful speaker-hearer relationships in a variety of foreign languages-cum-cultures and with the endless problems of analytical interpretation posed by the texts he was labouring hard to establish. The denotative/connotative approach to meaning has led and could lead again to important insights but was insufficiently sensitive to the full meaningful employment of speech. No branch of linguistics was immutable and semantics, one of the younger branches, needed to grow.

Any adequate theory of language has to be apt to what people are doing when they are talking. It hardly does, for instance, to pay lip-service to the prior claims to attention of speech over writing and thereafter not to include in our books a single example of a recognizable spoken sentence. (The linguist's interest in written form, in its influence upon speech, in the special part it plays in koines and more generally in the creation and maintenance of standard languages, etc is not, of course, in question.) Speech functions or uses, among which denotation is merely one,[3] are the source of shared human experience, whatever our forms of cerebral organization; essentially contrary concepts of language 'cores', autonomous syntax, or 'language for the sake of language' are probably fundamentally fallacious. The reaction of the small French child to an adult failure in his language to use appropriate pronominal forms when addressing him is part of his *linguistic* competence or native knowledge of his language, and the complex differential employment of grammatical number in most Indian languages, for example, relates much more importantly to statuses and roles of interlocutors than to a 'logical' distinction between '1' and '1+'. The different, common enough denotative/connotative view is basically that of transformational-generative linguistics (TG), although it is true that, in reaction to earlier 'structuralism', the transformationalists have brought meaning back into the forefront of linguistic interest. Firth's 'Technique of semantics', however, appeared as long ago as 1935. TG has perhaps been too preoccupied so far with its understandable rejection of the view of us as speaking automata to attend to the many aspects of meaningful speech that at present it ignores and thus to live up fully to its laudable intention of asking and answering important questions about language which 'center upon the nature of the abilities displayed by human beings in acquiring and using a language'.[4] Neo-Firthianism, for its part, also seems to depart from the view of meaning inherent in the Firthianism of this book, to the extent that in spite of its acceptance of 'context and situation', in practice linguistic patterns seem to be studied in the abstract by neo-Firthians, that is 'without reference to how, where, when . . . they are used'; further, by the doctrine of 'autonomy of levels' semantics is regarded as essentially independent of grammar, grammar of lexicon, and so on.[5] Autonomy of levels, moreover, notwithstanding a permitted measure of cross-reference, is advanced as a *theoretical* tenet rather than a necessary condition of *descriptive* formulation. It is presumably from similar theoretical premisses that M. A. K. Halliday speaks not as here in favour of the close interdependence of lexical and grammatical analysis but rather of 'a lexical theory that will be complementary to, but not part of, grammatical theory',[6] and this is in turn consistent with the view that collocations, for example, can be determined statistically by the use of computers. The notion of central language cores – rejected by Firth but apparently accepted by neo-Firthians – leads logically on to notions of 'deviation' from the core and the belief that this is measurable. It is this belief that underlies the use of statistical procedures in lexical analysis, with the use of computers to count electronically what occurs on either side of a lexical item focused in one's attention. The Firthian view is rather that more

interesting results are likely to follow from the use of one's own knowledge in response to textual prompting, computer-aided or otherwise, and that the apparent objectivity of such quasi-mathematical procedures is illusory. Neo-Firthians have in the past claimed that they study 'language for its own sake',[7] which is an infelicitous form of words, since language has never existed for its own sake. Nevertheless, neo-Firthian recognition of 'institutional linguistics'[8] does betoken a willingness to face up to many aspects of meaning that go by default in other approaches to the study of language. The neo-Firthian term *register*, for example, carries with it the recognition that language is more than just form and it is this that makes the concept interesting and useful.

2 *The primacy of speech and the need to fully recognize the potential meaningfulness of phonetic minutiae*. Phonetics was the study of meaningful pronunciation. The parallel with some recent work in the sociolinguistic field is clear.[9] The plea was for a generally greater phonetic awareness than was evidenced in the confined 'phonemicism' of Bloomfield, Harris, and others, in relation to whom Firth should be seen in his place in time. 'One did not prick up one's ears just to catch a few sounds,' he would say in graphic indication of the linguist's need for phonetic competence in the everyday sense of that word before the infinite variety of speech. He felt that, although our built-in stabilizers suffice to filter out wholly random facts of variation, there were nevertheless many more meaningful facts of phonetic variability than our theoretical frameworks responded to and in any case, to change the sensory metaphor, we were not to allow ourselves to be blinkered by purpose-built viewfinders, especially those of a phonemic kind. He would not have shared the transformationalist's distrust of 'performance', which on the contrary seemed to provide the only means of access to linguistic knowledge, if we really mean what we say about the primacy of speech, and certainly involved much more than hesitations, false starts, and the like. 'We speak to live' was how he expressed things and he abhorred what he saw as the arid soil of post-Bloomfieldian structuralism. He would have agreed, for example, with Chomsky's strictures on Z. S. Harris's description of 'the over-all purpose of work in descriptive linguistics' as 'a compact one-one representation of the stock of utterances in the corpus'.[10] In a view of linguistics that saw as the linguist's principal aim the construction of inventories of elements with which to represent utterances Firth discerned the placing of a dead hand on his subject, and he found little to encourage him in the application of the earlier versions of *Methods in Structural Linguistics*[11] to Moroccan Arabic.[12] He certainly did not believe that any of the adequacies, observational,

explanatory, or descriptive, was satisfied by the collecting and subsequent chopping of merely extensive corpora, and one feels that he would have approved of the notion of *transformation*, though perhaps more of the later Harrisian type than of the Chomskyan, but in any case this can only be a guess and possibly a wrong one, since Firth never really commented on transformational linguistics of any kind. What one can be sure of is that, as far as the observer's need for a 'phonetics quorum' is concerned, he would not only have found deeply meaningful the forms of vocalic and consonantal pronunciation adopted for instance by elitist groups 'in anxious flight from hotly pursuing masses' but would also have expected to see contrastive possibilities of phonetic form given due place in addition to available grammatical criteria in disambiguating such English phrases and sentences as the following:

(i) *a pretty little house* (where the association of tonicity with *little* marks 'adverbial' *pretty* in contrast with the meliorative adjectival compound of superficially similar form);[13]
(ii) the reflexive *he shot himself* (where tonic *shot* entails *felo de se* and tonic *-self* the games-player who may or may not have scored with his shot – *cf: he fancies himself*=(a) conceited fellow that he is! versus (b) . . . to win);
(iii) *what's your name, Barbara?* (with tonic *your* and low-level *name*, where a rising tone pitched in the lower half of the voice register invites the small child called Barbara to tell a third person her name, in contrast with a similar rise in the top half, which may rebuke her for having answered to the name Barbara when it is not in fact hers to answer to);
(iv) *I like that* (where again different possibilities of tonal and tonic association serve to distinguish (a) a statement of positive liking from (b) a statement of qualified liking, *ie* . . . but I'm not mad about it, and both from (c) a protest).

Subtle as it may be, it is surely incumbent upon the linguist to detect and account for intonational differences, optional or obligatory, between, say, *you said he was coming*=(a) . . . and there he is! versus (b) . . . but where is he? And since speech is on-going, involving more often dialogue than monologue, who if not the linguist is to explain the difference between so-called 'double-stressed' forms like *disappear*, oxytonic in the context of isolation or 'first mention' in discourse but proparoxytonic in intensificatory 'second mention', *cf A: If you don't come soon, he'll disappéar. B: Let him dísappear*. The examples could be multiplied *ad infinitum*. Firthianism was concerned to evoke experience, to stretch its scope, which is perhaps another way of saying that it was concerned to prompt intuitions as well as validate them by bringing into conscious order what has been acquired at least in part unconsciously and stored subconsciously. In the latter process we were certainly not to be misled by an inadequate phonetics and an equally inadequate semantics into classifying, let us say, *John is a musician but Bill plays the piano* as ungrammatical, when a falling-rising tone and decelerando tempo on *musician* and a high-falling tone on *plays* bring the sentence, so to speak, to life.

It will be seen, therefore, that the Firthian view of spoken language as meaningful pronunciation, with the close phonetic study of speech given its rightful place in the linguist's attention, is at variance with the doctrine of 'double articulation', embraced in its essentials by linguists as far apart as, for instance, Martinet in France and Chomsky in America.[14] It would have seemed to Firth that, with due adaptation of metaphor, 'classical' phonemics/morphemics, with its 'minimum sames of vocal feature', its meaningless phonemes and meaningful morphemes, could claim, with TG, that 'phonetic manifestations' (at the surface) are 'a system of instructions governing the movements of a physical system – the speech apparatus'.[15] Is it really 'a primary fact that sentences consist of pairings or associations of information about meaning with information about pronunciation'?[16] This may conceivably be said of a practical way in which we can formulate findings, but it seems that a more fundamental claim is being made as to human linguistic organization. The answer to the question no doubt derives ultimately from one's own conception of the scope of semantics, but it is undeniably true that phonology has a much greater relevance to syntactic analysis than the mere provision of (ortho-) phonemic shape, featurized or not, for sentences and their parts.

3 *The need for a basically inductive approach to analysis in the present state of knowledge*. This is how Firth's 'ad hocism' should be interpreted, not as the restriction of interest to a given corpus of data, however extensive, nor as an expression of disinterest in valid generalizations or even in universals. It is in the nature and refinement of the universals recognized that differences lie between linguists and Firth was also concerned that his subject should have something of interest to say about particular languages. True, linguistics sought to establish a general theory of language, a framework of theoretical concepts within which to approach the study of any given language, but it was also indisputable that individual languages or groups of languages were interestingly characterized by features that were *sui generis*, and an adequate linguistics should envisage the need to provide insights into the internal mechanism of particular languages. There was, moreover, no blinking the apparently infinite complexity of languages and the fact that we still have a lot to learn. Firth accordingly dis-

tinguished between what he called 'a general theory for particular application' and 'a theory of universals for general application'. He was himself more interested in the former, while in practice transformationalists seem primarily committed to the latter.

Insistence on a basically inductive approach to analysis should not, of course, be thought to preclude theoretical expectations and the need for predictive power in the classes and categories recognized in analysis. One can never be wholly inductive or exclusively deductive but it is possible at a given time to be more one than the other, and when there is still so much to know of meaning in its formal linguistic aspects around the world, then it seems reasonable to believe that at least for the time being it is desirable to treat texts and part-texts on their own merits. This is all that is implied by a 'basically inductive' approach, namely that reasonably free, though properly controlled, rein should be allowed to the development and exploitation of contrasts arising out of close observation and textual analysis. This does not run counter to the need for explanatory adequacy, objectivity, and rigour of statement but, in an understandable wish to meet these requirements, some linguists have tended to jump to general conclusions ahead of time. Many in the past have even wished to limit their linguistic statements to those based on a corpus of collected texts, in the belief that a sufficient number of such texts will capture all that is worth capturing. This procedure not only denies by implication the value of inescapable introspection in the analytical process but has led to excessive reliance on aprioristic grids of hierarchically ordered categories, imposed *deductively* on texts and carrying all the 'risks' that linguists in what one might almost call 'the old days' fervently recognized in their unanimous condemnation of forcing English facts into a Latin mould.[17] Rather should one see the recorded utterance as a device to prompt the observer towards the making of 'worthwhile' comparisons and contrasts. Clearly, one starts with all sorts of expectations, which noticeably obtrude if, for example, instead of leaving the first recording of spoken utterance to a machine, one immediately seeks to reduce it to writing in whatever form, including that of phonetic transcription. Clearly, too, one must avoid the oddities and particularities of speech 'on the air', but the meaning of a text and its parts does not lie *in* the text itself but rather in the networks of differential relations between texts; meaning is not part of the text but part of the linguistic organization of the speaker-hearer, who, as far as the practice of linguistics is concerned, is usually also the observer-analyst. Meaningful distinctions are not in any absolute sense 'signalled' in utterance as per an older structuralist view – for example, it does not seem reasonable to believe that one hears absolutely and on any particular occasion a given level of pitch or value of 'junctural time' between lexical items; more plausibly, one locates what one observes in relation to other comparable features in their absence. Linguistics is 'scientific' insofar as it seeks to order linguistic experience in terms of some theory, insofar as it is concerned with regularities, conditions, systems, structures, etc, insofar as it permits predictions to be made, insofar as it is descriptive not prescriptive. Sensitiveness, doubt, and speculation are as important to, say, the natural scientist as to the linguist, but the subject matter of language is such as to lead one to agree with Firth that an adequate general theory has to come to terms with the untidiness of language and languages and that we should be prepared to settle for somewhat tentative generalizations and assumptions, for systematic postulates rather than laws. In view of the part played by introspection in analysis and of the apparent impossibility of mounting experiments at all comparable to those of the natural sciences, it is to say the least unlikely that linguistics will ever become an 'exact science'. It is not just that a unidimensional explanatory hypothesis, such for example as that apparently implicit in the concept of 'autonomous syntax', does not seem apt to the totality of linguistic facts requiring explanation, but also that experience tends to suggest that the most appropriate linguistic rules are of a *variable* kind.[18]

Perhaps in the matter of inductive emphasis, there is more in common between TG and Firthianism than might at first seem. It is noticeable that among the most insightful work in TG terms is that often described as 'fragmentary', *ie* based on selections of bits of language (almost invariably English) that are presumably felt to cohere semantically and/or syntactically, notwithstanding the further impression given that a monolithic TG grammar (?of English) will one day follow. When it does, will it contain chapters, one wonders? Firth advocated what he called 'partial studies', *eg* the study of newspaper headlines *per se*,[19] in which attention would be drawn to distinctive features of the 'restricted language' or language function. There is much in common between the Firthian 'restricted language' and the neo-Firthian 'register', now fairly generally accepted *qua* term. Although, as has been said, Firthians and neo-Firthians share a willingness to look at more aspects of meaning than most other kinds of linguist, they differ over the primacy and logical priority accorded by neo-Firthians to linguistic form, in the sense that they have regarded a change of form as involving a potential change of register; this is to see the linguist among all specialists as best equipped to recognize meaningful variation in language, since language variety is seen as first and foremost formal variety. This appears to contrast with Firth's willingness to treat on equal terms what scholars in other disciplines, not least in social anthropology in Firth's case, had to say about language from their standpoint. As was said earlier, it is because language is more than form that the notion of register or restricted language is useful.[20]

Transformationalists today speak of 'evidence for the existence of rules'[21] and of 'what may be going on in the heads of native speakers concerning their knowledge of their language'.[22] The claim is sometimes made that the theoretical model of their allegiance is an all-embracing reflex of the brain or nervous system. Firth made no such claims. He was unconvinced of the interest of available universals, especially perhaps those of an abstract typological or statistical kind, although he would certainly have recognized the 'operations' of linguistic analysis, *ie* permutation, substitution, etc, as formal properties of language and probably universally applicable. Interesting universals have been said to be formal principles – 'formal', that is, in a logical sense – that one can easily imagine violated in a natural language, so that presumably it does not matter when the Indian or Pakistani with a poor knowledge of English uses *he* in reference to his wife – he will be 'understood'; but in what sense does it not matter, and in the service of what discipline? Firthianism endorsed rather the traditional view of grammar as the art and science of getting things right. We return to the topic in the essay on gender below. In practice, putative universals of language can seem to be something of a small mixed bag – Langacker's *Language and its Structure*, to take a random example, included the posing of questions, the giving of commands, the expression of negation, syntactic processes of embedding and conjoining, and a few word-classes like noun and verb.[23] The search for language universals so conceived, Firth felt, could lead to an inappropriate, even totalitarian process of standardization, when there is nothing more intimately human and therefore more subject to flux and change, nothing less transformable by force, the force of logic, into a Utopia than a language. Nor was this to deny 'innate specification' for language nor to say that logic and linguistics could not be mutually instructive. It is legitimate to question whether TG to date has measured up to its own high requirements of 'empirical adequacy' and 'truth',[24] and is the further requirement that 'individual grammars and general linguistic theory must meet'[25] so differently conceived among scholars accepting it as to leave different groups of them irreconcilably opposed? It is difficult to see how anyone could object to Postal's assertion that 'general linguistic theory must contain an explicit description of all those formal and empirical constraints to be imposed on individual grammars'[26] but how can this be achieved in advance of acquiring detailed knowledge of individual grammars? TG to date has effectively limited its interest to English, on which it has had some interesting things to say, but work on other languages has so far been mostly derivative and rather superficial. The test of a theory is sometimes said to be whether it enables us to state the facts, but if these are ultimately of meaning, then it must be required of a theory of language not merely that it facilitates the formulation of representations or even of rules – since rule-philosophizing easily degenerates into its own kind of 'phatic communion' – but that it accounts for the totality of linguistic aspects of meaning. It was said earlier that we need a theory adapted to what people are doing when they converse; if current theories fail in this respect, they should be discarded or modified, certainly not shored up by such apparently specious distinctions as that, for instance, which was lately drawn between language use and language meaning, with Firth's context of situation in particular consigned to a limbo of use.

4 *The priority of the syntagm and the resulting importance of finding the syntagmatic limits beyond which linguistic choice is unpredictable.* For Firth the consequences for analysis of the on-going nature of language were inescapable. As one acquires one's language/s in response to whole utterances, so phonological units, form-classes, and even sentences are first and foremost practical means of giving descriptive and mnemonic shape to more inclusive distinctive wholes that we use and respond to. This syntagmatic emphasis came to be labelled 'the prosodic approach', but the latter term is best reserved for Firthian phonology, since the syntagm is also at the heart of lexicogrammatical and situational analysis. The concepts of collocation and colligation, for instance, relate to a syntagmatic view of lexical and syntactic structure. TG's subcategorizations and selectional constraints are apparently similarly motivated,[27] but in practice are not taken very far. It is not clear, for example, whether transformationalists would want to concern themselves with the particular fact that the set of final nouns in the following English locative phrases relating to a temporal or spatial nucleus develop their individual collocational associations with preceding nominal or 'adverbial' forms – *at the height of summer*, *in the depths of winter*, *right* (or *full* or *slap*) *in the stomach*, *plumb in the middle* – and that English uses collocational variation in contrast with *eg* French *en plein été/hiver/ventre/milieu*, or again with the obverse of the coin as illustrated by, say, English *heavy breathing/rain/eater/drinker/body*/etc versus French (*respiration*) *pénible* / (*pluie*) *battante* / *gros* (*mangeur*) / *fort* (*buveur*) / (*corps*) *lourd*/etc. It does seem, however, that present subcategorization rules and selectional restrictions are open to benefit from the greater flexibility inherent in Firthian collocations. It is certainly not clear at which point TG wishes to cease examining what are in effect collocational and colligational dependencies and constraints in a language and

across languages, and one can be left with the misleading impression that the question is less answerable to the facts of language than to the needs of grammatical rule-writing.

As to linguistic analysis within a 'situational' framework, the Arabic of the region of Zagazig, a town in the Nile Delta, provides interesting exemplification of syntagmatic relations within addressive phrases and at the same time of the close association of 'situation' and grammar.[28] In this Egyptian dialect, the form 'ˈab' is translatable as 'father', as it is in the corresponding form 'ˈabu' in 'ˈabu ħasan' (Hassan's father). In the vocative context with the preceding particle 'ya', the form is 'ɑbɑ', so that one says 'yɑ ɑbɑ', but now not only to one's father but also to one's father-in-law. There are always marks in the total vocative syntagm, notably in terms of dependencies and constraints obtaining between subclasses of appellative noun, of the relationship of participants in the situation. Thus, if 'yɑ ɑbɑ' is followed by a proper name, for example '9ali' (Ali), and one says 'yɑ ɑbɑ 9ali', then the addressee is one's paternal uncle; if a title is interpolated, *eg* 'ˈilħajj', to which a man is entitled if he has made the pilgrimage to Mecca, and one says 'yɑ ɑbɑ ilħajj 9ali', then one is addressing an older male relative of whatever order or, possibly, a close friend of the family; and, finally, the inclusion of a further vocative phrasal component, marked by a further preposed 'ya', as in 'yɑ ɑbɑ ilħajj 9ali ya abu ħasan' (Haj Ali, son of Hassan), means that one is talking to an older man who is a close friend of the family and one cannot oneself be a child. In passing, we may contrast 'ya abu ħasan' (O Hassan's son) with 'ˈabu ħasan' (Hassan's father) and wonder in what consists any putative core of absolute meaning attaching to 'ˈab', but for the time being the purpose is simply to indicate that not only is grammar involved at all times in the phrasal type illustrated and in its constituent classes but that analysis can only be satisfactorily undertaken on a syntagmatic basis. Moreover, of course, with regard to such material, to ignore the interrelationship of interlocutors and the social values involved is considerably to impoverish the analytical statement. The need to consider such parameters tends to be obscured in native language study, where so much knowledge on the part of the reader or listener is usually taken – mistakenly – for granted, but the need is immediately apparent when one is confronted with a foreign language, especially with one whose cultural background is 'exotic'. Further extensive illustration is provided below.

In the manner of its emphasis on the syntagm, Firthian linguistics is very much on its own. Syntagmatic analysis aims at avoiding, for example, what are seen as errors and pseudo-problems that attend the splitting of unitary associations like collocations and the forcing of parts of the meaning of such wholes into fictitious 'sememes', to use

Bloomfield's term, which are then attributed in particular to words and bits of words. Recognition of the on-going nature of language and of sentences as at least in part definable on the basis of transsentential relations also reveals this syntagmatic orientation. It is necessary to separate the 'appreciation' of what is meaningful and how it is so from the subsequent manner in which findings are presented. 'Lexical meaning' is not denied but neither it nor 'semantics' are self-explanatory terms, and lexical items and their classes (not necessarily equated with words and word-classes) should first be shown within the syntagmatic associations whence so much of meaning derives. Once syntagmatic analysis has been completed, it may perhaps be otiose to deal again in a narrow paradigmatic way with the discriminations recognized and it is certainly unjustifiable to take such narrow paradigms as the basis of a semantico-syntactic theory of speech. It is also perhaps because of a preoccupation with 'units' and their relevance to formulation that few linguists to date have considered at all closely the facts of linguistic patterning within suprasentential domains. There is no apparent reason why the sentence should not continue to serve as the principal unit of statement.

In phonology, too, Firthianism rejected the phoneme in favour of a syntagmatic concept, which was termed – perhaps not too happily – the 'prosody'. The mainspring of prosodic analysis in phonology was the recognition of phonetic features whose domains extended beyond those of the (more practical) phoneme as well as of constraints and dependencies which, as in the case of lexico-grammatical study, had to be examined first before deciding what, if anything, was left to be dealt with paradigmatically under 'phonematics' (a term bearing only 'etymological' resemblance to phonemics). Subsequently, the syntagmatic basis of the prosody came to be confused rather with other aspects of Firthian thinking and especially with the need not to identify – in the phonemic manner – terms in what was recognizable as one system with those in another. A polysystemic approach to linguistic analysis is wholly justifiable at all levels but belongs rather to the Firthian inductiveness already spoken of. As to relationship between Firthian phonology and TG, Postal's indictment of what he termed the 'autonomous phonemics' of earlier structuralist phonology in accordance with which phonological structure concerns nothing more than brute phonetic fact (whatever that may be) plus word-contrastive distributionalism to the exclusion of morphophonological considerations,[29] would certainly have found favour with Firth, as would the reminder that 'neither articulation nor the acoustic signal has the discrete, segmental properties which phonetic representations manifest.'[30] Approval would certainly have been forthcoming in response to TG opinion on the relevance to phonological structure of morpheme boundaries, morphological and syntactic categories, morphophonological alternations, etc. To the extent, however, that feature analysis in generative phonological terms seems for practical purposes to be confined to phonemic, morphemic, and lexical domains, Firth would probably have felt that its adherents had not yet carried their reservations about 'autonomous phonemics' to their logical conclusion. In spite of quite often recognizing interesting new paradigms of related word-forms, generativists rarely look beyond the word and can also recognize in the process of formulating rules so-called underlying forms that are unmotivated (save as contributing to a uniformity of presentation), thereby obscuring or ignoring features that interestingly characterize particular languages (accentuation in Arabic is an example to which we return below). Moreover, the equation that has been made by TG protagonists between Z. S. Harris's 'long components'[31] and Firth's 'prosodies' is far too facile,[32] as it is hoped the phonological essays in this book will demonstrate. Indeed, it is time we turned to the promised exemplification of the aspects of Firthianism we wish to stress and first to what was termed above its basic inductiveness. Before doing so, however, perhaps one should say that any reservations expressed above on the subject of TG do not extend to its generally admirable manner of formulating findings; it is to be desired that the insights of any given approach could be accommodated within something like the TG framework of presentation, although it is not clear whether this can be done without at least considerable recasting of attendant theoretical premisses.

Notes

1 *Cf*, for example, B. Bloch, 'A set of postulates for phonemic analysis', *Language* 24 (1948), *pp* 3–46, and his earlier 'Phonemic Overlapping', *American Speech* 16 (1941), *pp* 278–84, reprinted, together with subsequent editorial comment, in *Readings in Linguistics I*, ed M. Joos, *pp* 93–6. See, too, B. Bloch and G. L. Trager, *Outline of Linguistic Analysis* (Baltimore, Waverly Press, 1942), *p* 68. For brief general comment, see F. R. Palmer, *Grammar* (Penguin, 1971), *pp* 109–110.

2 For example, in *New Horizons in Linguistics*, ed J. Lyons (Penguin, 1970), under the definition attached to *cognitive meaning* (*p* 318), which should be compared with the entry under *stylistic* (*p* 326). This twofold view of meaning is a traditional one and, with minor modifications, appears to be espoused by a majority of linguists and semanticists.

3 Notwithstanding an apparent measure of acceptance of the unsatisfactory twofold division into (1) referential or denotational and (2) stylistic, the following extracts from D. H. Hymes's editorial introduction to the journal *Language in Society* (1/1, 1972) are in close accord with the principles of 'Firthianism': 'If we begin, not with formalisms and the autonomy of a discipline as overriding considerations, but with language as it is commonly used, we find the referential function only one among the bases on which

discourse is organized and often a minor or peripheral one. We find completeness or explicitness of reference itself a dimension of appropriateness. We find conventional stylistic features and patterns used for emphasis, clarity, appeal, expression and the like. And we find referential and stylistic dimensions organized together within conventionally recognized ways of speaking, acts of speech, and speech events. We find, in short, that language is not solely an instrument for naming and describing and conducting rigorous argument. We find it to be an instrument of expression and appeal, of persuasion and command, of deference and insult, of gossip and rebuke; we find it an instrument preferred, eschewed, enjoyed, distrusted, pervasively evaluated, not only in terms of referential adequacy and logical validity, but also in terms of aptness, pleasure, rewards and costs, self-identity and community respect. And we find it to have these roles, not by some wholly external process, some mysterious and magical insertion into social reality, once it has left the grammarian's hand, but in virtue of properties partly specific to it, of features and patterns, as has been said, that serve such meanings, and that have been developed and adapted, often differently and to different degree in different communities, to do so.... The greatest challenge... is to develop the methods, concepts and findings that will enable one ultimately to approach language... not only as grammar but also as language organized in use.... The point, of course, is not to reject the possibility of generalizations and general theory, but to recognize that the only path to valid generalizations and theory lies *through* the sphere of the diverse, socially specific forms of speech that men and women actually have available and use.... What is essential... is a functional perspective comprehensive enough to support a general theory of language as part of social life, yet specific enough to orient empirical research.'

4 R. A. Jacobs and P. S. Rosenbaum, *English Transformational Grammar* (Ginn, 1968), *p* vii.

5 For a clear statement of the position, see, for instance, Geoffrey N. Leech, *Towards a Semantic Description of English* (Longman, 1969), *p* 28 *ff*; the preceding quotation is from the same author's *Linguistic Guide to English Poetry* (Longman, 1969), *pp* 40–1.

6 M. A. K. Halliday, 'Lexis as a linguistic level', in *In Memory of J. R. Firth* (Longman, 1966), *p* 148. *Cf*, too, the treatment of *collocation* in M. A. K. Halliday, Angus McIntosh, and Peter Strevens, *The Linguistic Sciences and Language Teaching* (Longman, 1964), *p* 33 *ff*.

7 M. A. K. Halliday *et al*, *The Linguistic Sciences and Language Teaching*, *p* 4.

8 *ibid*, Chapter 4.

9 *Cf*, for example, W. Labov, *The Social Stratification of English in New York City* (Center for Applied Linguistics, Washington, DC, 1966), and the same author's 'Social motivation of a sound change' *Word* 19 (1963), *pp* 273–309. For its relevance to the 'variationist' approach referred to elsewhere, see also Labov's 'Some principles of linguistic methodology', *Language in Society* (1/1, 1972), *pp* 97–120.

10 N. Chomsky, 'Some methodological remarks on generative grammar', *Word* 17 (1961), reprinted in *Readings in Applied English Linguistics*, ed H. B. Allen (Meredith, 1964).

11 Later reprinted as *Structural Linguistics* by Z. S. Harris (University of Chicago Press, 1951).

12 See Z. S. Harris, 'The phonemes of Moroccan Arabic', *Journal of the American Oriental Society*, 62/4 (1942), *pp* 309–18, and the critical and contrary views of the late J. Cantineau in his 'Réflexions sur la phonologie de l'arabe

marocain', *Hespéris*, 37 (1950), *pp* 193–207 and his *Etudes de linguistique arabe* (Klincksieck, 1960), *pp* 241–55.

13 Other criteria for the recognition of a 'meliorative-pejorative' class of English adjectival compound are to be found in the Firth memorial volume (Longman, 1966), *pp* 349–50.

14 *Cf*, for example, A. Martinet, 'Arbitraire linguistique et double articulation', *Cahiers F. de Saussure* 15 (1957), *pp* 105–16, also his *Linguistique synchronique* (Presses Universitaires de France, 1965), *p* 21 *ff*; and J. Lyons, *Chomsky* (Fontana/Collins, 1970), *pp* 22–3.

15 P. M. Postal, in *Epilogue* to R. A. Jacobs and P. S. Rosenbaum's *English Transformational Grammar* (Ginn, 1970), *p* 276.

16 *ibid*, *p* 275.

17 As to hierarchies, the Firthian and transformationalist positions are close with regard to the arguments that once waxed hot over 'mixing of levels'; Firth was quite uninterested in devising step by step phonological and grammatical procedures on the way to knowledge of this or that language and saw no sense in asking whether analysis proceeded from top (sentence) to bottom (phoneme) or *vice versa*, since recourse is constantly had to a mixture of phonological, morphological, lexical, and syntactic considerations in arriving at an understanding of the internal mechanism of a language. The manner in which findings are presented is a secondary matter. Rather would Firth and Chomsky have parted company over what seems a transformationalist preoccupation with rule-ordering and satisfaction with what may be an overstated theory of mental structure in preference to an adequate theory of meaning.

18 In this connection, see, for example, Charles-James N. Bailey, *Variation and Linguistic Theory* (Center for Applied Linguistics, Washington, DC, 1973), and my 'Something more than "writing with the learned, pronouncing with the vulgar", investigating the Arabic koine' (to appear in the Mont Follick series, edited by W. Haas and published by Manchester University Press).

19 See H. Straumann, *Newspaper Headlines* (Allen & Unwin, 1935).

20 It follows from the view of the priority of linguistic form that linguistics is taken to be the primary discipline among those with an interest in language, but – differences of training and experience apart – such pre-eminence is no more tenable than that apparently claimed for psychology by the statement, *pace* Chomsky, that linguistics is a branch of cognitive psychology (see N. Chomsky, *Language and Mind* (enlarged edition; Harcourt Brace Jovanovich, 1972), *p* 1). The fact that our meaningful uses and responses to language are organized in the brain (perhaps better, the nervous system) is of no special relevance to the diverse areas of scholarship to which language is of concern. In today's situation, in which such different disciplines as linguistics, anthropology, sociology, psychology, philosophy, communications engineering, computer science, etc, as well as the very many particular language disciplines, all have their contribution to make to linguistic knowledge, no one discipline can be considered prior. Although most linguists, conscious of their own limitations and anxious to welcome the insights of other specialists, nowadays very properly seek the occasions to hear other points of view, it is nevertheless highly unlikely that many will achieve Chomsky's quite remarkable familiarity with a whole congeries of disciplines and more probable that they will be obliged to remain content with a thorough acquaintance with one or at most two specialized areas of study. In such circumstances, an inductive approach of a different kind is indicated – is indeed a practical necessity – namely that by which the individual scholar may hope to make his own contribution according to his own lights.

21 Marina K. Burt, *From Deep to Surface Structure: an Introduction to Transformational Syntax* (Harper & Row, 1971), *p* 9.
22 *ibid, p* 10.
23 R. W. Langacker, *Language and its Structure* (Harcourt, Brace & World, 1968), *p* 242. As it happens, the author has now expanded his treatment of the topic in a revised (1973) edition which, unfortunately, was unavailable to me at the time both of writing and of proof-correcting.
24 *Cf* P. M. Postal, *Constituent Structure* (Mouton, 1964), *p* 1.
25 *ibid, p* 2.
26 *ibid, p* 5.
27 See N. Chomsky, *Aspects of the Theory of Syntax* (MIT Press, 1965), especially Chapters 2 and 4.
28 A detailed statement of the facts is to be found in S. M. Badawi's '"Ya"-particles in the Egyptian dialect of El-Nakhas (Sharqiya Province)' (unpublished MA thesis, University of London, 1960). Strictly, the facts given relate to El-Nakhas village, which is six miles from Zagazig.
29 See P. M. Postal, *Aspects of Phonological Theory* (Harper & Row, 1968).
30 *ibid, p* 6.
31 Z. S. Harris, 'Simultaneous components in phonology', *Language* 20 (1944), reprinted in *Readings in Linguistics I*, ed M. Joos, *pp* 124–138.
32 See, for example, D. T. Langendoen, *The London School of Linguistics* (MIT Press, 1968), *pp* 54–5.

One

'*Caveat* to the general'

The linguist discovers much of the meaningful organization of a language by the observation and exploitation of contrastive relations of several kinds between overt and potentially overt texts. The inaccessibility of 'mind' and the processes of language acquisition to any present experimental method capable of accommodating the rich material of meaningful linguistic distinctions precludes any other procedure. The implied need for a theory of 'performance' as well as 'competence', to use the TG terms, seems inescapable. The facts impose a division of 'competence' into at least 'grammatical' and 'functional' competence, both subsumed under a total 'communicative' competence. Moreover, should not a valid general theory take some account of what we do when we successfully translate? Firth spoke of 'a general theory for particular application' – there is much interesting relativity in language, even in the apparent 'absolutes' of phonetics, and it is all too easy to impose one's parti-pris deductively on facts that require other than aprioristic interpretation.

One approaches a language with 'expectations' as to meaningful discriminations it is likely to contain and in part, therefore, according to one's prior linguistic experience; nor is one always disappointed. Yet, in spite of the possibilities that exist for successful translation and even for 'language engineering', there is no reason to suppose that any language will recognize the same meaningful contrasts as any other, nor that any two languages will cater for – or wish to cater for – a given difference of meaning in the same way. It is not simply, for example, that the Bedouin's habitat is sufficiently *sui generis* to ensure that his geographical nomenclature in Arabic finds no parallel elsewhere but also, for instance, that in the 'general semantic' area of *intensification* the English difference represented by *too* (big) versus *very* (big) does not correspond to any clearly recognizable Arabic distinction. We find ourselves looking in a sense at the other side of the picture when we discover – as it were by chance but in the normal process of linguistic research – the particular fact that in Cyrenaican (Libyan) Arabic the difference of sequential order between *eg* 'hu (*he*) kill (*every*) yawm (*day*) yalbas (*wears*) fi (particle of habitual or continuative aspect) kabbuuT (*coat*)'[1] and 'hu yalbas fi kabbuuT kill yawm' carries with it the fact that in the case of the first order only, the person referred to wears a *different* coat every day. There is absolutely nothing in one's prior knowledge of English or any other language including other forms of vernacular Arabic, as far as I am aware, to lead one to suspect this fact *a priori* and clearly translation is only possible *a posteriori*. The discovery is made, of course, by such indications as the extensibility of the first order but not the second by, say, 'u killhin ħumur' (and all of them red) and by such supporting examples as 'hi (*she*) kill yawm utTabbux (*cooks*) fi makaruunih (*pasta, ie* in general, not specifically macaroni)', extensible by the Arabic equivalent of, *eg, on Mondays she cooks spaghetti, on Tuesdays vermicelli*, etc, a distinctive implication absent from the contrastive order 'hi utTabbux fi makaruunih kill yawm'. Similarly, no grammar book leads one to expect for Arabic in this and other of its colloquial forms that the so-called 'active participle', morphologically nominal, has temporal relevance in regular contrast with the two Arabic verbal tenses, and corresponds more or less to English perfective aspect: Thus,

1 'hu 9aaTi (active participle) kilmih' (he has given his word)
2 'hu 9aTaa (perfect tense) kilmih' (he gave his word)
3 'hu y9aTi (imperfect tense) kilmih' (he gives/will give his word)

It is again by contrasts between potential extensions that one finds that the active participle 'refers to a past act creating a state *that has remained unbroken up to the present*'. The important thing at (1) – and it *is* important to a Bedouin, given the force of the oath and the practice of oath-taking in his society – is that the person in question gave his word *and has not gone back on it since*. This is in contrast with the use of tenses at (2) and (3). How should one translate (1), one may relevantly ask? Perhaps by such a form of English words as *he has not retracted his word*. The example could be multiplied a thousandfold and translation will take multifarious forms, having regard to constraints in English as well as Arabic. Thus,

1 'hu liebis [active part] kabbuuT' (he is wearing a coat)
2 'hu libas [perf] kabbuuT' (he put on a coat)
3 'hu yalbas [imperf] fi kabbuuT' (he wears/is putting on a coat)

or again,

1 'ilgiitih mieʃi [active part]' (I found him gone)
2 'ilgiitih yimʃi [imperf]' (I found him going)

Clearly, the Arabic active participle, like participles in other languages (*eg* Urdu, Greek), merits the attention of those linguists who find it of interest to discuss the relative priority of noun and verb, with or without adjective, in universal grammar. Priority must first be given, however, to the textual comparisons on which recognition of the category rests.[2]

None of the foregoing should be taken to imply that it is not perfectly legitimate to compare the 'modes of expression' of, *eg*, *perfectivity* in this and that language. There are, however, real risks of language being lost sight of in the process, of confusion between language of explanation and linguistic data proper, and of the kind of insecurity inherent in so-called 'contrastive' linguistics other than of a superficial, phonemic kind. Interlingual comparisons usually bring with them loss of the terra firma, so to speak, provided by the overtly comparable texts with which it seems possible to operate intralingually. Nor, in the absence of verifiable definitions, do universals of a 'deep structural' kind offer at present any surer footing. The need appears for a balance to be struck between that which is universal or more or less so and the greatly ramifying networks of particular linguistic organizations. The latter, it might be noted, are to many linguists interesting for their own sakes. So, too, are particular devices of linguistic form – reduplication, let us say. Indeed, for research purposes one must start with such devices, not with 'deep structures'. Is it not legitimate to examine the use made of reduplication in a language or, for that matter, over a sample of the world's languages? Take the North Indian languages, for instance. One obviously cannot know in advance whether or how Sindhi or Panjabi or Hindi or Urdu recognizes categories of 'distributive', 'repetitive', 'intensive', 'approximative', etc and once again, as it happens, the grammar books are rarely helpful in respect of sets of relevant forms. It is experimentation with comparisons between comparable items, distinguished *inter alia* by varied forms of reduplication, that *forces* the recognition of such categories and incidentally facilitates subsequent translation. When all is done, the languages of India and Pakistan are found to be notably specialized in the uses they make of reduplicative patterning. Let us consider, for example, Sindhi and at first the particular noun 'churii'[3] (table-knife). Subsequent examples will show that a syntax based on a word-class point of departure with little or no attention paid to extended syntagms can be as misleading as a word-based semantics. For the time being, however, attention is drawn to the fact that the common run of grammars tell us that there is no class in Sindhi to which the term 'article' can be properly applied and leave the question of definite versus indefinite reference at that. Now, from appropriate textual comparisons it appears that 'churii' in, say, the imperative sentence 'churii (*knife*) saaf (*clean*) kar (*make*)' is in fact referentially definite and the sentence therefore to be translated 'clean the knife'. Reduplicative possibilities are among the contrastive relations meaningfully accreted by the 'unmodified' form. Thus, *cf*

'churii saaf kar' (clean the knife)
'churii-churii saaf kar' (clean every knife)
'(kaa) churii-b'urii saaf kar' (clean a knife or something *or* clean the knife and the rest of the things)
'kaa churii saaf kar' (clean a knife)
'kaa-kaa churii saaf kar' (clean some of the knives)
'kaa-na-kaa churii saaf kar' (clean any (old) knife)
'hik(iṛii) churii saaf kar' (clean one of the knives)
'sabh churiiãa saaf kar' (clean all the knives)

Taking for granted the textual operations (substitution, transposition, interpolation, expansion, etc) necessary for the proper justification of the classification recognized – and providing their own kind of interesting universals – we might perhaps plausibly divide the above examples semantically as follows:

DEFINITE

singular	'churii' (the knife)
singulative	'hik(iṛii) churii' (one of the knives)
distributive	'churii-churii' (every knife)
totalitive	'sabh churiiãa' (all the knives)

INDEFINITE

singular	'kaa churii' (a knife)
singulative	'kaa-na-kaa churii' (any (old) knife)
partitive	'kaa-kaa churii' (some knives)
approximative	'(kaa) churii-b'urii' (a knife or something, the knife etc)

Different classifications are possible from other points of departure but these will not detain us. The object so far has been simply to indicate the irrelevance of such a statement as that by which no class of 'article' is said to be recognizable for Sindhi. Let us, however, look a little more closely at some of the categories involved, in particular those relating to complete reduplication (churii-churii) and to the partial reduplication pattern illustrated by 'churii-b'urii'.

Most word-classes in Sindhi and cognate languages are associable with reduplication but several kinds of syntagmatic constraint would have to be considered in any thoroughgoing analysis of what is a fascinating and very wide-ranging area of study. The numeral, for example, is reduplicated in Panjabi 'mũdee tin-tin san' (the boys were in threes) but may not be within the phrase structure Numeral-Adjective-Noun, *eg* 'tin kaalee aadmii' (three black men). Again, most Sindhi 'fractional' numerals, *eg* 'savaa' ($1\frac{1}{4}\times$), differ from cardinals in respect of reduplicability, *cf* 'savaa saoo-saoo' (a hundred and a quarter at a time) (not '*savaa-savaa saoo') versus 'doo-doo saoo' (two hundred at a time). Yet again, in the adjective-noun phrase, there are restrictions on the co-occurrence of adjectival and nominal reduplicates, but in spite of such manifestly interesting restrictions, it is possible to recognize generalized meaningful functions for the types of reduplicate in question, so much so in the case of complete reduplication, for example, that one can plausibly regard reduplication and its absence as morphologically on all fours with, say, singular and plural affixes; the categorial distinction may be labelled 'distributive' versus 'non-distributive'. Once again, the following examples in a thoroughgoing analysis would require 'proving' by reference to extended or otherwise modified texts; *cf*, however, for present purposes:

'chookiɽoo-chookiɽoo (*boy*) ãdar (*inside*) acee (*may he come*)'
(let each boy come in (in turn))
'chookiɽee-chookiɽee (*boy* [indirect or agentive case]) joo (*'s*) kitaab (*book*) khaɳ (*take*)'
(take each boy's book)
'chookiɽee joo kitaab-kitaab khaɳ'
(take the boy's every book)
'chookiɽee-chookiɽee khee (*to*) kitaab ɖ'ee (*give*)'
(give the book to each boy (in turn))
'chookiɽee-chookiɽee khee kitaab-kitaab ɖ'ee'
(give a book to each boy)

And for good measure:

'g'ooʈha-g'ooʈha (*village*) jee ghara-ghara (*house*) jee maaɳhuu-maaɳhuu (*person*) aayoo (*came*)'
(every person of every house of every village came)

Tonal and other phonological features (for example those of a rhythmic kind affecting vowel and consonant length) also regularly relate to meaningful differences involving reduplication, notably to the contrast between complete reduplication, on the one hand, and repetition or mere juxtaposition, on the other. Thus, for instance, a falling tone would be associated with the first 'b'aara' in sentence (1) below but with the second in sentence (2):

1 'b'aara-b'aara (*child*) khee inaam (*prize*) milyoo (*obtained*)'
(a prize was obtained by every child)
2 'b'aara b'aara khee inaam ɖ'inuu (*gave*)'
(the child gave the boy a prize)

Similarly, a repeated rise or a continuous rise is uniquely characteristic of the repetition of, say, 'pakhii' (bird) in 'pakhii, pakhii (pakhii . . .$_n$) pee (continuative aspect marker) ɖ'isana (*see, seeing*) mẽe (*in*) aayaa (*came*)' (birds were to be seen (flying) everywhere). Intonation may also distinguish between different cases of reduplication, even where the sentence is otherwise ambiguous; thus, tonal contour (1) below relates to a translation 'give all the pice to (all) the children', while (2) is to be interpreted 'give a pice to each child':

b'aara-b'aara khee paiisoo-paiisoo ɖ'ee

1 \ - - - ‾ \ - - - -

2 ‾ ‾ ‾ ‾ ✓ ‾ ‾ \ - -

If 'b'aaran' (*children* [indirect case]) is substituted for 'b'aara-b'aara', then the intonational possibilities of the sentences do not match (1) and (2) absolutely but the same relative distinctions remain between

b'aaran khee paiisoo-paiisoo ɖ'ee

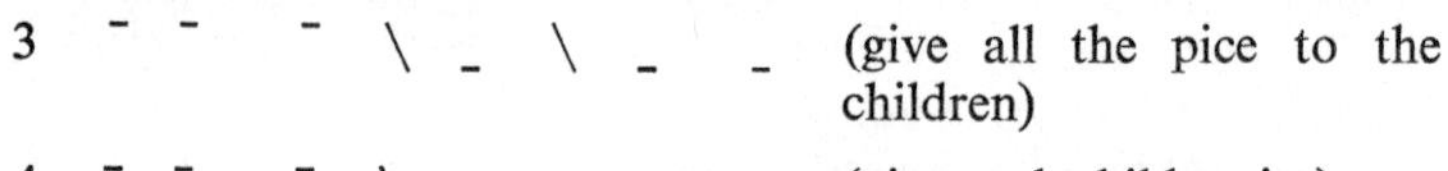

3 (give all the pice to the children)

4 (give each child a pice)

Much more research is needed in this area of the 'reinforcement' provided by phonological differences to the syntactico-semantic distinctions in question, but no theory can be considered adequate that does not recognize them.

We might perhaps note in passing that, apart from certain kinship terms and in poetry, the vestigial case-endings of Sindhi nouns survive only in reduplication, at least in my informant's speech. Thus, 'tar(a)hẽe' or 'qismẽe', for example, do not occur in isolation or in non-reduplicated form, *cf* 'tar(a)hẽe-tar(a)hẽe jaa maaɳhuu' (all manner of people), 'qismẽe-qismẽe gula' (every kind of flower). It is sometimes just the ending that provides the formal reduplicating mark as in the following example of a type of reduplication which is only one among many that space precludes us from considering here: 'hã̃dhẽe (*place*) -maag'ẽe (*habitable place*) maʃahuur (*famous*) aahee (*is*)' (he is famous everywhere). Reduplication in its many forms is, in fact, so common in the languages of the region, so sought after for instance in poetry, that I am personally convinced that the repetitiousness felt to inform 'Indian English' by the user of British and I dare say American English, is due to this single feature in the Indo-Pakistan languages.

Let us now turn to our second type of reduplication, known, I believe, as *muhmal* in Urdu and involving, as far as Sindhi is concerned, the replacement of the first consonant or zero consonant of the first element of a reduplicate by 'b'' in the second element, *eg* 'churii-b'urii' (a table-knife or something; the table-knife etc).[4] Uncertainty, indefiniteness, and interrogation are semantically related areas and it is not surprising to find that this type of reduplication concerns them all. You are, for example, not sure of the fact of a man's wealth if you say of him in Sindhi 'paiisee-b'aiisee (*money* [indirect case]) vaaroo (*possessing*) maaɳhuu (*man*) aahee (*he is*)'; this is in contrast with the comparable case of non-reduplication and therefore translation should take some such form as 'he is a pretty rich man (I think)'. Similarly, 'pretty' would be better included in an English translation of the interrogative sentence 'kiiã [interrogative sentence marker] huʃyaar-b'uʃyaar (*intelligent*) aahee (na (*not*))?' (is(n't) he pretty intelligent?). Translation is bound to take as many forms as are appropriate for the rendering of, *eg*, *uncertainty* and in the Sindhi source language itself the marks of this semantic category will be rarely if ever limited to *muhmal*. Thus, for example, the form 'miʈaii' – untranslatable in word-by-word terms – and the indefinite particle 'kaa' [feminine singular] both 'reinforce' reduplication with 'b'' in, say, 'miʈaii kaa maiza-b'aiza (*table*) vaʈhaɳii (*buyable, meet to buy*) aahee' (I must buy some sort of table). Again, the combination of the 'future' modal 'hũdoo' together with 'koo' [masc sing] and 'b'' in 'hũdoo koo ʈikhiʈaaii-b'ikhiʈaaii' (perhaps he will (have) be(en) a man from Tikhir or somewhere (of the sort)) provides syntagmatically the marks of uncertainty in answer to *eg* 'ãauu (*I*) kaalha (*yesterday*) hik(ka) maaɳhuu khee milyus (*met*) jãh (*who*) "aahĩi" ("*you are*") jee badirãa (*instead of*) "aiihẽe" pee [continuative marker] g'aalhaayoo (*said*)' (I yesterday met a man who kept saying 'aahĩi' for 'aiihẽe').

The dependencies and constraints of on-going discourse in on-going situations have always to be recognized. In the following exchange, B is searching high and low for something lost:

A: 'peeʈin-b'eeʈin mẽe g'oolh' (Look in the bags and things!) (*or* 'kẽeh peeʈii-b'eeʈii mẽe g'oolh' (Look in some bag or other!))
B: 'peeʈiia-b'eeʈiia mẽe g'oolhiyoo atham' (I've looked in the bag and so forth)

This exchange is quite appropriate to circumstances in which only one bag is concerned and is visible to both participants. Collocational accompaniment as well as the on-going circumstances of use will impose an interpretation of 'b'' varying between 'N or something (like N)' and 'N etc'. For example, 'diloo' is used both as a 'chati' or water-jar and as a drum, so that, for example, 'diloo-b'iloo khaɳii aa' is ambiguous between (1) 'bring a chati or some other jar' and (2) 'bring the (jar-)drum and the other things (*sc* the 'yaktaaroo' ((one-stringed) guitar), the 'khaɽtaala' (clappers), etc)'. Translation will again, of course, take many forms. Because 'maanii-b'aanii (*meal*) khaaii (*eaten*) poo (*after*) acijaĩi (*come*)' (come after you've eaten and things) 'means' that the addressee may come not only having eaten but also having subsequently washed, rested, and changed, *ie* not immediately after his meal, the contrastive sentence without 'b'aanii', *ie* 'maanii khaaii poo acijaĩi' is to be translated 'come as soon as you've eaten'. Collocability will naturally differ between the two sentences, so that *eg* 'jald, hikidam, sighoo, turt' (quickly, at once, etc) exclude 'b'aanii'. The latter is also excluded by *eg* 'sãa' or 'ii' in the alternative sentence-forms 'maanii khaaiɳa sãa acijaĩi' *or* 'maanii khaaĩidee ii acijaĩi' (come immediately after eating). Thus, the sense of 'etc' in 'b'' spills over into the contrastive time-reference of the sentences concerned. There are numerous other examples in this book of the frequent futility of trying to force the whole of meaning into the straitjacket of words and word-classes. In the following examples – on which further research is necessary – an adjectival form 'ɖ'aaɖhiiũu' (thorough, complete) not only develops interesting associations with 'b'' but is also pluralized in common with the whole noun phrase, although reference is to a single place or object:

'ɖ'aaɖhiiũu karaaciiũu-b'araaciiũu (*Karachi*) ghumii (*having visited on foot*) aayoo (*come*) aahĩi (*you have*)' (So you're back after a (thoroughly) good look round Karachi!)
'ɖ'aaɖhiiũu maizũu-b'aizũu vartiiũu athaii' (That's a very fine table you've bought!)

No uncertainty or indeterminacy is involved in the last example, say, which might therefore be contrasted with 'maizũu-b'aizũu vartiiũu athaii' (*sc* with 'ɖ'aaɖhiiũu' omitted), which must be interrogative, indeterminate, and of plural reference, *ie* 'Have you bought any tables or whatever?'

There is also room for research into the facts of exclusion between the several speech functions involved as well as the manner of their distribution over the parts of sentences. The distributive notion of 'every, all, in turn' that often characterizes complete reduplication is in some sense an *intensification* of the noun to which it is applied, although intensification is as a rule more frequently associated with adjectives and adverbs, *cf* 'varii-varii (*again*) samjhaaoomãas (*I explained to him*)' (again and again I explained (it) to him), 'mũhjaa (*my*) ghaɳaa-ghaɳaa (*good*) salaama (*wishes*) ɖ'ijaĩis (*give to him*)' (Give him my very best wishes). Let us look briefly at adjectival reduplication in the adjective-noun phrase, wherein both complete reduplication and 'b''-reduplication regularly occur. Simultaneous reduplication in both the adjectival and the nominal place is rare and inadmissible with reduplication of the same type.

Reduplication with 'b'' is 'approximative', *eg* 'thuloo-b'uloo (*fat*) mard (*man*)' (a fattish man), complete reduplication is 'intensive' *eg* 'thuloo-thuloo mard' (a very fat man). A complete reduplicate cannot be preceded by the intensifying adjectival form 'ghaɳuu' but the latter may itself be reduplicated, *ie* 'ghaɳuu-ghaɳuu thuloo mard' (an extremely fat man). It appears that word-order – probably in association with unexplored phonological features – is important to the distinction between 'approximative' and 'intensive'. Thus, the order '*mard thuloo-b'uloo aahee' was not accepted by my informant, for whom nevertheless 'mard thuloo-thuloo aahee' was acceptable in the attenuated sense of 'he is rather a fat man' in comparison with 'thuloo-thuloo mard aahee' (he is a very fat man).

With certain adjectival forms, *eg* 'nãɖhoo' (*small*), 'b'' contrasts with 's', which marks greater intensification, *cf*

'nãɖhoo-b'ãɖhoo b'aar' (a smallish child)
'nãɖhoo-sãɖhoo b'aar' (a small child)
'nãɖhoo-nãɖhoo b'aar' (a very small child)
'ghaɳuu nãɖhoo b'aar' (an extremely small child)

Such possibilities of distinction are reduced by one when the isolated adjective itself begins with 'b'', *eg* 'b'uɖhoo' (old). In this case, 'b'uɖhoo-suɖhoo' does duty for 'oldish man' and 'any kind of old man' according to context. The prefix 's' is also used for the chiming component of 'b''-beginning *nominal* reduplicates, *eg* 'b'akirii-sakirii' (a goat or something). As a rule, however, 's' is specialized for adjectival reduplicates. In the presence of the diminutive ('affectionate') suffix 'ɽoo', however, no meaningful difference appears to attach to the threefold difference of form

'nãɖhiɽoo-b'ãɖhiɽoo b'aar'
'nãɖhiɽoo-sãɖhiɽoo b'aar' } (a dear little child)
'nãɖhiɽoo-nãɖhiɽoo b'aar'

Complete reduplication of a noun with '-ɽoo' does not occur; in contrast with adjectival 'nãɖhiɽoo-nãɖhiɽoo', we only find, *eg* 'kitaabiɽii (*little book*) -b'itaabiɽii'.

Meaning will depend *inter alia* on the particular noun accompanying the reduplicated adjective and on the cultural values of the society. As a subdivision of the category 'intensive' there has to be recognized on cultural grounds a distinction 'meliorative/pejorative' in accordance with whatever is liked or valued, feared or despised. 'kaaroo-kaaroo (*black*) deev (*devil*)' is translatable as 'a horrible black devil'; in contrast, 'parii' ((good) fairy), say, is never collocated with 'kaarii', but 'sũdar' or 'hasiina (*beautiful*) parii' will please and reassure the child listening to the fairy-tale. Similarly, black hair and eyes as well as pink cheeks are much valued in Sind, so that 'kaaraa-kaaraa vaara (*hair*)', 'kaariiũu-kaariiũu akhiiũu (*eyes*)' and 'g'aaɽha-g'aaɽha (*red*) g'illa (*cheeks*)' are properly translated 'nice black hair, nice black eyes, nice pink cheeks', while 'kaarii-kaarii' in similar association with 'ʃakil' can only be translated 'a nasty black face'. A noun like 'maiza' (table), for example, is neutral as to the 'meliorative/pejorative' distinction, thus 'kaarii-kaarii maiza' is 'a very black table'. It will be seen, therefore, that a good deal hangs on the apparently trivial distinctions represented in English by *-ish*, *nice* (*and*) –, *nasty* (*and*) –, *very*, etc. We must remember, too, that socio-cultural relevance also extends to the type of speaker and speaker-hearer relationship. Thus, differences in forms of reduplication correspond to differences of region, educational standard and class, and a given speaker may use different forms in what he considers to be necessary adjustment to the relationship obtaining between him and his interlocutor(s). Sindhi 'b''-reduplication, for example, is generally used to inferiors and peers, not to superiors; again, a Panjabi speaker with a knowledge of Urdu would sometimes prefer 'meez-veez' and sometimes 'meez-ʃeez', but would be unlikely ever to use 'meez-muuz'. These forms never occur in writing, whence the scornful designation of the feature in Urdu as 'muhmal' (slovenliness).

As has been said, it is not possible here to consider the innumerable patterns of reduplication in the language as a whole. Not only are verbal reduplicates greatly diverse in the nature and number of their patterns, but nouns and adjectives, too, would require much more to be said about them in any reasonably full treatment of the subject. With adjectives, for instance, we should need to consider the interpolation of particles like 'intensive' 'ii' (*eg* 'ughaaɽoo-ii-ughaaɽoo' (stark naked), 'akeeloo-ii-akeeloo' (utterly alone) , 'kaaroo-ii-kaaroo' (as black as black)) or the selection between the negative prefixes 'naa-', 'aɳa-', 's-', and 'a-' (*eg* 'vaakif-naavaakif' (efficient or not), 'paɽhiyalaɳapaʈhiyal' (literate or illiterate), 'abharoo-sabharoo' (thin or fat), 'sũuhũu-asũuhũu' (expert or fool)) or the comparable discontinuous prefixation of 'ɖ'-' and 's-' (*eg* 'ɖ'ukhiyoo-sukhiyoo' (uncomfortable or not) as in 'ɖ'ukhiyoo-sukhiyoo vakt (*time*) pioo [continuative aspect marker] guzaariyãa (*I pass*)' (I'm just about managing, *sc* neither impoverished nor well-off)). The prefix in such cases may be 'su-', which marks a meliorative antonymous relationship with the prior component of a reduplicate, *cf* 'ɖ'ukaar' (famine) -'sukaar' (abundance). Most commonly, 'su-' 'negates' a preceding pejorative 'ku-', *cf* 'kulachaɳuu' (ill-mannered) -'sulachaɳuu' (well behaved), 'kupat' (dishonesty) -'supat' (honesty). Sindhi makes endless play with antonyms of this kind and 'ku-' regularly occurs also in nominal reduplicates, *eg* 'mahla' (aptness, opportuneness) -'kumahla' (unsuitability, lateness), 'riit' (family custom) -'kuriit' (violation of custom), 'veej'' (country doctor) -'kuveej'' (quack). Elsewhere patterns of morphological relationship are more complex, *cf* 'ɖ'ukh' (grief) -'ɖ'aakhiʈoo' (difficulty), 'mũh' (face) -'muhãaɖoo' (features, appearance), 'ghaʈii' (street) -'ghoobii' (path), etc. In some cases, otherwise independent quasi-synonymous forms are juxtaposed, *cf* 'coor-cakaar' (thieves and vagabonds), 'sabhaag'oo-sadooroo' (of good character), 'nibhaag'oo-nidooroo' (of bad character). Some reduplicates of this kind – possibly borrowed from cognate languages with their own form of *muhmal* – are very similar to those with Sindhi 'b'', *eg* 'kam kaar' (any kind of work) versus 'kam' (a specific task) (*cf* 'vaɲii (*go*) pãhjoo (*own*) kam kaar kar (*do*)' (go and do some work of your own) versus 'vaɲii pãhjoo kam kar' (get on with your work)).

I shall not attempt to 'formalize' or write rules for the above facts of Sindhi reduplication, even if I were able to do so. There are in any case probably too many gaps in the data for this to be profitably undertaken at present. I like to think that the distinctions recognized could be accommodated within a transformational-generative mode of presentation but it is not for the time being clear to me whether or not this is feasible. Moreover, the raison d'être of this fairly lengthy exposé of reduplication in an Indo-Pakistan language has simply been to indicate something of the kind of phonological, lexical, and grammatical distinctions that need to be accounted for among others in fully meaningful linguistic analysis. There is no point in formalism for formalism's sake.

Turning now to phonetics, 'brute' phonetic fact is unknowable and consequently adherence to a 'general', *a*-linguistic phonetics is misplaced. It would, for instance, be wrong to consider the chart of the International Phonetic Association as embodying general categories of phonic experience rather than amalgamating *grosso modo* phonemic distinctions of individual languages and conceivably of English and French in particular; distinctions, that is, of graphic form as much as anything within the amplified framework of the roman alphabet. If in a practical phonetics class the Arabic word 'qɑssam' is dictated for ear-training purposes to a group of English-speakers with no knowledge of Arabic, one may feel reasonably confident that most if not all of them will indicate length for the intervocalic consonant and equally confident that this will at least partly be attributable to their regular discrimination between short and long consonants in similar English intervocalic environments, albeit usually at morphological boundaries. However, had they been given the sentence 'atəf dəttəqqəsʃ əlbab' [æ·tf dttqqʃʃ lbæ·b] (come in and don't shut the door) from the Berber dialect of the town of Zuara in (Libyan) Tripolitania near the Tunisian frontier,[5] then they would have been hard put to know whether to write short or long in a number of places, if the question ever occurred to them. It can be plausibly maintained that phonetic transcription can be successfully undertaken only after appropriate comparisons have been made and meaningful discriminations established, so that the foregoing transcription in square brackets depends for its form on contrastive relations which centrally concern the investigator from the very outset of work with the informant. Reading conventions of the coarsest mesh – as for example those relating to θ, s, t, and T in our transcription – must have regard *ab initio* to interdependencies between phonetic complexes so labelled.

Relativity in language is, then, phonetic and phonological as well as lexical and grammatical, and, since it is sometimes supposed that there are phonetic 'facts' of a universal kind other than those appertaining to the phonatory and auditory potential of the human mechanism of utterance and perception, let us stay briefly with phonology. Consider, for instance, the syllable. It is often thought that most people are able to say without difficulty how many syllables are contained in a given word or sentence, but who are the people in question? Sindhis, say, spell 'juld' (binding, book-cover) and 'amb' (mango) – both monosyllabic to the English ear (and eye) – as if these words comprise three and two syllables respectively, and no Englishman would be likely to agree with the native speaker of Japanese that the Japanese pronunciation of *Nippon* contains four syllables. It would be much nearer the mark to say that 'syllable' has so far defied attempts at definition in any 'general phonetic' sense, and more profitable to stress the difference between a phonetic (generalized phonological?) syllable, probably perceived in terms of one's native language and at most its cognates, and the syllables and patterns of syllables one finds oneself recognizing in the process of analysing and presenting in the simplest, most economical way the systematic phonology of this or that language or part language. Where, one wonders, is the 'general phonetic' criterion by which one may recognize in Zuara Berber the form 'asəttas' [æˈsttæ·s] as trisyllabic. True, one perceives (by self-reference, of course) a considerable increase of breath-force during the voiceless phase of articulation also characterized by successive sibilance and dental closure ([-stt-]), and a diminution of such force subsequently. But one is aware *at the same time* of the shortness of the vowel in the first syllable and of the low monotone at which the vowels preceding and following [-stt-] are both pitched. Moreover, one feels that this awareness does not derive from anything inherent in the single form itself but rather from the meaningful contrastive relationships into which the form enters with the grammatically comparable forms 'asdətas' [ˈæːsttæ·s], in which not only is the pattern of breath-force different but the first syllable is longer and associated with falling tone, and 'asəddyas' [æˈsɪd·jæ·s], in which a voiced phase of articulation succeeds the sibilant, while the pitch pattern is low-high-low. If on these grounds, supported by such evidence elsewhere as the behaviour of ə in contrast with other vowels, it is reasonable to recognize 'asəttas' as phonologically trisyllabic, it will be seen among other things that neither intercostal chest 'pulses' nor vowels nor 'liquid' vowel-like consonants are necessary as syllabic determinants in any 'general phonetic' sense to underpin syllabic structures we may posit in phonological terms. The inclusion of 'ə' in 'asəttas' carries with it all the implications for the contrastive relations accreted by the form and which we have attempted to describe. The transcribed form 'asəttas', and for that matter [aˈsttæ·s], too, is a long way from 'brute phonetic fact'. These are simply ways of writing one end-point of a relational network in the speaker's linguistic organization.[6]

Firth used to warn, too, against those *faux amis* of the linguist, terms which, while apparently similar in related languages or even different disciplines, tend to conceal considerable differences of interpretation. It appears that we do not even 'see' the same phonetic facts or talk the same phonetic way as between France and Great Britain, for instance. Some research is necessary before one discovers that Martinet's *spirante vélaire profonde* in his *Description Phonologique* (*avec application au parler franco-provençal d'Hauteville* (*Savoie*))[7] corresponds to the British 'uvular fricative' and that the use of *profond* derives from the French (? continental European) tendency to view the mechanism of utterance vertically, so to speak, in contrast with the British side view. One may suppose that, strictly speaking, translation between French and English in the field of elementary phonetic description is impossible when the French divide the tongue simply into *la pointe* and *le dos* in comparison with the British 'tip, blade, front, back'. And what corresponds in current English terminology to the usual French division of palatal, pre-palatal, and post-palatal articulation, not to mention *la voûte du palais*, at some vertical remove from the depths of the uvula? Yet linguists bandy such terms about as if they 'mean the same' to all of us. The physical processes of peristalsis and anti-peristalsis are no doubt uncomfortably familiar to Arabs, Frenchmen, and Englishmen alike, and it is certainly useful for non-Arabs to learn something about these processes if they wish to master certain features of Arabic pronunciation, notably pharyngalization. But we should not suppose that we shall all talk about the facts in the same way. It is, for example – on the different topic of 'emphasis' in Arabic – the segmentation implied and imposed by our roman ways of notation and description that tends to obscure for the Englishman and the Frenchman the fact that the initial consonants and the vowels of, say, the Arabic letter-names 'taaˡ' and 'Tɑɑˡ' share positive contrastive features of tongue and lip articulation, *ie* 'ta' must be considered as a whole in contrast with 'Tɑ'. We shall return to this topic. In the meantime, it seems clear enough that we need greatly to sharpen our awareness of such matters and to seek new and less confusing modes of observation and description. As far as phonology is concerned, Firth hoped to meet the need by his 'prosodic approach', to which attention is paid in the following essay. In the meantime, we have to define even our supposedly 'general phonetic' terms; it is, for example, remarkable how much overlap there is in the literature between such terms as breath, voicelessness, aspiration, lenition, etc.

'Phonic data' might reasonably be considered to derive from the extra-linguistic sound-making capacity of the human phonatory apparatus and nothing that has been said above should be held to imply that it is not incumbent upon the linguist to sensitize himself in this 'general' sense to the limit of his ability. Failure to do so accounts, for example, for the present quite unsatisfactory use that is made of the term *pharyngalized* in British and American linguistic usage. It is a noticeable feature of languages like Arabic and Berber that they make systematic use of consonant articulations that are characterized in important part by the 'fusing' of the epiglottal fold with the rest of the tongue and by the drawing down and back of the whole tongue mass within the pharynx in such a way as to restrict the passage of air between the base of the tongue and the pharynx wall. It is also possible to restrict the air passage between the top of the trachea and the under-surface of the epiglottal fold, leaving a comparatively open pharynx, and it is the writer's belief that this type of articulation occurs in the Berber speech of Zuara in Tripolitania. Neither of these articulatory complexes is easy to control if one is not to the manner born and this may explain the confusion that has arisen in the classificatory schemes of British and American phoneticians and linguists, who seem to regard any degree of restriction of the pharyngal cavity – as, for example, in the pronunciation of a fully back open vowel – as 'pharyngalization'. Now Arabic and Berber are also characterized, as we have seen, by what are sometimes called 'emphatic' consonants, which are distinguished *grosso modo* by lateral expansion of the tongue and by its flattening in the mouth in contrast with the lateral contraction and forward tongue raising appropriate to 'non-emphatic' correlative consonants. It so happens that the 'flattening' referred to carries with it a concomitant reduction of the pharyngal cavity in contrast with the open pharynx that accompanies 'forward raising' and this has led 'Anglo-American' linguists to talk – quite inappropriately – of the emphatic consonants as 'pharyngalized'. This term has tended to replace an earlier, equally unsatisfactory 'velarized', used in response to a belief that the articulatory types in question were significantly characterized by the raising of the back of the tongue towards the velum. Properly termed pharyngalization, regularly occurring in these languages and cursorily described above, is a feature with which it is perfectly possible to imbue one's speech *passim*, as with, say, 'a nasal twang', so that a properly pharyngalized 'l' is greatly different from the 'emphatic' 'L' of *eg* 'ˈɑLLɑɑh' (God) in Arabic, notwithstanding the frequent reference to 'L' nowadays as pharyngalized. 'Emphasis', moreover, as we shall see, always relates to a complex of features, consonantal and vocalic, and cannot be located within a minimal consonantal segment in any meaningful way.[8] The linguist's need, then, for what Firth used to call 'a phonetics quorum' as well as for the recognition of a measure of 'relativity' in the supposedly meaningless areas of 'general' phonetics would appear to be indisputable. Nor do we need the abnormality of the misquoted Hamlet of the title to discern the interesting particularities that in sum make up, not 'shreds and patches', but often enough the very fabric of a language.

Notes

1 Reading conventions for Arabic examples are to be found at the beginning of the book (*pp* xiii–xiv).

2 A detailed account of the facts as they relate to Cyrenaican Bedouin Arabic can be found in my 'Active participle in an Arabic dialect of Cyrenaica', *Bulletin of the School of Oriental and African Studies*, 14/1 (1952).

3 See the beginning of the book for Sindhi reading conventions. The spoken Sindhi on which statements here and elsewhere are based is that of Mr A. S. Hussaini, who acted as my informant at the School of Oriental and African Studies approximately twelve years ago. Mr Hussaini was a speaker of the important Lāṛī dialect of Sindhi, belonging to a region extending south-westwards towards the sea from a point near Hyderabad (Sind). He came from

Ţikhiŗ on the left bank of the Indus, 16 miles SSW of Hyderabad, but had resided in Hyderabad from the time he was 15 years old in 1947. Although Hyderabadi and so-called standard Sindhi had influenced him in minor ways, his speech was still clearly recognized and recognizable as belonging to the region of Ţikhiŗ. However, it is not our purpose to draw attention to, say, Mr Hussaini's use of 'ãauu' (I) for 'maa' elsewhere; for practical purposes, what is said here of Sindhi can be regarded as applicable to whatever form of the language.

4 The form of the 'replacement' varies considerably from one language to another in the area and even between dialects of the same language; *cf* Urdu and Panjabi 'meez-veez', Panjabi 'rooţii-ʃooţii', 'standard' Sindhi 'maanii-b'aanii', northern Sindhi 'maanii-dhaanii', etc. Nor is it always the initiating *consonant* on which the change is rung: *cf*, for example, Panjabi 'meez-muuz'. Reduplication in these languages, including that involving the verb, is extremely complex in its exponency.

5 Reference to Berber in this volume is exclusively to this dialect and is based on the speech of Mr Ramadan Hadji Azzabi, with whom I worked for approximately two years in the early 1950s. Mr Azzabi was then 25, a native of Zuara, having lived there almost continuously from birth. His mother and father, brothers and sisters, were all natives of Zuara, and Berber was the language of the home. Appropriate reading conventions are given at the beginning of the book (*pp* xiv–xv).

6 Nor does the foregoing represent a complete account of relevant facts. Differences in the 'realization' of 'ə' correspond to various differences of contextual factor, for example the number of surrounding consonants – *cf* 'as(ə)tməl' (she will tell him) versus 'asəttməl' (she will tell it to him).

7 Geneva. Droz, 1956.

8 It is with regret that I am compelled to say of Roman Jakobson's article 'Mufaxxama: the emphatic phonemes of Arabic' (in *Studies Presented to J. Whatmough* (The Hague, 1957), *pp* 105–15; lately reprinted in *Phonolədʒi*, ed E. C. Fudge (Penguin, 1973), *pp* 159–71), that it is seriously misleading in the treatment it accords to 'emphasis' in Arabic, partly because of the confusion with pharyngal articulation referred to here and, more importantly, because 'emphasis' is *not* reducible to a single feature. Misconception is understandable since Jakobson has had to rely on others' earlier observations, which in my opinion are inadequate.

Two

'Not of the letter, but of the spirit; for the letter killeth, but the spirit giveth life.'

The narrow segmentalism of phonemics entailed the ignoring or at best obscuring of many regularities of phonetic form extending beyond the domains of written phonemes. Phonological analysis in prosodic terms covers not only cases of homogeneous features, fluctuating or stable, continuous or discontinuous as to domain, but also relationships of dependency and constraint. These relationships involve homogeneous and heterogeneous features in (mutual) accompaniment as well as selectional constraints between features.

A rose by any other name would smell as sweet, they say, but it is poor advice, and it may be that Firth's use of 'prosody' (*anima vocis*, as he sometimes saw a particular prosody) came to bear so little resemblance to the more traditional use of the term in reference to such features as accentuation, length, quantity, pitch, and the like, as to verge on arbitrariness. This, however, is by no means to diminish the importance of those features to which he wished attention to be drawn in terms of his 'prosodic approach'. As we shall see, prosodic features are of several kinds, all of them sharing relatability to domains *in extenso* in the speech continuum, both to 'concord of sweet sounds' and accompaniment of 'strange bedfellows'.

Firthianism lays great stress not only on 'pervasive' features of linguistic form, 'threads', as it were, of the fabric of speech, but also on dependencies and constraints of a syntagmatic kind, grammatical and lexical no less than phonological. In many languages, certain possibilities of *eg* phonetic form are either determined or excluded at given structural places or over given domains by the occurrence of this or that feature or complex of features elsewhere. It is this simple fact that underlies Firth's insistence on the need for what he called a 'polysystemic' approach to analysis, by which he intended that for instance in phonology we should recognize systems of unitary distinctions appropriate to *initial* consonantal and vocalic elements in contrast with those applicable to *final* and variously *medial* counterparts, or relevant to *tonic* syllables in opposition to *atonic* syllables, or again apt to *short* vowels versus *long* vowels, etc, and this to the utmost degree of refinement consistent with the facts in given cases. Yet such considerations apply as much to other levels as phonology, and 'prosody' would probably have been best reserved for syntagmatic features and relations of phonetic form. True, since we are first and foremost concerned to study spoken language, the use and comprehension thereof must constantly be referred to phonetic categories and we should clearly expect to find frequent congruence and interaction between phonological and lexico-grammatical analysis. After all, we use the resources of our phonatory and auditory capacity to be meaningful in a predominantly systematic manner. It is not surprising, therefore, that the prosodic phonologist wishes to undertake his analyses 'within a grammatical framework', so that for instance the distinction between final close and half-close back rounded vowels following a nasal consonant in Sindhi, a distinction that is applicable to certain form classes and not others (*eg* proper names versus adjectives), is seen as 'prosodic'. But it is only so in a polysystemic sense, and 'polysystemicity' is not an exclusively phonological concept, although it has clear advantages in phonological statement. Firth himself considered a prosodic feature – no example of which is discernible in the example just quoted – as an 'integrating feature', whether integration was seen as between parts of a structural whole or between levels of analysis. He held that statement at whatever level must be 'referred to phonetics', but this neither suggests that the polysystemic is exclusively prosodic nor that phonology is – as seen by some – a 'bridge to grammar'. All speech is in an obvious sense phonetic form, but it is seemingly structured in such a way as to enable us to talk about it in recognizably grammatical versus lexical versus phonological terms, notwithstanding a measure of overlap and even dependence between these 'levels'. It should, therefore, be possible to restrict the terms 'prosody' and 'prosodic feature', if we wish to use them at all, to phonological discourse. This would not, of course, preclude us from closely examining the exploitation of particular prosodies in languages, from seeing for example how 'vowel harmony' is used in various language-specific and grammatically specialized ways. Uses may be many and diverse, embracing the morphological, the syntactic, even the functional and situational, as well as the purely phonological. Although one may wish to confine 'prosodics' to phonology and even to formulate prosodic facts 'within a grammatical framework' where appropriate, nevertheless this may not suffice and we shall often need to be more specific about the use made of a given feature or features. Nor, *a priori*, should we expect phonological features, prosodic or otherwise, to be specialized in grammatical use. They may be, but they may also not be.

Polysystemicity, then, is logically no particular part of the Firthian 'prosodic approach', except insofar as it answers the need to account for the manifold syntagmatic features overlooked by an explanatorily inadequate phonemics, obsessively concerned with minimal segmentation and often enough confusing an alphabetic-type simplification with analytical simplicity.[1] Those interested in the more theoretical aspects of prosodic analysis may refer to recent writings on the subject.[2] Here we are concerned rather to exemplify some of the regularities of 'phonetic form' common in languages of the writer's experience to which prosodic analysis is apt in contradistinction to any other form of linguistic analysis to date.

It is, of course, well known that the glides to and from consonants and vowels are in all cases *sui generis* according to the articulatory types involved, and it is even conceivable that we may respond to differences between such glides rather than to any supposed inherent properties of consonantal and vocalic type. Prosodic phonology, however, does not seek to substitute new minimal segments (glides) for old (consonants, vowels) but rather to stress that segmentation of the phonemic – and often enough subphonemic – kind is misleading, since features are clearly determined mutually or shared by consonants and vowels. Nor, as we shall see, do such features have to be continuous. Every language or dialect makes its own use of all the potential minutiae of phonetic form and no less in a maximally segmental way than any other. There is no physical reason why what is labelled /t/ in phonemic manner in the Arabic letter-name /taaʔ/ should be followed by a phonetically *front* vowel, nor that /T/ in corresponding /Tɑɑʔ/ should be followed by a *back* vowel; it is perfectly possible to pronounce the complexes concerned in contrary fashion but it would be quite un-Arabic to do so. Nor is it just a matter of regularly different accompaniment; articulatory features are in both cases shared by consonant and vowel. It is not only that there is no single feature that can plausibly or usefully be singled out and labelled 'non-emphatic' or 'emphatic', not only that /t/ as pronounced in high Classical style in Egypt, for instance, must be recognized from the beginning of research not simply as plosive, denti-alveolar, and voiceless but also – in contrast with comparable features of /T/ – as characterized by lateral contraction of the tongue along its length, by front and forward raising of the tongue with concomitantly open pharynx as for a close front vowel, and by lip-spreading; it is not only these things, be it said, but also that the front raised component characterizes the whole segment labelled /ta/ in contrast with the 'flattened' component characteristic of /Tɑ/. This 'sharing' of articulatory feature is positively obscured by our roman terminological and notational habits of segmentation. The same 'blinkers' no doubt have limited European and American linguists to believing that /T/ alone requires special descriptive effort and that there are no relevant 'non-emphatic' features of /t/, which is typically categorized as a 'voiceless dental plosive' *tout court*. A prosodic approach would ascribe the accompanying characteristics of consonant and vowel to the prosodic features of emphasis [+e] versus non-emphasis [−e] and residual properties to what are termed phonematic units, which do not in the least resemble phonemes. The initial consonantal feature-complexes of the two letter-names – to the limited extent to which we are at present considering them – comprise voicelessness, denti-alveolarity and plosion, in addition to either emphasis or non-emphasis. Once the latter have been abstracted as prosodies, then the symbols /t/ and /T/ would be precluded from any prosodic transcription, and a different method of transcribing phonematic units – employing, say, Greek letters – would be advantageous. Disregarding length and other regular contrastive relations into which the two forms enter, we might transcribe them in preliminary fashion as $\underset{.}{\tau}\alpha^{\pm e}$.[3]

It will be seen from the foregoing that for Arabic among other languages the conventions on which, for instance, much of the International Phonetic Association's chart is based, are often inadequate even for the limited purpose of establishing the reading conventions to be attached to a set of roman alphabetic symbols. For example, in order to disambiguate the necessary instructions to the reader, such terms as 'sulcal' and 'non-sulcal' are needed for some forms of Arabic in relation to symbols /s/ and /θ/, representative of articulatory complexes which include voicelessness, friction, denti-alveolarity, and non-emphasis. While there is an obvious requirement for the linguist to familiarize himself as best he may with the processes of spoken utterance in general human terms, what can 'general phonetics' be but 'generalized phonology'? Are there taxonomic categories of any real linguistic interest that are applicable to the identification, description, and explanation of the elements of any utterance without regard to meaningful discriminations maintained in the particular language in question? It should, however, perhaps be observed in passing that prosodic phonology has sought to break loose from phonemic alphabetic fetters by insisting less on subphonemic features than on broader-than-phonematic domains, and in particular on that of the syllable, as frames of prosodic reference. It is true, for example, that the domain of emphasis versus non-emphasis in Arabic and Berber is never less than syllabic, but nevertheless to enshrine a somewhat unsatisfactorily defined entity as the basic unit of prosodic analysis is to beg questions, and all that can surely be said is that by definition the domain of any prosodic feature or interdependence of feature must extend beyond that of any single phonematic unit.

We should distinguish between, on the one hand, prosodic features and associated complexes of features and, on the other hand, prosodic relationships of compatibility and, probably more importantly, incompatibility between entities, in brief between syntagmatic inclusion and exclusion. Moreover, one is as much concerned in prosodic analysis with complex accompaniments of interdependent features, that is with structural dependency of feature, as with homogeneous features, continuous or discontinuous, spread over a given syntagmatic domain. When one looks in greater detail at the facts of Arabic or Berber emphasis versus non-emphasis, for example, one finds that consonantal and vocalic form are mutually determining in ways unrelated to the occurrence of any homogeneous phonetic feature. Such 'relationship' is more directly comparable with, say, incompatibility between consonantal features in successive places and, therefore, differs logically from, shall we say, nasality or breath found to be characteristic of a particular domain. Prosodic relationships, then, concern the numerous syntagmatic (inter-)dependencies and constraints, compatibilities and incompatibilities that are regularly discernible as much between phonetic features as between lexical items and grammatical classes in the organization of a language. They involve, for example, the consonantal incompatibilities within an Arabic root that are briefly reviewed below as well as those features that are characteristic of, let us say, initiality or finality in utterance and therefore in special relationship with the feature of pause.

Prosodic analysis in the writings of the so-called London school of linguists is closely tied to the syllable and syllable features that (i) run through the whole syllable and 'modify' the articulation of all segments in the syllable, marking them as components of a larger unit (lip-rounding or spreading are fairly typical examples) or (ii) mark a particular type of syllable (*eg* the association of tonicity with length in Arabic oxytones) or (iii) characterize one or more segments in relation to a given position in a syllable (*eg* initial, medial, final). Thus, syllable features do not occupy places within the syllable but rather belong to the whole or part of it, marking its unity or boundaries. As was said earlier, however, there seems no reason why the syllable should be given any pride of place in prosodic analysis; it may well be that much will depend upon the facts of particular languages. It is not only that there is no agreed definition of syllable in any general phonetic sense, or that it often appears necessary to distinguish between phonetic and phonological syllables (as, for example, when [ˈfɪlu] 'foal' in Cyrenaican Arabic is 'interpreted' as /filw/ or, more generally, CVCC, in order to facilitate the generalization of rules of accentuation and the accommodation of such forms as *eg* [ˈfɪlwʌ] 'his foal'), or again that in literate societies syllabication is closely bound up with habits of spelling, not only these matters require consideration but also the fact that regularities of accompaniment often do not correspond to syllable divisions; *cf*, for example, the voicelessness characteristic of the final cluster in *eg* Cairene 'sabt' (Saturday), which belongs to easily statable regularities in the distribution of voice and voicelessness over consonant clusters in the language, or the homorganic plosive-nasal clusters of the Devonian English forms [ɛbm] 'hasn't, haven't; heaven', [dɛbm] 'Devon', [ɪdn] 'isn't', [twʌdn] 'it wasn't', etc, or again the nasality which before plosive consonants within the same indigenous Urdu root takes forms varying between a long nasal vowel when the plosive is voiceless (*eg* 'sãap' [sãːp] (snake)), a combination of half-long nasal vowel and half-long nasal consonant homorganic with a following *voiced* plosive (*eg* 'sãaɖ' [sɑ·ⁿɖ] (buffalo)), or a less than fully nasal vowel and a longer homorganic nasal consonant when the vowel is short (*eg* 'rãg' [rʌŋg] (colour), 'lãbaa' [lʌmbɑ·] (long, tall), 'ãɖaa' [ʌɳɖɑ·] (egg), etc). The following are important Urdu contrasts, in more or less logical 'pecking order':

1 indigenous [−loan] versus loan material.

2 ~C versus n+C, where ~ = varying forms of nasality preceding C, and + = morphological junction (*cf* 'lãbaa' above but 'an+paɽh' [ʌnp−]).

3 C^{+p} versus C^{-p}, where plosivity [+p] and its absence [−p] are prosodic relational features referable to C, since the phonetic forms of nasality and their morphological exploitation differ between C^{+p} and C^{-p} (*cf* C^{-p} = s, *eg* 'hãs-'[hʌ̃s][4] (stem of 'hãsnaa' (to laugh)) versus 'hans' [hʌns] (swan)).

4 $C^{\left[\substack{+p\\+v}\right]}$ versus $C^{\left[\substack{+p\\-v}\right]}$, where the features of voice [+v] and voicelessness [−v] located at C are likewise prosodic relational features but here lack any morphological implications.

5 C^{+s} versus C^{-s}, where shortness [+s] and length [−s] are relational features of V, prosodic since C is typically long after V^{+s} and short after V^{-s}. Lengthening of C takes the form nC (n = nasal

consonant) in the context of the nasality prosody (see 6).

6 $\overset{+n}{\overline{VC^{+p}}}$ versus $\overset{-n}{\overline{VC^{+p}}}$, where the several forms of prosodic nasality [+n] and its absence [−n] involve V and C simultaneously.

The threefold distinction recognized for nasality can be expressed as follows:

$$\overset{+n_3}{\overline{V^{+s}C^{+p}}}$$ (*eg* rãg)

$$V^{-s}C^{\left[\substack{+p\\-v}\right]}$$ (*eg* sãap)

$$V^{-s}C^{\left[\substack{+p\\+v}\right]}$$ (*eg* sãaḍ)

There are doubtless other things to be said on the subject but perhaps sufficient indication has been given of the fact that the syllable is of no particular relevance to the prosodic features and relationships in question. Again, lip-rounding – a favourite candidate for prosodic status elsewhere – characterizes in the Arabic of Marrakesh in Morocco not only the whole of the first syllable but also the whole of the velar phase of *eg* 'sukkaan' (inhabitants) and contains a marked labio-velar off-glide from the velar phase to that of the long open vowel. In the same form of Arabic, there is no 'phonic' justification for recognizing any vocalic element between the first two consonants of either verbal 'tqaal' (he became heavy) or adjectival 't(u)qaal' (heavy [pl]); in the latter case, however, the cluster 'tq-' is pronounced with strong lip-rounding throughout and labio-velar off-glide from the uvular plosive, in contrast with the 'neutral' lip action and lack of comparable glide in the verbal correlative form. For the purposes of a reading transcription and, as it happens, pan-Arabic simplicity (synchronic and diachronic), it is reasonable to write the adjectival form as 'tuqaal'. The two forms are, however, better indicated – in somewhat rough and ready prosodic transcription – as follows: (+w = lip-rounding, and −w its absence)

$$\overset{+w}{\overline{\text{tq}}}\ \overset{-w}{\overline{\text{aal}}}\ \text{[adj]} : \overset{-w}{\overline{\text{tqaal}}}\ \text{[vb]}$$

There are innumerable similar contrasts in Marrakshi Arabic; *cf*

$\overset{+w}{\overline{\text{kəbb}}}\ \overset{-w}{\overline{\text{a}}}$ 'skein' : $\overset{-w}{\overline{\text{xərba}}}$ 'hovel, ruin'

$\overset{+w}{\overline{\text{xf}}}\ \overset{-w}{\overline{\text{aaf}}}$ 'light [pl adj]' : $\overset{-w}{\overline{\text{xfaaf}}}$ 'became light'

+w −w −w
'gazelle' : 'tribal name'
ɣ zaala glaawa

+w −w −w
'just now' : 'tribe'
gb iila qbiila

+w −w −w
'baggage' : 'it (fem) has been fried'
təq laat ttəqlaat

+w −w −w
'pomegranates' : 'buttermilk seller'
Rəmm aan ləbbaan

+w −w −w
'rapping, tapping' : 'jeweller'
dəgg aan dəggaag

+w −w −w
'fodder' : 'large conical laundry basket'
nəxx aal bəxxaaRa

+w −w −w
'antimony' : 'black'
k ħəl kħəl

+w −w
'come in! [masc]' : 'he came in'[5]
dxəl dxəl

The foregoing left-hand examples of 'mixed' prosodic form are all of a sequence +w∼−w. There may well be some grammatical specialization of sequence but −w∼+w also occurs and even −w∼+w∼−w (as, for instance, in the loan from Berber

−w +w −w
'perverseness').
aa ɣ naan

The passive participle (məCCuuC) is characterized by rounding in the ultimate syllable and illustrates the sequence −w∼+w. Length apart, backness and closeness are also associated with the vowel of this ultimate syllable in other forms of Arabic, but variation between front (centralized), close to half-close quality in the context of non-emphasis, on the one hand, and back (centralized), half-open quality in that of emphasis, on the other, is strikingly characteristic of a Moroccan pronunciation of the final syllables of *eg* 'mədfuun' [−øːn] (buried) versus 'məjbuuR' [−ɔːr] (found (by accident); compelled). The syllable is nevertheless rounded in both cases.[6] It will be seen from this comparatively straightforward example that the sorting out of prosodic features and their 'correct' apportionment among categories is not a simple matter. The reader will probably have already formed a hypothesis from perusal of the above examples as to the restriction of the rounding versus non-rounding contrast – in contexts not involving vowel length – to the environmental occurrence of consonantal velarity and/or labiality. Clearly, such facts would have to be accounted for in any thoroughgoing analysis; we shall not do so here but shall return below to somewhat similar considerations in regard to Cyrenaican Arabic. In passing, the comment should perhaps be made that it is behaviour of this kind that enables one usefully to distinguish broad articulatory categories in the analysis of Semitic languages and justifies an otherwise unspecifiable 'liquidity' attaching to nasals, laterals, and 'r'-consonants (their own kind of laterals) in the language. We return to the topic later. In the meantime, let us notice again from the Moroccan examples cited that the nature of the environmental consonant/s has important implications for the *extent* of the +w or −w domain, that, in all the above cases of +w∼−w 'mixture', initiating +w does not extend to include the second consonant within its domain unless this consonant is characterized by either velarity or labiality; other examples would include

+w −w
xf aaf 'light [pl adj]' versus +w −w
ɣ Rɑɑb 'crow';

+w −w
ɣb ɑɑR 'dung-heap' versus +w −w
ɣ Lɑɑ 'dearness';

+w −w
rukb ɑ 'knee' versus +w −w
lək ħəl 'the antimony'.

+w −w
ff aaqa 'people upstairs', +w −w
bb aaqəl 'parts of well', and +w −w
mm aagən 'watches', plural forms corresponding to *eg* 'jwaaməɡ' (mosques), 'ʃwaarəb' (lips), 'ħwaanət' (shops) elsewhere in the dialect, are characterized morphologically among other things by the infixation of '–w–' after the first consonant of the root, *ie* 'f', 'b', 'm', 'j', 'ʃ', 'ħ' in the examples given. Phonologically, the prosodic gemination and rounding of the initial consonant (+labio-velar off-glide) is associated with its labiality. Once more it is behaviour of this kind that serves to mark off a labial group among Arabic consonants; further east in the Bedouin Arabic of Cyrenaica, the plural pattern miC1aC2iiC3, for instance, is 'subject' to the omission of the first vowel and consequent initial clustering when C1 is labial, *cf* 'mfatiiħ' (keys) versus 'mikatiib' (letters). Of course, the CVC– sequence (mik–) is determined by interrelationship of consonantal feature and is therefore as much a matter of prosodic pattern as CC– (mf–). To return to Marrakesh, we also find there among the invariably interesting Arabic nouns of relationship such forms as

$\overset{+w}{\text{bb}}\ \overset{-w}{\text{ɑ}}$ '(my) father', $\overset{+w}{\text{bb}}\ \overset{-w}{\text{eeh}}$ 'his father',

$\overset{+w}{\text{mm}}\ \overset{-w}{\text{i}}$ '(my) mother', $\overset{+w}{\text{mmo}}$ 'his mother'.

It seems clear from the behaviour of labials elsewhere that here too we are concerned with the morphological association of 'w' and a labial consonant. For other transcriptional purposes, it would be unambiguous to write *eg* 'bwa' (or even 'wba'), 'mwi' (or even 'wmi') and in such guise the apparently somewhat outlandish Marrakshi forms do not seem so far apart from *eg* 'ˈabu' and 'ˈum(m)' encountered elsewhere. It is noteworthy too that in the case of 'mmo' (his mother) and in contrast with all preceding examples, the domain of +w extends to include the final (rounded) vowel; nor does pronunciation include a labio-velar off-glide from the bilabial nasal phase. Switching the grammatical category, another example of such extension would be, say, $\overset{-w}{\text{itt}}\ \overset{+w}{\text{fukkoo}}$ (they free themselves), again without the labio-velar off-glide from the velar plosive, a glide characteristic of other vocalic environments. These facts of prosodic domain suggest that, in transformational-generative terms, prosodies would belong to 'surface structure', but we must not allow ourselves to be misled by the association of 'surface' with 'superficial' into detracting from the inherent interest of prosodic analysis. The many hitherto disregarded regularities of pronunciation to which it draws attention are not simply interesting for, say, any typological implications they may have, nor do they belong only to the increasingly important sociolinguistic field that Firth was anxious to cultivate; they are meaningfully relevant 'across the board' of linguistic analysis, which ignores them at the risk of its own impoverishment. But we should return now to the outline classification of types of prosody that was spoken of earlier.

Classification, then, is in terms of phonology rather than specifically of the grammatical, lexical, dialectal or functional exploitation of prosodic features, and takes the following broad lines:

A. (presence or absence of *feature*)
Covers cases of homogeneous features (*eg* breath, tone, openness, etc), which may be either continuous (and fluctuating or stable as to domain) or discontinuous.

B. (structural *relationships* of dependency and constraint)
Subsumes both homogeneous and heterogeneous features in mutual accompaniment (dependency) (*eg* consonant and vowel in

Arabic or Berber) and that of selectional constraints operative between features, so that 'x' precludes 'y' (*eg* incompatibility of consonantal features within Arabic or Berber roots).

Let us look at some further examples.

Firstly, those features that cannot be allotted linear 'place', however much we find ourselves compelled to do so by the irrelevant constrictions of writing. It is sometimes instructive to consider spelling practice in this or that language. Sindhi spelling reflects the influence of the Devanagari syllabary and is as well adapted to the phonological structure of the language as its specially contrived form of the Persi-Arabic script permits. My informant regularly spelled Sindhi words in the form of a succession of syllables, individually spelled and pronounced before the whole word was pronounced. Pride of syllabic place went to the syllable-opening letter and reference to a particular syllable was terminated by the name of a vowel sign, either a letter ('alf', 'yee', 'vaa') or, more often, a diacritic ('zabara', 'zeer', 'peeʃ'). Thus, with 'siin' (s) opening the syllable, the possibilities were:

siin + zabara = sa
„ + zeer = si
„ + peeʃ = su
„ + alf = saa
„ + yee = see
„ + vaa = soo

Vowel letters and diacritica may combine in that order, so that

siin + yee + zabara = sai
„ „ + zeer = sii
„ + vaa + zabara = sau
„ „ + peeʃ = suu

Now the interesting thing is that nasality ('nuun' = letter n) and breath ('hee' = letter h) are treated as syllable features in the same way as the foregoing vowels. In common, and *only* in common with 'alf', 'yee', and 'vaa', they precede the name of a diacritic before the pronunciation of an individual syllable and are even interposed between a vowel letter-name and the terminating diacritic (written, incidentally, above the initiating consonant). Both features are illustrated in the first and last syllables in the spelling of *eg* 'pahriyũu'[7], *viz* 'pee hee zabara' [p$\overset{\text{ɦ}}{\text{ɛ}}$ɦ], 'ree zeer' [rï], 'yee vaa nuun peeʃ' [jũː] – [p$\overset{\text{ɦ}}{\text{ɛ}}$·ɦrijũ]. The form of homorganic nasality alluded to elsewhere is illustrated by *eg* 'mãɖ' (incantation), *viz* 'miim nuun zabara' [mɛ̃], 'ɖee peeʃ' [ɖø̈] – [mʌɳɖᵊ]. But breath and nasality are more-than-syllable

features and the facts of their occurrence and indeed co-occurrence are not by any means accounted for by Sindhi spelling, however significant the hints it provides. Both features are coterminous in monosyllabic ‘b’ãah’ (arm), for example, but spelling has to reflect grammar and lexicon as well as phonology and Sindhi nouns are subject to final short vowel inflection in terms of gender, number, and case; there are no monosyllabic nouns in Sindhi spelling, whatever the phonological facts of *eg* Lāṛī speech. Thus, the ‘alf’ (aa) of ‘b’ãah’ cannot be the final vowel in spelling and it is necessary to devise some means of spelling the word as a disyllable. For this purpose, ‘h’ – never a minimally segmental consonant in the language – is treated as opening a second syllable, and ‘nuun’ – the sign both of a nasal prosody (labelled ‘sung nuun’) and of a nasal segmental consonant – is repeated for both syllables, *ie* ‘b’ee alf nuun’ [b’ɑ̃ː], ‘hee nuun zeer’
ɦ
[ɦɪ̃] – [b’ɑ̃ːɦ].[8] It will be seen from these examples that nasality and breath are features often characterizing a whole syllable or sequence of syllables, whole words or sequences of words in Sindhi and related languages, features therefore that the usual type of linear analysis in terms of phonemes or subphonemic features can only distort. Undiminished breath and nasality belong *passim* to such Sindhi words as ‘aayhãa’ [spelled as if aa-hi-yãa] (I am) and breath only to ‘aahee’ (is), however we find ourselves obliged to place appropriate symbols in a transcription. Similarly, Urdu ‘voh aa rahaa hai’ (he is coming) is breathy from start to finish.

There is more than one way in which a feature cannot plausibly be tied to a given notational ‘place’. Breath and nasality in Sindhi are not only characteristic of at least the syllable but they are also subject to interesting positional fluctuation. In isolation, ‘heeḍ’ãah’ (here, hither) is pronounced as might be expected from the notation taken in conjunction with the foregoing expatiatory comments but nothing
ɦ ɦ ɦ
said so far would lead us to expect [ɦe·ɖ’ʌɦɑ̃ːc] as the regular pronunciation of ‘heeḍ’ãah + ac’ [ʌc] (come here!). Again, ‘hoaa’ (was) in isolation appears as ‘ohaa’ in *eg* ‘mũu vaṭ ohaa’ (it was with me, I had it). The well-known Hindi/Urdu aspirated plosives also exhibit fluctuation in the incidence of relevant aspiration; for instance, the imperfective participle ‘deekhtaa’ of the verb ‘deekhnaa’ (to see) is typically pronounced with what Daniel Jones somewhat quaintly termed ‘incomplete plosion’ of ‘k(h)’, *ie* with close transition ‘–kt–’, and noticeable breathiness *preceding* the velar closure, *ie* [de·^{h}ktɑ·]; on the other hand – and for no obviously compelling phonetic reason – the velar component of the corresponding complex ‘–khn–’ in the infinitival form is typically pronounced as a velar affricate, *ie* [de·k^{x}nɑ·].

Thus, both forms are markedly different in phonetic terms from the perfective participle ‘deekhaa’ [deːkɦɑ·]. Clearly, it would be advantageous to present such facts within the verbal paradigm but the differences indicated are a matter of the phonological implications of plosive + plosive sequence versus plosive + nasal sequence versus non-sequence and as such, prosodic. The point at present being made, however, is that of the positional fluctuation of the feature of breath, even when this is associated with the distinction between aspirated and unaspirated plosives in the languages of the area. For a change of scene, though not of topic, the Berber of Zuara illustrates an interesting fluctuation in the domain of emphasis in nominal and verbal forms that include ‘t–’ ‘–t’, ‘(–)tt–’, ‘–d’, mostly affixal. Fluctuation in this case is optional between freely variant forms, but the fact has not been reported elsewhere as far as I know. Thus, ‘tamuRt’ (city, town; Tripoli) varies between what may be represented as $\overset{-e}{\text{t}}\ \overset{+e}{\text{amuRt}}$ and $\overset{+e}{\text{tamuR}}\ \overset{-e}{\text{t}}$, ‘tiRəDəd’ (you dressed) between $\overset{-e}{\text{t}}\ \overset{+e}{\text{iRəDəd}}$ and $\overset{+e}{\text{tiRəD}}\ \overset{-e}{\text{əd}}$, ‘tamZit’ (grain of barley) between $\overset{-e}{\text{t}}\ \overset{+e}{\text{amZit}}$ and $\overset{+e}{\text{tamZi}}\ \overset{-e}{\text{t}}$, ‘təzRid’ (you saw) between $\overset{-e}{\text{t}}\ \overset{+e}{\text{əzRid}}$ and $\overset{+e}{\text{təzRi}}\ \overset{-e}{\text{d}}$, etc. Prefixal ‘tt–’ and suffixal ‘–d’ fluctuate likewise between the $\overset{-e}{\text{tti}}\ \overset{+e}{\text{RaDəd}}$ and $\overset{+e}{\text{ttiRaD}}\ \overset{-e}{\text{əd}}$ variants of ‘ttiRaDəd’ (you wear), but ‘–d’ is not a suffix in *eg* ‘yttaZəd’ (he hands over), which is nevertheless subject to similar variation between $\overset{-e}{\text{ytt}}\ \overset{+e}{\text{aZəd}}$ and $\overset{+e}{\text{yttaZ}}\ \overset{-e}{\text{əd}}$. Once again, word boundaries constitute no barrier to the ‘spread’ of a particular prosody; in the same Berber dialect, the isolated forms ‘ɑMMi’ [ʌm̶·m̶ï] (like, as), ‘aman’ [æ·mæ·n] (water) and, say, ‘iləl’ [iːlɪl] (sea) combine in the form [ʌm̶(m̶) ɑmɑn niːlɪl] (like sea-water), wherein not only is the vowel ‘–i’ regularly elided before a following open vowel[9] but the domain of emphasis includes ‘aman’, non-emphatic in isolation and in other environments. The area is one in which further research is necessary in order to establish the regularities appertaining to the forces at work in such cases, but the example suffices here for the purpose of indicating the need for prosodies to be accounted for in any analysis that claims to be adequate.

The foregoing are instances of fluctuation, 'metathesis', or what one wills, apparently freely variant within the speech of an individual or group of individuals. 'Substitution' is doubtless to be preferred terminologically to 'fluctuation' when one prosody replaces another, as for example when frontness versus backness or non-emphasis versus emphasis in one and the same lexical item characterizes a female pronunciation of *eg* Arabic 'garraaħ' (surgeon) versus male 'gɑrrɑɑħ' or Marrakshi regional 'tibbaax' (cook) corresponds to 'Tubbɑɑx' elsewhere in Morocco. Are not such distinctions worthy of attention, indeed eminently meaningful? But we must not leave the impression that only 'fluctuations' and 'substitutions' are common around the world; on the contrary, the prosodic feature which is stable as to domain is much commoner. Illustrations were provided in passing in the earlier parts of this section, but here are some more examples, mostly from Arabic, a language that requires so much to be said about it in prosodic terms.

Let us consider what at first seems to be 'vowel harmony' in the Bedouin Arabic of the Cyrenaican Jebel and, in order to be reasonably brief, let us limit ourselves mostly to forms involving long open vowels and qualitative variations among the latter. In pre-pausal open syllables a distinction in terms of the usual contrast front (aa) versus back (ɑɑ) is sufficient to account for the long vowels in question, and the vocalic difference is regularly relatable to features of the *consonantal* environment and therefore to the whole syllable. In gross terms, b(ackness) is particularly associated with emphasis (S, T, Đ), uvularity (x, ɣ), 'r'-ness (r), voice-cum-velarity (g), and labiality-cum-velarity (w); *cf*, for example,

f ⊢—⊣ laa 'no, not' versus b ⊢—⊣ rɑɑ (attention-directing particle)

f ⊢—⊣ miʃaa 'he went' versus b ⊢—⊣ 9ɑTɑɑ 'he gave'

f ⊢—⊣ simaa 'sky' versus b ⊢—⊣ suwɑɑ 'same'.

Post-pausally such a distinction is extremely rare, yet in keeping with its pre-pausal counterpart; *cf* f ⊢—⊣ aaðan 'he permitted' versus b ⊢—⊣ ɑɑmɑr 'he ordered'. In polysyllables, however, it is exceptional for relevant distinctions to be confined to a single syllable; the whole form 'miʃaa' is front, '9ɑTɑɑ' back. The interplay of consonantal and vocalic feature is, moreover, extremely intricate, greatly more complex than can be accounted for by a simple distinction between front and back; it is not only that short vowels following consonantal gutturality+friction (x, ɣ, ħ, 9, h) are open in contrast with other consonantal environments (*cf* '9ɑTɑɑ' versus 'miʃaa/luwɑɑ' (he wound round)) but also that consonantal features and sequences of feature regularly contrast in relation to differences of total vocalic pattern. Thus, for example, metaphorically speaking, the key of backness set by uvularity in the first syllable of *eg* 'ɣɑfɑɑ' (he took a nap) is 'permitted' to continue throughout the form in the presence of intervocalic labiality; in contrast, frontness characterizes *eg* '9afaa' (he pardoned) throughout, and a mixture of back and front is illustrated by 'ɣɑzaa' (he raided), where 'z' does not 'permit' backness to continue. Nor should it be thought that such relationships between syllables are only of the left-to-right, earlier-to-later kind. Consider 'miʃaa+ibkan/ubkɑm' (with you [fem pl/masc pl]) → 'miʃaabkan' versus 'miʃɑɑbkɑm'. The latter form (miʃɑɑbkɑm) resembles 'um9ɑɑkɑm' (with you [masc pl]) but *cf* (ruddu) 'baalkɑm' ((take) care, look out [masc pl]). Any complete account, such as is beyond our present scope, would need to recognize at least intervocalic difference of potential between '–bk–' and '–Vk–', on the one hand, and '–lk–', on the other, and this is not to mention the implicational differences of preceding consonants (*cf* 'ɑTfɑɑlkɑm' (your [masc pl] infants) versus 'baalkɑm'). Ignoring, therefore, for brevity's sake, the initial portions of the foregoing examples, the following possibilities obtain in terms of front versus back contrast:

f	b	f b	b f
(miʃ)aabkan	(miʃ)ɑɑbkɑm	(b)aalkɑm	(ɑTf)ɑɑlkan
(b)aalkan	(ɑTf)ɑɑlkɑm		

Clearly, dependency 'looks both ways'; variation in the quality of the penultimate vowel in 'miʃɑɑbkɑm' and 'miʃaabkan' corresponds to that of backness and frontness in the suffix, but due regard must at the same time be paid to the earlier consonantal context, since it is the latter that 'determines' the backness of the corresponding vowel in 'ɑTfɑɑlkɑm' (*cf* 'baalkɑm') or 'Tu9ɑɑmkan' (your [fem pl] food); at the same time, as we shall see below, '–kɑm/–kan' preclude the possibility of 'ie', *cf* 'biel+kɑm → baalkɑm'.

(In spite of the illustrations given so far, it cannot be said that the differences concerning us are closely relatable to grammatical distinctions. It is an interesting fact of Cyrenaican Arabic that 2nd person pronominal suffixes are characterized by backness in masculine forms versus frontness in feminine forms, but the prosodic differences extending over and beyond a domain that includes the suffixes are in fact applicable on a much broader grammatical front in the dialect. This is not, of course, to deny the interest of examining the ways in which such differences are turned to grammatical account.)

We have seen that long open accented vowels bounded by pause are monophthongal (miʃaa, 9ɑTɑɑ, etc), but accented and non-pausal, and in the absence of environmental emphasis (T, S, Đ), uvularity (x, ɣ), or labiality-cum-velarity (w), or such other constraints as that illustrated above by '–kɑm/kan' in *eg* 'baalkɑm/baalkan', a falling diphthong 'ie' [ɪɛ] regularly occurs, comprising a feature of openness with concomitant reduced aperture (*ie* closeness) in contrast with long open vowels elsewhere. *Cf* 'bieb' (door, entrance) versus 'bɑɑT' (armpit), 'i9gieb' (mountain passes) versus 'u9gɑɑb' (falcon), 'siemiħ' (forgive [masc sing imp]) versus 'saamaħ' (he forgave), etc.[10] Accentuation or prominence is shown to be relevant by such facts as 'síemiħ+–ni → samíħni' (forgive me!). The relatability of 'ie' to 'aa' and 'ɑɑ', as well as the dependence of these qualities on features elsewhere in the context, appears in the following examples, which contain 2nd person singular pronominal suffixes in contrast with the corresponding plural suffixes illustrated earlier:

'(ikt)ieb' (book)
'(ikt)aabɑk' (your [masc sing] book)
'(ikt)iebik' (your [fem sing] book)

The cumulate contrast of openness-cum-backness versus closeness-cum-frontness of the two suffixes is interestingly maintained in their combination with forms ending in '–aa', *eg* 'im9áa' (with); *cf* 'im9aa +-ɑk → um9ɑ́ɑk' (with you [masc sing]) versus 'im9aa+-ik → im9íek' (with you [fem sing]), a clear case of 'phonology become grammar' and of the fact that the distinctive features of gender ascribed for practical morphemic purposes to the suffixes are more often than not spread over the whole of a given form. The neutralization following '–ɑɑ' of the contrast '–ɑk/–ik' appropriate to other environments is further evidence of the need to take phonology into account in grammatical statement, *cf* '9ɑTɑ́ɑk' (he gave you [masc sing/fem sing]).

Elsewhere[11] I have distinguished between 'V' and 'v' as categories of *sonant* in response mainly to the elision or non-elision of short vowels in paradigms of related forms. Briefly, 'V' is not elided in potentially open syllables, whatever the vocalic quality that correlates with it; in comparable circumstances, 'v' is elided. In closed syllables and in those marked for gutturality and friction, 'V' corresponds to a qualitatively open vowel but, in general, vowel quality must be considered quite separately from sonant status. 'saamaħ' (he forgave) is an example of CV:CVC on the basis of *eg* 'síemiħih (< saamaħ + -ih)' (he forgave him), in which, irrespective of its quality, a vowel occurs penultimately; 'siemiħ' (forgive [masc sing]), on the other hand, is 'interpretable' as CV:CvC from the evidence of *eg* 'síemħih (< siemiħ + -ih)' (forgive him!), with absence of vowel in comparable place. The vowel quality that correlates with 'V' is prosodically related to the nature of the preceding consonant, so that, in the environment of preceding gutturality-cum-friction, V appears as 'a/ɑ' in *eg* 'yafhamɑw' (they understand) while any other complex of consonantal feature entails 'i/u' as in 'yamsiħɑw' (they sweep), 'yaʃrubɑw' (they drink). Qualitatively, therefore, 'V' and 'v' may completely overlap, *cf* 'ilfáf (-Vf)' (envelopes) versus 'ilfífih (also –Vf–)' (his envelopes) versus 'iktíb (-vb)' (books) (*cf* 'kítbih' (his books)).

A short vowel alternation of the kind exemplified in the ultimate syllables of 'rɑɑbɑT' (he tied) versus 'rɑɑbuT' (tie!) is a separate matter from the distinction between 'V' and 'v'. This vowel alternation may be symbolized α:ι, *ie* -C2αC3 versus -C2ιC3; other examples, with and without C3, are

–C2α(C3):	laagɑ	'he found'
	saamaħ	'he forgave'
	ħɑɑrɑb	'he fought'
–C2ι(C3):	liegi	'find!'
	siemiħ	'forgive!'
	ħierib	'fight!'

It will be seen that important differences in the form of 'α:' in such forms remain to be accounted for. The difference between 'saamaħ' and 'ħɑɑrɑb' is proportionate to that between the last two syllables of 'miʃaabkan' versus 'miʃɑɑbkɑm', and may be represented $\frac{\text{f/b}}{\text{C1}\alpha\text{:C2}\alpha\text{C3}}$, while that between ħierib and rɑɑbut, $\frac{\text{f/b}}{\text{C1}\alpha\text{:C2}\iota\text{C3}}$, is comparable to the corresponding syllables of 'miʃiebhin' (with them [fem]) versus 'miʃɑɑbhum' (with them [masc]). 'bielik', 'liegi', 'siemiħ', like 'ħierib', are examples of $\frac{\text{f}}{\text{C1}\alpha\text{:C2}\iota\text{(C3)}}$.

Not all consonants behave alike; 'r' and 'g' are notably subject to greater distributional variation than 'S', 'T', 'Đ', 'x', 'ɣ', 'w'; moreover, the succeeding consonantal context is as relevant to the form of 'α:' as what precedes, *cf*, for example, $\frac{\text{b}}{\text{gɑɑlɑb}}$ 'he knocked over'

versus $\overset{f}{\vdash\!\!\!-\!\!\!-\!\!\!\dashv}$ gaasam 'he divided'. In such forms as 'laagɑ' (he met, found) or 'baalɑk' (look out!; perhaps [male addressee]), the intervocalic consonant in the first example, the grammatical category of the suffix in the second, determines the backness of vowel in the ultimate syllable; the latter, in turn, determines the form of 'α:' in the preceding syllable. Both examples are of mixed front/back type, *ie* f b laagɑ, f b baalɑk.
The exclusion of 'ie' following C1, in contrast with 'liegi' and 'bielik', again indicates the interdependency of the vowels as well as the need to recognize contrastive prosodic categories of openness and closeness. '–ɑk' is cumulately and invariably open-cum-back; the variable quality of accompanying 'α:' reflects the consonantal environment. The latter is such in the case of 'baalɑk' as to block additional backness in the penultimate syllable. The whole form, however, is open, suggesting the priority of the open: close distinction over its front: back counterpart. Although 'baalɑk' is mixed as to frontness versus backness, it is classifiable with both 'saamaħ' (front) and 'ħɑɑrɑb' (back) as open, *ie*

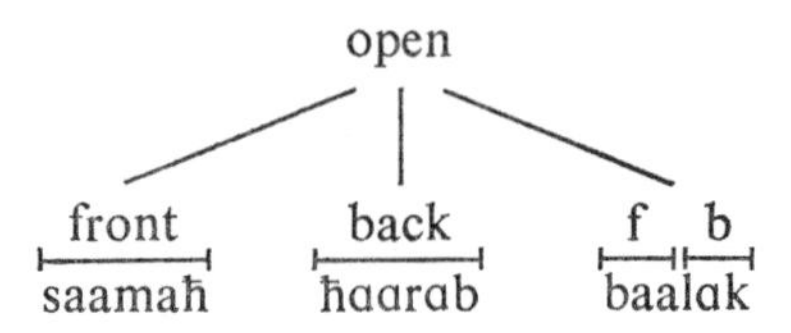

in contrast with

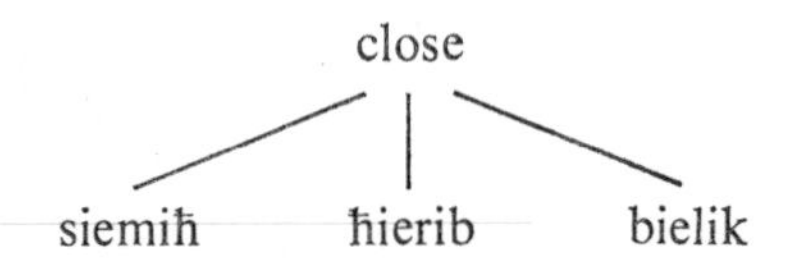

Front versus back phonetic differences relatable to consonantal context are also discernible in forms that are close, and indeed between vowels other than 'α', but are phonetically less striking than in the case of open forms. What is more, to consider the phonetic, phonological, and grammatical distinctions involved would take us far beyond the scope of the present objective, which is to indicate in fairly general terms the need to recognize pervasive distinctions of a syntagmatic, otherwise prosodic kind. If at the same time, something of the complexity of linguistic organization is underlined, no harm is done.

In the foregoing examples contiguous syllables have constituted the domain of a particular prosody but this need not be so. Although there is some difference of quality between the penultimate vowels of 'saamiħɑk' (he forgave you [masc sing]) and 'siemiħik' (he forgave you [fem sing]), it is expressible in terms of the distinction front versus back and is slight in comparison with the striking difference of vocalic form in the antepenultimate syllables, relatable for its part to the prosodic difference between open and close. It will be seen that, in accordance with familiar practice, the terms open and close have been used indiscriminately with reference both to segmental vowels (α and ι) and to prosodies; it would clearly be desirable to distinguish these categories terminologically, and the terms 'low' and 'high' suggest themselves as suitable replacements for the two terms in the phonematic, segmental system. If we were concerned only with a distinction of the type 'saamaħ' versus 'siemiħ' or 'ħɑɑrɑb' versus 'ħierib', the difference could be accounted for wholly in terms of an open versus close prosodic distinction, but we have to account not only for the comparable minimally differentiated 'rɑɑbɑT' versus 'rɑɑbuT', 'ɑTfɑɑlɑk' versus 'ɑTfɑɑlik', but also for the difference between 'saamiħɑk' and 'siemiħik'. The prosodic relationship between ultimate and antepenultimate syllables in the latter pair of forms is something apart from distinctions made elsewhere between 'C' and 'V', 'α' and 'ι', and 'V' and 'v'. On the other hand, unlike its 2nd person counterparts, the 3rd person singular masculine suffix has no 'inherent' vowel quality and is wholly accountable in prosodic terms, notwithstanding its qualitative variation from close-cum-front (–ih) to open-cum-back (–ɑh); *cf* 'siemiħih (<saamaħ+ih)' (he forgave him) and 'ħɑɑrubɑh (<ħɑɑrɑb+ɑh)' (he fought him), or again 'islibih' (he robbed him) versus 'uTlubɑh' (he asked him), 'uTrudih' (he dismissed him) versus 'uTlugɑh' (he released him), etc. That the matter is one of phonology rather than grammar is shown by the fact that the nominal feminine singulative suffix behaves in exactly the same way; *cf* 'isbilih' (ear of corn) versus 'iʃjurɑh' (tree), 'iʃħamih' (spot of grease) versus 'iʃ9ɑrɑh' (a hair), 'i9nibih' (a grape) versus 'u9gubɑh' (mountain pass).

One has to look a long way in Cyrenaican Arabic to find segmentally minimal distinctions of short vowels. The vocalic difference between, say, 'dukkɑɑn' (shop) versus 'kittieb' (Koranic school), 'rukbɑh' (knee) versus 'rikbih' (ride) is totally formulable in prosodic terms, *ie*

	b	f
C1ιC2C2α:C3	dukkɑɑn	kittieb
C1ιC2C3vh	rukbɑh	rikbih

Cf 'miʃɑɑbħum' versus 'miʃiebħin', where the suffix 'dictates' the form of the preceding syllable. In 'ɑTfɑɑlhum' versus 'ɑTfɑɑlhin', however, the feature of 'emphasis' takes precedence over the prosodic implications of the suffix vowel, all such prosodic features taking precedence over residual phonematic alternations. Even in such cases as 'ɑTfɑɑlhum/–hin', moreover, there obtains a regularity of syntagmatic relationship between suffix vowel and suffix-final consonant (back ɑ/u + labial m, front a/i + denti-alveolar n) and, although space precludes us from dealing with such matters, they too are of a prosodic order, though closely tied in this case to the grammatical categories of gender and number. Once again, such evidence may suggest the desirability of undertaking phonological analysis within a grammatical framework, yet prosodic distinctions spill over grammatical confines; for example, 'n' equally does not 'permit' the extension of backness in *eg* 'ɑSnief' (kinds), with which *eg* 'ɑSbɑɑħ' (mornings) contrasts, so that phonological generalization beyond the earlier grammatical paradigm is possible. Other examples of grammatical *correlation* for prosodic distinctions of the kind exercising us include, say, 'fiirien' (mice) (in which '–ien' is suffixal) versus 'miirɑɑd' (path) (in which '–ɑɑd' belongs to the root of the form in question), or again 'dɑɑri (< dɑɑr + i)' (my house) versus 'dieri' (take care of!), or 'uħmɑɑri (< uħmɑɑr + i)' (my donkey) versus 'iħmieri' (reddish [of horse]), etc. But grammatical specification is once more not crucial to the recognition of prosodic distinctions, which are by nature phonological. The non-emphatic:emphatic contrast focused, so to speak, on 'ð' in 'iðrieʢ' (fore-arm) is prosodically marked throughout the form in the way that the contrasting prosody informs, say, 'guTrɑɑn' (pitch, tar), but is of no particular relevance to the nominal class.

As we have seen, the suffix in 'rukbɑh' (knee) and 'rikbih' (ride) is grammatically the same but, phonologically, it is the whole form that is back in one case and front in the other, not just the vowels of the first syllables. The contrast, therefore, would not justify the recognition of a short vowel alternation in the first syllable; it is the further contrast with 'rɑkbɑh' (stirrup) that provides some justification. 'rɑkbɑh' and 'rukbɑh' are identical in terms of backness but minimally distinguished by the short vowels of the first syllables. Yet this minimality is, as it were, due to the 'accidental' circumstances of the consonantal environment, and it might be plausibly maintained that the distinction between the first vowels is more consistently attributable to a prosodic difference of openness versus closeness (referred to the first syllables) than to a low versus high alternation of short vowels. This would also be true of the ultimate syllables of the corresponding plural forms 'urkɑb' (stirrups) versus 'urkub' (knees), both of which contrast with (front) 'irkib' (he mounted); all three forms are oxytonic. Contrast, of course, is between the distinguishing vocalic marks of particular roots or of generalized grammatical categories, but it seems that there is a choice available between ascribing these marks to phonematic short vowels 'α' and 'ι' (with prosodic implications) or to prosodies of openness and closeness. We have chosen earlier, on the basis of minimal segmental contrast and for other unstated reasons, to regard the difference of vowel in the ultimate syllables of 'saamaħ' and 'siemiħ', as well as of 'rɑɑbɑT' and 'rɑɑbuT', as a phonematic matter and to speak subsequently of the prosodic implications of phonematic short vowels; equally, and some may think more consistently, we might have considered syllable-based prosodies of openness and closeness as carrying the grammatical distinctions involved. This would also apply to monosyllables, in which the need to recognize short vowel alternation seems most clear-cut, *cf* 'lamm' (he collected) versus 'limm' (collect!), 'ħɑgg' (he looked) versus 'ħugg' (look!), distinctions minimally located in the vowels. Yet here, too, extended forms ('lammih', 'limmih', 'ħɑggɑh', 'ħuggɑh') would support a prosodic as opposed to phonematic view of things. Provided, however, that the 'prosodic implications' of the phonematic distinction adopted between 'α' and 'ι' are recognized and fully accounted for, no harm seems to be entailed by the adoption, which is suggested by pan-Arabic relevance as well as transcriptional convenience among other considerations. It is perhaps hardly surprising, in view of the facts we are discussing, that the devisers of the Arabic script chose not to include letter symbols for short vowels but to rely on the use where appropriate of specially designed diacritica.

In most consonantal environments the distinction spoken of in the preceding paragraph would never be more than twofold. Certain environments, however – and especially those in which 'r' and 'g' figure – seem to permit a *prima facie* threefold distinction. Yet features of phonetic form other than a minimal vocalic difference are invariably involved, so that prosodic analysis again offers the best opportunity of accounting fully and systematically for the facts. 'ħigg' (young camel), for example, is marked by a noticeably fronter off-glide than 'ħɑgg/ħugg', and in the somewhat 'concocted' case of 'lumm' (the mother), which does not include 'r' or 'g', the whole form is 'darker' than the earlier 'lamm/limm'. Phonemically versus prosodically speaking, indeed, a fourfold discrimination would have to be made, to include that between 'a' and 'ɑ', not only in, say, the suffixes '–kan/ –kɑm' but also in such contrasts as 'ʃakk' (he doubted; doubt) versus 'ʃɑkk' (he scraped, struck (a match)). Once again, a prosodic account is more economical and greatly more adequate explanatorily, whatever the readability (and write-ability) of its accompanying transcriptions. Often enough, distinctions of the kind we are illustrating could not be related to phonemic differences of short vowel without distortion to phonological distinctions recognized elsewhere. For reasons that appear in the following essay, the initial vowels of *eg* 'i9gieb' (mountain passes) versus 'u9gaab' (falcon) are ascribable to a sonant category of anaptyctic vowel (ə) versus V/v; prosodies of frontness and backness then account for the manifold differences of vocalic and consonantal feature between the forms.

We have seen something of the manner in which consonantal features are closely interwoven with vowel quality in a given form. The facts are exceedingly complex. In general, voice-cum-velarity (g) is associated with back 'ɑɑ' in a prosodic context of openness and variously with back 'ɑɑ' or front 'ie/aa' in a context of closeness(-cum-frontness), *cf* '9agɑɑb' (cigarette-end) versus 'i9gieb' (mountain passes). Other examples are 'gɑɑbɑl' (he met) versus 'giebil' (meet!), 'bɑggɑɑl' (grocer) versus 'miigies' (bracelet), 'bɑggɑɑt' (bugs) versus 'digiigiet' (thin [fem pl]), etc. Yet other consonantal features have to be considered, as for instance non-emphasis in 'gaasam' (he divided) versus 'gɑɑlɑb' (he knocked over), which is neutral as to the emphasis:non-emphasis distinction. Yet again, sequential order of vowel and consonant has to be taken into account; '*–ieg#' (also '*–ier#') does not occur, so that, notwithstanding the close front nature of the first syllable, the long open vowel is back in *eg* 'ʃillɑɑg' (small herd of goats). It is only to be expected, therefore, from such interplay of features, that the domain of a particular prosody will vary considerably. Most of our examples have been restricted to two syllables, but 'umgɑɑbulɑh' (meeting), for example, develops contrastive prosodic relationship of back versus front with *eg* 'imbiedilih' (arbitration) throughout the tetrasyllabic structure of the forms. 'imnaawiʃih' (quarrel) is a 'mixed' example of the fact that 'ie' – close-cum-open, so to speak – does not occur in the immediate environment of 'w'. Something of the complexity of things is shown by variation in the form of 'α:' in such structural patterns as CιCCα:C, CαCCα:C, CιCα:C, and αCCα:C; *cf*

b		f	
rukkɑɑb	passengers	9immiel	workmen
Ðullɑɑm	cruel (pl)	ħijjiej	pilgrims
rummɑɑn	pomegranates	daffiel	spitter
burhɑɑn	proof	ħalliem	dreamer
xɑbbɑɑz	baker	kiliem	speech, talk
Tɑbbɑɑl	drummer	b f	
rɑffɑɑs	propeller		
Sɑllɑɑħ	repairer	rɑddiem	burier

ɣɑlbɑɑn	seriously ill	wɑzzien	weigher, measurer
bɑTlɑɑn	tired	ɣɑʃʃieʃ	deceiver
Subɑɑħ	morning	Tɑyyieb	cook
Tu9ɑɑm	food	Sɑyyieħ	bleater
ɑSħɑɑb	friends	Ɖɑnnien	thinker, procrastinator
ɑrkɑɑn	corners	ɑSnief	kinds
ɑwhɑɑm	habitat	ɑwlied	boys, young men

It will be seen from a cursory inspection of such examples that palatality and palato-alveolarity (y, ʃ, j), for example, though not entering into 'specific' non-emphatic:emphatic contrasts, behave as non-emphatic in relation to the form of an environmental long open vowel; laterality (l), labiality (f, b, m), on the other hand, are 'neutral' as to the extension of backness or frontness over domains that include them, *cf* 'rɑffɑɑs' versus 'daffiel'. As we saw in the case of velarity-cum-voice (g), any thoroughgoing analysis would have to consider right-to-left as well as left-to-right relations and the sequential interrelation of consonant and vowel; for instance, final consonants in the above examples do not seem to affect the prosodic category of the syllable in which they occur, although of course they retain their implications for extended forms; *cf* 'rummɑɑn' (pomegranates) and 'rummɑɑnih (not *–nɑh)' (a pomegranate), 'rɑmmɑɑy' (thrower [masc]) and 'rɑmmɑɑyih' (thrower [fem]).

Variation, then, between the qualities of 'α:' (aa, ie, ɑɑ) is always a matter of prosodic relationship of one kind and/or another. Stated informally and within the present somewhat constrained limits of analysis, regularities are broadly as follows: *'r'-ness* . . . in the contextual absence of emphasis (T, S, Ɖ), uvularity (x, ɣ), and labiality-cum-velarity (w), 'ɑɑ' follows word-initial 'r' (*eg* 'rɑɑs' (head), 'rɑɑmi' (having thrown)); both 'ie' and 'ɑɑ' occur in the immediate vicinity of 'r', 'ie' precedes when the following syllable is close (*eg* 'ħierib' (fight!), 'jieri' (running, flowing), 'baggieri' (cattle)), unless the closeness is suffixal (*eg* 'jɑɑri' (my neighbour) <jɑɑr+i); elsewhere 'ɑɑ' precedes medial 'r' (*eg* 'ħɑɑrɑb' (he fought)); 'ɑɑ' is the commoner form of 'α:' following syllable-initial 'r' (*eg* 'Suurɑɑt' (verses, suras), 'miirɑɑd' (path), 'bɑrrɑɑd' (teapot)), except when 'α:' is suffixal and closeness or elision characterizes the preceding syllable (*eg* 'niirien' (fires), 'mitwɑxxriet' (late) [fem pl] <mitwɑxxir+α:t; *cf*, too, the unusual form 'imrieyih' (mirror), also close *passim*); final 'r' is preceded by 'ɑɑ' (*eg* 'nɑɑr' (fire)). *Labiality-cum-velarity* . . . while 'aa', therefore, does not occur in the environment of 'r', 'ie' is excluded from that of 'w', which is followed by 'ɑɑ' (*eg* 'wɑɑjid' (much, very)) but preceded (in the absence of emphasis, uvularity, 'r'-ness, and velarity-cum-voice (g)) by 'aa' (*eg* 'di9aawi' (curses), *cf*

'miðieri' (pitchforks, winnowing forks)). *Velarity-cum-voice* . . . in the absence of emphasis, uvularity, 'r'-ness, and labiality-cum-velarity (w), and unlike 'r' or 'w', initial 'g' is followed by 'ɑɑ' when adjacent syllables are open (*eg* 'gɑɑlɑb' (he overturned)) but by 'ie' when such syllables are close (*eg* 'gielib' (overturn!)) and by 'aa' when non-emphasis follows 'α:' in the general environment of openness (*eg* 'gaasam' (he divided)); in the same environment of surrounding open syllables, medial 'g' is preceded by 'aa' (*eg* 'laagɑ' (he found, met)), but 'ie' is the rule when closeness follows (*eg* 'liegi' (find, meet!)); final 'g' is preceded by 'ɑɑ' (*eg* 'ʃillɑɑg' (small herd of goats)). *Emphasis and uvularity* . . . are always flanked by 'ɑɑ'. But immediate contiguity is far from providing the only relevant domain, *cf*, for instance, 'Subɑɑya' (women), 'xɑbbɑɑz' (baker), nor is dependency one-way only, *cf* 'gaasam' versus 'gɑɑlɑb', 'xɑbbɑɑz' versus 'ħɑɑmuĐ' (sour). 'Implications' differ between consonantal features, *cf* the tripartite contrast between emphasis, uvularity, and the absence of both of these features in *eg* 'jɑɑluT' (silly, stupid) versus 'baaluɣ' (of age, adult) versus 'bieyiɡ' (having sold). The permutational possibilities of consonantal features within roots are, of course, very great. In the absence of emphasis from the following examples, the occurrence of 'aa' is clearly tied to following backness-cum-openness, 'ie' to comparable closeness:

laagɑ	he found	baalɑk	look out [masc sing]	baalkɑm	look out [masc pl]
liegi	find!	bielik	look out [fem sing]	mielhin	their [fem pl] property

ysaamħɑk	he will forgive you [masc sing]	saamiħɑk	he forgave you [masc sing]
ysiemħik	he will forgive you [fem sing]	siemiħik	he forgave you [fem sing]

It is clear from such contrasts as 'saamiħɑk:siemiħik' that, despite the presence of an intervening syllable, the quality of 'α:' following 's' depends not only on the preceding consonant but also on the suffix; notwithstanding the 'morpho-phonematic' status of 'α:', 'siemiħik' (like 'siemiħ', the unsuffixed imperative) contains a prosodic feature of closeness throughout, *ie* 'ie' is at once close (prosodically) and low ('morpho-phonematically'). Contrariwise, the first syllable of 'saamiħɑk', in accord with open '–ɑk' versus close '–ik', is prosodically open, though not back because of the relationship developed by ‘ɑ:’ with preceding ‘s’. Forms like ‘saamaħ’ and ‘siemiħ’ comprise syllables agreeing for openness and closeness respectively, and both for frontness, while the syllables of ‘ħɑɑrɑb’ agree for openness and backness, those of ‘baalɑk’ for openness but not for frontness or backness, those of ‘jɑɑluT’ for backness but not for openness or closeness, etc.[12] Forms like ‘mitwɑxxriet’ or ‘Đɑɑhriet’ (in sight [fem pl]) resemble the earlier ‘im9iek (<im9aa+ik)’ (with you [fem sing]) and are particularly interesting as illustrations not only of the regular elision of sonant ‘v’ but also of the fact that close vowel quality correlating with the sonant category may remain in the elided form, if remaining features of the environment ‘permit’.

It has been sufficiently indicated that forms like ‘ɑTfɑɑlhum’ and ‘ɑTfɑɑlhin’, minimally differentiated in a short vocalic segment (disregarding the difference of nasal consonant), are the accountable exception to the general rule of vocalic differences extending over much wider domains. The grammatical exploitation of such features can often be very striking, as perhaps the implications of pronominal suffixation have already demonstrated. Another interesting example is that by which the type of minimal conjugational difference between ‘yifham’ (he understands) and ‘yiktib’ (he writes) in Egypt and elsewhere corresponds to Cyrenaican ‘yafham’ [open throughout] versus ‘yiktib’ [close throughout], an open:close proportion that embraces even the suffixes of the imperfect tense paradigm; thus,

	open	close
1st pers sing	nafham	niktib
2nd pers sing masc	tafham	tiktib
2nd pers sing fem	tafhamay	tikitbi
3rd pers sing masc	yafham	yiktib
3rd pers sing fem	tafham	tiktib
1st pers pl	nafhamɑw	nikitbu
2nd pers pl masc	tafhamɑw	tikitbu
2nd pers pl fem	tafhaman	tikitban
3rd pers pl masc	yafhamɑw	yikitbu
3rd pers pl fem	yafhaman	yikitban

Once a verb has been identified as of open or close type, subsequent distinctions are wholly phonological, as too are those between, say, ‘yiktib’ and ‘yuTlub’ (he asks), front and back exemplars of the close imperfect type. Yet once again, although clearly one needs to account for such grammatical exploitation of prosodic features, the fact is that they are not rigidly tied to grammatical classification. For instance, the Cyrenaican nominal form is 'majlas' (council) (open throughout) corresponding to Classical 'majlis', Egyptian 'maglis', etc.

It will in general be seen, therefore, that, although it makes no reference whatever to phonemics, prosodic analysis shares with TG's 'systematic phonemics' the recognition that phonetic structure does not contribute all the information necessary for the determination of phonological structure and that some recourse must be had to lexical and grammatical information. Nevertheless, that Firthian and transformational linguists do not see facts in the same light is illustrated by differences of interpretation placed upon the facts of prominence or accentuation in Arabic. Lately it might seem, TG has become so concerned with the ordering of rules that in the process it can generate quite unmotivated forms in what may be a failure to see a prosodic wood for phonemic trees. It has been held that it is because of a need to 'protect the prefinal high vowel from deletion' that Cairene 'Dubúɡa' (hyenas) is paroxytonic versus *eg* proparoxytonic 'búxala' (misers),[13] but I do not think this is the fundamental question. May not one rather believe that prominence here is part and parcel not only of the syllable structure of the form but also of its vocalic pattern –u–u–a versus other comparable patterns? Not dissimilar implications of vocalic pattern are discernible in Zuara Berber and the Egyptian Arabic dialect of Tahwēh in Munufiyya province and no doubt also elsewhere; *cf* Tahwēh 'ɡudúla' (members of the 'Adli family) versus 'ɡúgala' (wise men) versus 'ɡídila' (straight [fem sing]), examples capable of indefinite multiplication. The fact that Tahwēh 'ɡídila' is treated differently from Cairene 'ħiSína' (horses) is immaterial. Again, to say of Cairene Arabic that 'stressed short high vowels in open syllables are not elided' is true but begs the question of why certain relevant forms are paroxytonic. For my part, I think it a most interesting feature of many forms of Arabic – most unequivocally of Classical Arabic as pronounced in Egypt – that prominence is a function of the *total* structure of a form in terms of the quantitative pattern of its syllables. Thus, CVCCVCV can only be paroxytonic within the framework of rules set out in the following essay. Rules of the kind seen elsewhere in transformational-generative work on Arabic, by which, for example, Cairene 'wíSlit' (she arrived) is explained as derived from Classical or Literary 'wɑSɑlat', are by no means convincing; they are roughly as follows:

wɑSɑlat (stress assignment) → wɑ́Sɑlat
wɑ́Sɑlat (vowel raising) → *wíSilit
*wíSilit (short vowel elision) → wíSlit

For the second of these rules there seems to be no justification beyond that of a somewhat dubious wish to pan-Arabize the facts and to propose 'solutions' in quasi-mathematical manner. Similar attempts to derive *eg* Cairene 'musa9da' from Classical 'musaa9ida', which is arbitrarily allotted proparoxytonic prominence prior to vowel elision, *ie*

musaa9ida (stress assignment) → musáa9ida
musáa9ida (short vowel elision) → *musáa9da
*musáa9da (long vowel shortening) → musá9da

fail to take account of the fact that typically Egyptian (Cairene) accentuation of literary 'musaa9ida' is paroxytonic, not proparoxytonic. For reasons explained subsequently, 'musaa9ída' is completely parallel to 'yiktíbu', sharing the same syllabic structure from the standpoint of accentuation, namely (from rear to front) short-short-not short. The occurrence of a fourth syllable in one case and not the other is irrelevant. The genuinely interesting fact is again that prominence is part of the total syllable pattern of the form in terms of short and not-short syllables in a way that, as far as I am aware, is not paralleled in any other language or language family. Linguistics, as has been repeated at the risk of boring the reader, is not only concerned with universals but also with providing a general theory of language capable of demonstrating what is interestingly *sui generis* about particular languages. It is also an interesting fact that one is best able to state rules for accentuating Classical Arabic words as pronounced in Cairo by taking the ultimate syllable as one's point of departure and moving towards the front. Another interesting fact is the special treatment invariably accorded (not only in Classical Arabic but also, for example, in Cyrenaican) to sequences or potential (underlying) sequences of short open syllables,[14] but enough of Arabic for the time being.

Perhaps other languages have less to be said about them of a kind appropriate to Arabic, but that some statement of a prosodic order will be necessary in response to the facts of any language is probably beyond question. It is not so much that a prosodic conception of things will be more relevant to some languages than others but rather that the features involved are likely to differ quite considerably from one language group to another. Let us remember, too, that 'prosodic analysis' is genuinely attempting to come to grips with what we do when we *speak*; the norms it seeks to state by editing out the hesitations, false starts, etc of so-called 'performance' are *spoken* norms, not those of the largely *written* grammaticality in whose terms 'competence' has so far been mostly formulated. Be this as it may, there is no doubt that the kind of prosodic statement relevant to, say, Thai[15] differs from that appropriate to Arabic, though both are equally necessary. In relation to European languages, 'prosody' has been used to refer to features of pitch, rhythm, quantity, loudness, and the like, which are too often seen as marks of a supererogatory 'fury' added to the 'sound' that really matters. Yet much of a prosodic kind remains unnoticed in these areas, not only through the present lack of a suitable framework within which to observe, say, meaningful differences of voice quality but conceivably also through the aforementioned unconscious bias towards written norms. Should we not pay attention, for example, to the (? universal) use of high voice register, even falsetto, when addressing small children – by women particularly, I dare say, but often enough by men. 'Careful! Mind your head!', uttered in this way, responds functionally as much to self-gratification as to reassurance, and what is to be done intonationally with the 'split-level' tone (¯ –) on which the 'short' vowel of 'head' is typically pronounced? Not swept under the carpet, one hopes. Such features are distinctly inconvenient to phonemics, whether autonomous or systematic, and the phoneme, of course, is essentially a device of *written* relevance. Are prosodies of this kind mere 'subtleties' of no great concern, in brief meaningless? Can we seriously believe that there is anything of interest to be said in purely referential, denotative terms about such a sentence as '(Oh), Robert!', uttered – as I recently heard it uttered – with long-drawn out, falling tones on both syllables of the name (\rɔːːː\bəːːːt) by a young girl *remonstrating* with her brother over the tediousness of his behaviour? The child's intention ('Robert, stop playing the fool'), crystal-clear in the circumstances and very much part of her linguistic 'competence', was rebuke or remonstrance, the function similarly marked by falling tones peppered over such a sentence as 'You \might at \least have \said so'. Perhaps some measure of definition of 'appellation' can be achieved but hardly without appeal to the kind of prosodic, phonological behaviour to which attention is being drawn. It will not do to respond to the forms of intonation and rhythm which are available to Robert's mother – when subsequently she calls him into a meal – by means of the !, ?, or !? of an earlier structural linguistics, if we wish our claims to attend to the facts of spoken language to be taken at all seriously. Nor will it do to resort to the arbitrary labelling of such matters variously as 'sociolinguistic', 'stylistic', 'paralinguistic', 'connotational', 'usage', or by any other means to suggest that they should not be of direct concern to the linguist with an interest in spoken language. The recognition of the manifold differential uses made of time and timing (*rallentando* versus *accelerando*, for instance) must also pass beyond the gross distinctions of the structuralist's *juncture* if it is to encompass, say, the contrast between the 'protraction' in time appropriate to an aggressive, bullying 'Do you mind?' and the 'contracted' enquiry in the same 'form of words' as to the interlocutor's readiness or not to accept a given proposal. Is not the equal distribution of rhythmic weight over all the syllables of 'Will you shut up?' a sure sign of the final exasperation of the speaker? It should perhaps be said in passing that such features have nothing to do with the speaker's 'attitude', as stated by some phoneticians; so used, 'attitude' is just another word for 'style', 'connotation', etc elsewhere and is better reserved for use in relation to the attitudinal studies of the psycholinguist. We are concerned rather with *regular*, meaningful distinctions of spoken form. Do we, at any rate in this country, not share the belief that the speaker does not wish to leave his fireside if he pronounces '. . . or not bother' in the sentence 'Shall we go – or not bother?' *rallentando* and on a sub-vocal fall (*ie* terminating below the musical range of the voice), in contrast with the positive request for instructions contained in his utterance of the same form of words *presto* and at a higher pitch-level, though with the same pitch contour? Such features, and many like them, go largely unnoticed at present and prosodic analysis seems more likely than other phonological frameworks to encourage an increasing awareness of these areas of meaningful speech.

With the exception of the repeated falling tones in 'You ⸜might at ⸜least have ⸜said so', the foregoing prosodic features have all been continuous over a stretch of discourse, and it is possible so to regard even the exceptional case if we think in terms not of falling tones on discontinuous syllables but of tonal patterns over sequences of syllables. Similar exemplification is provided by, say, the use of isochrony (*sc* the occurrence of strong stress at *regular* intervals of time) in nursery rhymes ('⸜Jonathan ⸜Jo had a ⸜mouth like an ⸜O', etc), or of intonational 'echoes' that seek to jog the memory in, say, 'Do you remember old Harry ⸝Bell, the chap who used to deliver our ⸝coal, and do a bit of ⸝gardening for us?' or to avoid the absurdity of suggesting the existence of two works of the same name by different authors in *eg* 'Have you read 198⸝4 by George ⸝Orwell?'. Tonicity, too often misleadingly associated with stress and/or intonation and meaningful in such abundant measure in English, provides even clearer indication of discontinuous dependencies within English discourse and was sufficiently illustrated in the Introductory.

In a not dissimilar way, the 'thread' of interrogation is marked in the Zuara Berber sentence 'ləktab (*the book*) dajdíd (*is new*) iziɣ (*or*) daqdím (*is old*) a (question marker)?' (Is the book new or old?) by the manner of accentuating 'ajdid' and 'aqdim' in contrast with the corresponding uncompounded affirmative sentences 'ləktab dájdid' (the book is new) and 'ləktab dáqdim' (the book is old). A corresponding difference in a non-alternative type of interrogative sentence involves the speech functions of information-seeking versus incredulity, as between, for example, 'tafúnast dtmɑDúnt a?' (Is Tafunast ill?) versus 'tafunást dtmɑDúnt a?!' (You don't mean to say Tafunast is ill?). Elsewhere locatives, for example, reveal accentual differences of a grammatical order, for instance in forms containing the prefixed particles 's–' and 'l–', apparently in parallel with a directional distinction, *cf* 'səjjáj' (from inside) versus 'lə́jjaj' ((towards) inside). From the prosodic standpoint, the interesting fact of my informant's speech was that accentuation in particles of this kind varied in accordance with the part of the verb they accompanied; thus, with the perfect tense, 'yzə́wwqit səjjáj dəsbəRRɑ́' (he painted it inside and out) contrasted markedly with the imperative 'zə́wwqit sə́jjaj dəsbə́RRɑ' (paint it inside and out). As we have seen, the verbal form itself may be accented contrastively as between 'yzə́wwqit' in 'yzə́wwqit səjjáj dəsbəRRɑ́' (he painted it inside and out) versus 'yzəwwqít' in the interrogative 'yzəwwqít səjjáj dəsbəRRɑ́' (Did he paint it inside and out?). To the extent that it may not occur in isolation, it is the second form that is marked in such contrasts. To speak of 'threads', 'dependencies', etc is to recognize that language is on-going in association with the circumstances of its use. The fact has been illustrated elsewhere by the English sentence 'That'll do'[16] and might equally have been exemplified from the same Berber dialect, in which 'əkkər ssyin /kəkkər ssyin/kkəkkər ssyin' (Get up from there)[17] represent a crescendo pattern of exasperation with the male child ('k–'=male addressee; 'm–'=female) who will not do as he is told. 'k–/m–' is a kind of emphatic attention-drawing particle, which might also have been illustrated by, say, '[k(k)]aʃbik?' (What's the matter with you?).

The examples of prosodies that have been given so far, and which might have been greatly extended, have been of homogeneous features or of mutually dependent heterogeneous counterparts. To conclude this treatment of 'prosodics', otherwise phonological 'syntagmatics', let us return to Cyrenaican Arabic in order to demonstrate the frequent fact of selectional constraints obtaining between phonological features, in particular the incompatibility of certain consonantal features within Arabic roots. We should, however, perhaps first say something of what is meant by 'root'. Briefly, in any account of Arabic morphology it is necessary to recognize *inter alia* a category of *root* and to consider the relation of the root to more abstract concepts such as *base*. The root is lexical and particular, common to all forms within a given lexemic scatter or paradigm; for example, the root '√ktb' is common to Cairene 'katab' (he wrote), 'kaatib' (clerk), 'maktab' (office; desk), 'maktaba' (library), etc. A category *schema* also requires recognition in order to explain certain aspects of morphological alternation to which roots are subject in the syntactic process, excluding morphemes of tense, gender, number, and person, for which the term *inflection* may be reserved. A pronounceable *word* is thus made up of (root + schema + inflection), *eg* (root k–t–b + schema –a–a– + inflection –t) = 'katabt' (I/you [masc sing] wrote). Schema and inflection are general and grammatical in contrast with the particular and lexical root. Base is likewise grammatical and generalizes from numerous scatters of the kind briefly illustrated for '√ktb'. Following the traditional practice of Arabic grammar and using the symbolization '√f9l' for the generalized root or base, we add schemas and inflections to it in whose terms morphological scatters may be stated, having regard to syntactic and other syntagmatic contextual factors. 'katab' (he wrote) is an example of the base 'fa9al', 'simi9' of the base 'fi9il', while both 'kattab' and 'samma9' are, so to speak, to the base 'fa99al'.[18]

To return now to phonology, the complex symbol 'f9l' is doubtless deliberately chosen, probably not so much for its semantic implications of 'doing' ('fa9al' (to do), 'fi9l' (verb), etc) as for the fact that the consonantal features of labiality, gutturality, and laterality it serially embodies may be freely permutated. We shall see that elsewhere incompatibility of consonant feature is as often the rule. Prosodic analysis is once more particularly suited to the handling of the facts of compatibility and incompatibility; indeed, no recognizable theory of phonemes could possibly provide a satisfactory account. Twenty-six phoneme-letters are needed to write Cyrenaican Bedouin Arabic in roman form but no such set of discriminations can be referred to any single consonantal place in a given structural pattern. Although we are concerned here with a different type of syntagmatic ordering from that by which features uniformly characterize extended segments, nevertheless it could not be represented by a coarse-grained, over-simplified, 'letter'-type segmentation of a phonemic kind. The following observations concerning Cyrenaican Bedouin Arabic were made twenty-five years ago independently of Greenberg's interesting paper 'The patterning of root morphemes in Semitic'[19]–the point of departure is nevertheless importantly shared, together with certain findings.

In the following tabulation, Cyrenaican consonant phonemes are displayed principally as stops and continuants, voiced and voiceless, within zones of articulation. The labio-dental zone extends from the lips to the cutting edges of the teeth, the denti-alveolar from the cutting edges of the teeth to the front of the hard palate behind the alveolum, the palatal from the front of the hard palate to the velum, and the guttural zone rearwards from the velum:

LABIO-DENTAL ZONE	LABIAL		
	VOICED	VOICELESS	
STOP	b		NASAL
CONTINUANT		f	m
	LABIO-VELAR SEMI-VOWEL		
	w		

DENTI-ALVEOLAR ZONE	DENTI-ALVEOLAR						
	VOICED	VOICELESS	VOICED	VOICELESS			
STOP	d	t					
		EMPHATIC					
		T					
CONTINUANT	NON-SULCAL		SULCAL		NASAL	LATERAL	TRILL
	ð	θ	z	s	n	l	r
	EMPHATIC			EMPHATIC			
	Đ			S			

PALATAL ZONE			PALATAL	
			VOICED	VOICELESS
CONTINUANT			j	ʃ
			SEMI-VOWEL	
			y	

GUTTURAL ZONE	VELAR/UVULAR		PHARYNGAL		GLOTTAL
	VOICED	VOICELESS	VOICED	VOICELESS	
STOP	g	k			
CONTINUANT	ɣ	x	9	ħ	h

The phonemes of the above ready-reference table are better seen for analytical purposes as complexes of features. For example, denti-alveolar /θ, ð, Đ, t, d, T, s, z, S/ can be categorized in terms of denti-alveolarity [+d], sulcality [+s], non-sulcality [−s], plosivity [+p], friction [−p], voice [+v], voicelessness [−v], emphasis [+e], non-emphasis [−e], so that /ð/, let us say, may be symbolized

$$\begin{bmatrix} +d \\ -p \\ -s \\ +v \\ -e \end{bmatrix}$$

Some features develop their own relations with others; thus, [+p], for example, implies [–s]. Other features relevant to the present concern include palatality [+y] (/j,ʃ/), velarity/uvularity [+u] (/k, g, x, ɣ/), pharyngality [+ph], glottality [+h]. Features do not combine freely with one another, and the facts are most simply stated in terms of mutual exclusion or incompatibility of feature. Reference below is primarily to examples of the favourite structural pattern C1VC2VC3 of the triconsonantal type of root, although by and large the rules stated are also applicable to other patterns. Two categories of feature exclusion are recognizable: (1) *complete*, when the occurrence of a given feature or complex of features at any consonantal place excludes the occurrence of itself or certain other feature/s at either of the remaining places, and (2) *partial*, when exclusion operates only between successive places, *ie* C1–C2 or C2–C3. Generally speaking, restrictions apply within zones of the table excluding the palatal zone, and also within a 'liquid' class (denti-alveolar, usually voiced, variously trilled [+r], lateralized [+l], or nasalized [+n]). Freedom of association is the general rule interzonally, but it is also most important to consider feature constraints without as well as within a given zone. Before doing so, however, discrimination has to be made between identity and non-identity of feature complexes.

The twofold occurrence, ungeminated, of a given complex (duplication) is only common at C2–C3, *cf* '9adad' (number), 'sibab' (reason, cause), 'Sɑħiiħ' (true), etc; in the scatter of morphological *relata* containing such 'duplicates', at least one form occurs with gemination. Elsewhere, duplication does occur at C1–C3, but rarely, and examples are mainly limited to denti-alveolarity and velarity (*cf* 'θieliθ' (third), 'gielig' (disturbed)). These are exceptions to the rule that duplication in indigenous Arabic roots containing three radical consonants does not include C1 within its domain.[20]

Let us consider now something of the constraints that obtain between non-duplicate complexes, and in particular those that are distinguished by a single contrast, *eg* voice [+v] versus voicelessness [−v], emphasis [+e] versus non-emphasis [−e], etc. There are seven correlative pairs of feature-complex in which the paired correlates are distinguished solely by [±v] (phonemic labels are included in round brackets for purposes of ready reference):

(1) $\begin{bmatrix} +d \\ -p \\ -s \\ -e \end{bmatrix}$ (/θ, ð/) (2) $\begin{bmatrix} +d \\ -p \\ +s \\ -e \end{bmatrix}$ (/s, z/) (3) $\begin{bmatrix} +d \\ +p \\ -e \end{bmatrix}$ (/t, d/)

(4) $\begin{bmatrix} +y \\ +s \end{bmatrix}$ (/ʃ, j/) (5) $\begin{bmatrix} +u \\ +p \end{bmatrix}$ (/k, g/) (6) $\begin{bmatrix} +u \\ -p \end{bmatrix}$ (/x, ɣ/)

(7) $\begin{bmatrix} +ph \\ -p \end{bmatrix}$ (/ħ, 9/)

The set of seven may be symbolized $C(7)^{\pm v}$. Now a given term of a subset that occurs [+v] excludes the same subset [−v] at any other place, and *vice versa*, with the notable exception of C(4), *cf* 'jayʃ' (army), 'ʃujɑr' (trees), etc. The only other counter-example I have found is of C(3) in 'wutad' (tent-peg).[21] Disregarding 'wutad', and using $\bumpeq$ in the sense of 'does not occur with' and X for any member of the set, we may summarize the facts as $C(X)^{+v} \bumpeq C(X)^{-v} - C(4)$. Ignoring the so-called 'glottal fricative' (/h/),[22] we can 'pair' on the grounds of similarity of phonetic feature any of the consonant phonemes tabulated earlier (/t, d/, /s, S/, /m, n/, etc) with the apparent exception of /b/ and /f/. The [±v] correlation set out above seemingly applies to all zones except the labial, *ie* there is neither a voiceless (bi)labial plosive nor a voiced labio-dental fricative. The disequilibrium suggests *prima facie* that the bilabial and labio-dental difference of articulation may be disregarded systemically and /b/ paired with /f/. This distributional criterion, however, would be inconclusive without the further strong justification supplied by the complete exclusion that obtains between the two complexes concerned and which does not obtain between *eg* /b/ and /w/ or /f/ and /w/.[23] There is, therefore, sufficient reason to extend this first set $[C^1(7)^{\pm v}]$ to include an eighth labial subset.

Similarly, there are three correlative pairs of feature-complex distinguished by [±e]:

(1) $\begin{bmatrix} +d \\ -p \\ -s \\ +v \end{bmatrix}$ (/ð, Ð/) (2) $\begin{bmatrix} +d \\ -p \\ +s \\ -v \end{bmatrix}$ (/s, S/) (3) $\begin{bmatrix} +d \\ +p \\ -v \end{bmatrix}$ (/t, T/)

Again, a feature-complex marked 'positively' for [e] excludes its 'negative' counterpart, and *vice versa.* Symbolizing this second set $C^2(3)^{\pm e}$, we may say formulaically $C^2(X)^{+e} \bumpeq C^2(X)^{-e}$.

Consider now the fricative feature within the denti-alveolar zone. Distinctions are recognizable in terms of [±s] as follows:

(1) [+s] $\begin{bmatrix} +d \\ -p \\ -v \end{bmatrix}$ (/s, S/) (1a) [−s] $\begin{bmatrix} +d \\ -p \\ -v \end{bmatrix}$ (/θ/)

(2) [+s] $\begin{bmatrix} +d \\ -p \\ +v \end{bmatrix}$ (/z/) (2a) [−s] $\begin{bmatrix} +d \\ -p \\ +v \end{bmatrix}$ (/ð, Ð/)

Sulcality present in the complexes labelled /s, S, z/ and non-sulcality in /θ, ð, Ð/ are once more mutually exclusive features, *ie* $C^3(X)^{+s} \bumpeq C^3(X)^{-s}$. In this case, however, it is not one member of the threefold sulcal or non-sulcal sets that excludes its opposite number; exclusion is between any member of one set and any member of the other (*eg* /ð/ $\bumpeq$ /s, S, z/). And there is more. If the complex labelled

/ð/ is expressed in terms of constituent features, *ie* [+d, −p, +v, −s, −e], it will be seen that it develops a relation of mutual exclusion or incompatibility through the contrasts [±v], [±s], and [±e] with at least those corresponding complexes labelled /θ, s, S, z, Đ/, and therefore that the abstraction of [±s] is otiose, since analysis may be considerably simplified by the recognition of a combined category of dentality or denti-alveolarity and friction ([df]) and the statement that [df] can occur only once in a given form. The sole qualification necessary is in respect of the above considered case of 'duplication', *eg* '9asas' (guard). The facts may thus be expressed as follows: $C(X)^{+df} \bumpeq C(Y)^{+df} - (2 \times X)$, where X and Y = any non-identical members of the set $C^3(6)^{+df}$. In passing it may be worth underlining the greater economy and clarity of such notational expressions in comparison with those imposed by a monosystemic phonemic approach, as for example

/θ/ ≏ /ð/, /Đ/, /s/, /z/, /S/
/ð/ ≏ /θ/, /Đ/, /s/, /z/, /S/
/Đ/ ≏ /θ/ /ð/, /s/, /z/, /S/
/s/ ≏ /θ/, /ð/, /Đ/, /z/, /S/
/z/ ≏ /θ/, /ð/, /Đ/, /s/, /S/
/S/ ≏ /θ/, /ð/, /Đ/, /s/, /z/

Other examples of complete exclusion among my data include, within the guttural zone, $C^{\begin{bmatrix}+u\\-p\end{bmatrix}}$ (/x, ɣ/) $\bumpeq C^{\begin{bmatrix}+u\\+p\\-v\end{bmatrix}}$ (/k/), $C^{\begin{bmatrix}+u\\-p\\+v\end{bmatrix}}$ (/ɣ/) $\bumpeq C^{\begin{bmatrix}+ph\\-p\end{bmatrix}}$ (/ħ, 9/), and $C^{\begin{bmatrix}+u\\-p\\-v\end{bmatrix}}$ (/x/) $\bumpeq C^{\begin{bmatrix}+ph\\-p\\-v\end{bmatrix}}$ (/ħ/) $\bumpeq C^{\begin{bmatrix}+h\\-p\end{bmatrix}}$ (/h/) $\bumpeq C^{\begin{bmatrix}+u\\-p\\+v\end{bmatrix}}$ (/ɣ/). Indeed, forms like '9ahid' (promise) and 'xɑda9' (he deceived) are very rare exceptions to a rule that gutturality-cum-friction can occur only once within the root.

The foregoing facts of exclusion apply equally to *immediate* consonant successions (C1–C2, C2–C3) and to *interrupted* successions (C1–C3). Considering now the facts of the former type only, we find that incompatibility is greatly extended. Not only do they support the earlier recognition of denti-alveolar and guttural zonal categories but clearly justify the additional recognition of further categories of labial (/f, b, m/) and liquid (/r, l, n/). A labio-velar semi-vowel (/w/) occurs regularly with labiality ([b]) in an adjoining consonant place, *eg* 'bɑwl' (urinating), 'mɑwt' (death), etc, but exclusion obtains not only, as we have already seen, between bilabial plosion and labio-dental friction but also between either and bilabial nasality, *ie* $C^{\begin{bmatrix}+b\\-n\end{bmatrix}} \bumpeq C^{\begin{bmatrix}+b\\+n\end{bmatrix}}$.[24] Other types of constraint are listed numerically below.

In the denti-alveolar zone, restriction obtains between plosion and friction as at (1) and (2) following:

(1) $C^{\begin{bmatrix}+d\\+p\\-v\end{bmatrix}}$ (/t, T/) $\doteqdot C^{\begin{bmatrix}+d\\-p\\\pm s\end{bmatrix}}$ (/θ, z, ð, Ð/) $- C^{\begin{bmatrix}+s\\-v\end{bmatrix}}$. The exceptional case is illustrated by 'tisi9' (nine), 'sitir' (curtain), 'wɑSuT' (middle).

(2) $C^{\begin{bmatrix}+d\\+p\\+v\end{bmatrix}}$ (/d/) $\doteqdot C^{\begin{bmatrix}+d\\-p\\+v\end{bmatrix}}$ (/z, ð, Ð/). Contrast the mixed [+v] and [−v] successions in *eg* 'θady' (breast), 'Sɑdir' (chest), 'sudɑg' (he told the truth), '9adas' (lentils), etc. NB The rule $C^{\begin{bmatrix}+d\\+p\\+v\end{bmatrix}} \doteqdot C^{\begin{bmatrix}+d\\-p\\+v\end{bmatrix}}$ holds for the triconsonantal structures we are considering but requires modification for the structure C1VC2C2, *cf* 'Ðidd' (against), etc, although $C^{\begin{bmatrix}+d\\+p\\+v\end{bmatrix}}$ (/d/) excludes $C^{\begin{bmatrix}+d\\-p\\+v\\-e\end{bmatrix}}$ and *vice versa* in such structures.

(3) Still within the denti-alveolar zone, $C^{\begin{bmatrix}+d\\+p\\+e\\-v\end{bmatrix}}$ (/T/) not only excludes – as already accounted for – the non-emphatic correlative complex $C^{\begin{bmatrix}+d\\+p\\-e\\-v\end{bmatrix}}$ (/t/) but also $C^{\begin{bmatrix}+d\\+p\\+v\end{bmatrix}}$ (/d/). The incompatibility of the last two complexes has already been noted, so that all the facts can be formulated as follows: $C^{\begin{bmatrix}+d\\+p\\+e\\-v\end{bmatrix}} \doteqdot C^{\begin{bmatrix}+d\\+p\\-e\\-v\end{bmatrix}} \doteqdot C^{\begin{bmatrix}+d\\+p\\+v\end{bmatrix}}$. In general, therefore, in this zone, compatibility is mostly between plosive and sulcal features.

(4) Some notice needs to be taken of the palatal zone of articulation in cases of immediate successions. Generally speaking, palatality is among the most freely combinable features of the language but it is noticeable that voicelessness in association with friction is not repeated in successive places when the remainder of the complex is either palato-alveolar or denti-alveolar. In brief, voiceless prepalatal or palatal friction (/θ, s, ʃ/) occurs once only in immediate succession.

(5) Of all consonant complexes, those we have written /r, l, n/ have by far the highest frequency of occurrence in my material, /n/ as C1, /r/ then /l/ as C2 and C3. This in itself suggests a need to recognize a category 'liquid', quite apart from some fairly obvious articulatory resemblances between the complexes in question (including, for instance, the 'complementarity' of /r/ and /l/ in terms of median and lateral contact versus aperture). The categorization

is more fully justified by the behaviour of such complexes in the matter of compatibility. 'Liquid' successions do occur at C2–C3, *cf* 'wurɑl' (snake), 'gɑrun' (horn; century), etc, but by no means all possibilities are exploited and C^{+n} noticeably does not occur as C2. The most striking fact, however, is that 'liquidity' may occur only once in the domain C1–C2.

(6) In the guttural zone, we have already seen that $C^{\begin{bmatrix}+u\\-p\end{bmatrix}}$ (/x, ɣ/)≏ $C^{\begin{bmatrix}+u\\+p\\-v\end{bmatrix}}$ (/k/), that $C^{\begin{bmatrix}+u\\-p\\-v\end{bmatrix}}$ (/x/)≏$C^{\begin{bmatrix}+u\\-p\\+v\end{bmatrix}}$ (/ɣ/), and that $C^{\begin{bmatrix}+u\\+p\\-v\end{bmatrix}}$ (/k/)≏ $C^{\begin{bmatrix}+u\\+p\\+v\end{bmatrix}}$ (/g/). Additionally, in immediate succession, $C^{\begin{bmatrix}+u\\-p\end{bmatrix}}$ (/x, ɣ/)≏ $C^{\begin{bmatrix}+u\\+p\end{bmatrix}}$ (/k, g/), so that velarity/uvularity can occur once only, a fact also true of (gutturality + friction) with the single aforementioned exception of '9ahid' (promise). Guttural friction is thus on a par with the earlier denti-friction and we may express the facts as follows:

$C^{\begin{bmatrix}-p\\+u\end{bmatrix}}$ (/x, ɣ/)≏$C^{\begin{bmatrix}-p\\+ph\end{bmatrix}}$ (/ħ, 9/)≏$C^{\begin{bmatrix}-p\\+h\end{bmatrix}}$ (/h/) – 9ahid.

In the light of the preceding fairly informal analysis, it will be seen that the 26 phoneme-letters needed to write this dialect of Arabic in roman form have no more than the status of practical devices giving transcribable shape to relevant feature-complexes and thereby orthoepic pronounceability to words. Firth's insistence on polysystemic analysis, as far as this appertains to phonology, is fully justified. Let us take a random example of the C1VC2VC3 pattern, *eg* 'ðibaħ' (he slaughtered), and pass it through the sieve of the rules and regularities of mutual exclusion that can be established. These may be summarized as follows.[25]

Duplication

1 Duplication is only common over the domain C2–C3, except when velarity, less often denti-alveolarity, is involved.

Complete exclusion (*ie* in both immediate and interrupted successions)

2 Voice≏voicelessness in otherwise similar feature-complexes (/b≏f, d≏t, ð≏θ, z≏s, g≏k, ɣ≏x, 9≏ħ/). (*Exception:* /j ~ ʃ/.)

3 Emphasis≏non-emphasis in otherwise similar complexes (/T≏t, S≏s, Ð≏ð/).

4 (Denti-alveolarity + friction) occurs once only (/θ≏ð, Ð, s, z, S; ð≏θ, Ð, s, z, S; Ð≏θ, ð, s, z, S; s≏θ, ð, Ð, z, S; z≏θ, ð, Ð, s, S; S≏θ, ð, Ð, s, z/).

5 (Velarity + plosion + voicelessness)≏(Uvularity + friction) (/k≏x, ɣ/).

6 (Uvularity + friction + voice) ≏ (gutturality + friction + voicelessness)
(/ɣ≏x, ħ, h/).
7 (Uvularity + friction + voice) ≏ (pharyngality + friction + voice)
(/ɣ≏9/).
8 (Gutturality + friction + voicelessness) occurs once only
(/x≏ħ, ≏h/).

Partial exclusion (in immediate successions only)
9 Labiality (excluding labio-velarity) occurs once only
(/f≏b≏m/).
10 (Denti-alveolarity + plosion) ≏ (denti-alveolarity + friction)
(/t, d, T≏z, ð, Đ/).
11 (Denti-alveolarity + plosion + voicelessness) ≏ (denti-alveolarity + non-sulcality + voicelessness)
(/t, T≏θ/).
12 (Denti-alveolarity + plosion + emphasis) ≏ (denti-alveolarity + plosion + non-emphasis)
(/T≏t, d/).
13 (Pre-palatality + friction + voicelessness) occurs once only
(/θ≏s≏ʃ/).
14 'Liquidity' occurs once only in the domain C1–C2 (/n≏l≏r/ as C1/C2).
15 Nasal ~ non-nasal 'liquid' successions do not occur at C2 ~ C3.
16 (Uvularity + friction) ≏ (Velarity + plosion)
(/x, ɣ≏k, g/).
17 (Gutturality + friction) occurs once only
(/x≏ɣ≏ħ≏9≏h/) (*Exception:* '9ahid').

Thus, returning now to the example of 'ðibaħ' considered phonemically:

(a) *C1 and C2 known:* ð–b–C3

The following phonemes could not occur at C3:
(i) *In relation to C1:*
/ð/ (rule 1), /θ/ (rules 2, 4), /Đ/ (rules 3, 4), /s/ (rule 4), /z/ (rule 4), /S/ (rule 4)
(ii) *In relation to C2:*
/f/ (rules 2, 9), /m/ (rule 9).

There are then only 18 *prima facie* possibilities of phonemic substitution at C3. By chance, the same number of quite different substitutions may be made at C1; thus

(b) *C2 and C3 known:* C1–b–ħ
   (i) *In relation to C3:*
      /ħ/ (rule 1), /9/ (rule 2), /ɣ/ (rule 6), /x/ (rule 8), /h/ (rule 8) cannot occur
   (ii) *In relation to C2:*
      /b/ (rule 1), /f/ (rule 9), /m/ (rule 9) are also excluded.

Finally, only 13 possibilities may potentially occur at C2;

(c) *C1 and C3 known:* ð–C2–ħ
   The following phonemes are inadmissible:
   (i) *In relation to C1:*
      /ð/ (rule 1), /θ/ (rules 2, 4), /Đ/ (rules 3, 4), /s/ (rule 4), /z/ (rule 4), /S/ (rule 4), /t/ (rule 10), /d/ (rule 10), /T/ (rule 10)
   (ii) *In relation to C3:*
      /ɣ/ (rules 6, 17), /x/ (rules 8, 17), /h/ (rules 8, 17), /9/ (rules 2, 17)

Let us turn now to quite a different area of phonology and consider something of the facts of accentuation and syllable patterning in various forms of Arabic.

Notes

1 It is strange to be asked to think of Firth as one of those 'easily frightened souls' referred to by M. Halle in an oddly ambiguous passage of his article 'On the bases of phonology' (in *The Structure of Language*, eds J. A. Fodor and J. J. Katz (Prentice-Hall, 1964), *p* 325). The passage reads: 'The inability of instrumental phoneticians to propose a workable segmentation procedure has, however, not resulted in a wholesale abandonment of the phoneme concept. Only a few easily frightened souls have been ready to do without the phoneme. The majority has apparently felt that absence of a simple segmentation procedure does not warrant abandoning the discrete picture of speech. The most important justification that could perhaps be offered for this stand is that almost every insight gained from Grimm's Law to Jakobson's distinctive features depends crucially on the assumption that speech is a sequence of discrete entities.' No linguist would deny that language submits to analysis in terms of structural entities but it is over the nature of these entities that deep divisions persist.

2 See, for example, *Prosodic Analysis*, ed F. R. Palmer (Oxford University Press, 1970); also E. W. Roberts, 'A critical survey of Firthian phonology', *Glossa* 6/1 (1972).

3 Contrary to the implication of this very simple example, a prosodic analysis of Arabic monosyllables and polysyllables is extremely complex, such is the intricacy of the relations developed between the parts of given patterns. Much more is involved than open vowels, emphatic and non-emphatic consonants, even for the two forms cited. Prosodic analysis, however, unhampered by any restriction to traditional phonetic powers of roman letters, permits such

complexities to be handled consistently, economically, and fully; it is not, as some may have thought, simply a means of counting a few more hairs on the (phonetic) animal's tail, nor indeed of splitting them.

4 Pronunciation is, in fact, breathy and nasal *passim*, but this is not our present concern.

5 This type of contrast within the verbal paradigm is, in fact, less common in Marrakesh than in *eg* Fez.

6 Outside the Maghrib, extensive vocalic difference of this kind is limited to open vowels, front and back, although 'smaller' phonetic differences between varieties of close vowel have still to be accounted for. In Morocco, the phonetic form of the long vowel of the passive participle varies greatly in proportion to differences of consonantal context and also in relation to dialect differences.

7 A spelling 'pahriiũu' is perhaps to be preferred for reasons of vowel sequencing possibilities that are not however germane to our present purpose.

8 The Sindhi spelling – ٻانهن – (b'aanhn) has no origin in Persian or Arabic practice.

9 A feature importantly shared, it may be remarked, with Cairene colloquial Arabic. A few vestiges of Hamitic influence are still in my opinion discernible in some forms of colloquial Egyptian Arabic.

10 The diphthong is reminiscent of that which is recognized orthographically in Maltese, as in 'kies' (cup), 'tlieta' (three), etc. In passing, mention may perhaps be made of an interesting case of open diphthong combining frontness and backness [aɑ] that occurs pre-pausally in western Algerian and Moroccan Arabic non-emphatic forms. Typically, the diphthong is followed by glottal closure. Thus, for example, 'slaa' [slaɑʔ] (Salé) (port at the mouth of the Bou Regreg river opposite Rabat) contrasts with 'Slɑɑ' [s̶ɫɑ·ʔ] (prayer).

11 In the following paper, 'Prominence and syllabication in Arabic'.

12 The features of emphasis and non-emphasis, usually stable within a root, sometimes fluctuate in relation to a contrast of frontness versus backness in association with other relevant consonantal features. Fluctuation is most noticeable in the case of sulcality + denti-alveolarity (S/s). As always, account must be taken of other features of the consonantal environment and 'r'-ness, for example, is relevant to the interesting contrast involving also short 'α' between 'kɑSSɑr' (he smashed) versus 'kassir' (smash!).

13 D. T. Langendoen, *The London School of Linguistics* (MIT Press, 1968), *p* 104.

14 Any such sequence is inadmissible in the Cyrenaican Bedouin Arabic we have spoken of; *cf* the use of incremental vowel length and of gemination in *eg* 'iktibat' (she wrote) + 'ih' > 'iktibietih', and 'iktiban' (they [fem] wrote) + 'ih' > 'iktibannih'.

15 See Eugénie J. A. Henderson, 'Prosodies in Siamese', *Asia Major* 1 (1949), *pp* 189–215; reprinted in *Prosodic Analysis*, ed F. R. Palmer (Oxford University Press, 1970), *pp* 27–53, and in *Phonetics in Linguistics: a Book of Readings*, eds W. E. Jones and J. Laver (Longman, 1973), *pp* 127–53.

16 See *p* 101.

17 Some account of the phonetic features of tense (kk–) and lax (k–) articulation in Berber has been given in my 'Long consonants in phonology and phonetics' in the Philological Society's special volume *Studies in Linguistic Analysis* (Blackwell, 1962), *p* 193 *ff*.

18 A similar analysis of the Berber *word* is to be found in the article by L. Galand in the *Encyclopaedia of Islam* (new edition, 1960), Vol I (A–B), *p* 1182.

19 J. H. Greenberg, 'The patterning of root morphemes in Semitic', *Word* 6 (1950), *pp* 162–81.

20 Duplication involving C1 elsewhere occurs with
(1) forms of monosyllabic structure CV:C, *eg* 'bieb' (door, entrance), 'sies' (wall), 'xuux' (peaches), etc;
(2) reduplicated quadriliteral forms, mostly of a phonaesthetic kind, *eg* 'TɑʃTɑʃ' (to spark), 'dabdab' (to call sheep), 'ʃakʃak' (to call goats), 'bɑxbɑx' (to drizzle), 'wɑkwɑk' (to stutter), etc;
(3) other phonaesthetic forms, *eg* 'rɑɑrɑ' (to drive a flock of sheep and goats) (derived from the shepherd's cry ['rr::'ħaʔ]). The Egyptian form 'ɣaaɣa' (to gurgle [of contented infant]) is a similar example known to the writer;
(4) loans, *eg* 'bunb' (bomb), 'bɑbuur' (ship, train; primus-stove), 'bimbieʃi [? superseded]' (corporal), 'ʃawiiʃ [? superseded]' (sergeant), 'kaɡak' (cake), 'sibsi' (cigarette), 'TumɑɑTum' (tomatoes), etc;
(5) forms belonging to a baby-talk register, including 'wɑwɑ' (warning to infant, *eg* against danger of fire), 'bɑbɑ' (anything nice), 'dada' (female Sudanese servant), 'bɑbbɑ' (slap), 'nanna' (sleep), 'guggɑ' (dirt), 'titta' (horse), 'ʃiʃʃa' (meat). 'mɑmmɑ' is also a form children are taught to say when they want food. I have also heard 'biibi' (father) and 'gɑɑg' (chicken). In general, these forms are more likely to occur in the speech of women, which in turn may possibly reveal something of a Berber substrate. 'nanna' and 'dada', for example, strongly recall similar Berber forms, and so also does 'biibi'. Berber nouns of kin relationship are a sub-class of nominals characterized by their own set of pronominal suffixes, and a noun of relationship does not occur without a suffix; thus, Berber 'baaba', for example, is 'my father' and '–i' (Arabic 1st pers sing pronominal suffix) in 'biibi' is perhaps to be interpreted in the same way. I have also heard the form 'ya yimmi' as a variant of 'ya ummi' (O my mother) (*cf* the use among Berber women of 'i yəmma' as an affectionate form of address to a child). Other examples of baby-talk that I recorded include: 'kuxxɑ' (warning to child to desist), 'umbuwwɑ' (water), 'aħħa' (fire), 'aɡɡa' (defecation), 'zaɡa' (camel), 'irrɑ' (donkey), 'baɡɡa' (sheep), 'biʃʃa' (cat), 'muu' (cow), 'ubwiyya' (milk [at breast]).

21 The rareness of the co-occurrence of $C(3)^{+v}$ and $C(3)^{-v}$ in one root is no doubt in part accountable from the grammatical use of $C(3)^{-v}$, to which categories of tense, number, gender, and person are referable in *eg* 'tidris' (you [masc sing] learn, study), 'guɡadit' (I/you [masc sing] sat down), etc.

22 *A propos*, in contrast with most Arabic dialects, there is no glottal stop in Cyrenaican colloquial Arabic.

23 We should notice in passing that the Cyrenaican Bedouin form 'fam' (mouth) is irregular in a number of ways, not least for its CVC structure, rare indeed in nouns, but also for the twofold occurrence of labiality in adjacent consonantal places. It is normally only /w/ that occurs in the vicinity of other labials.

24 The single exception 'fam' (mouth) (see preceding note) is irregular in other ways. The structure CVC, exceptional in nouns, occurs also in a few irregular verbs, *eg* 'xɑð' (he took), 'kal' (he ate); elsewhere it is characteristic of the particle class, *eg* 'min' (from), 'ɡan' (about). Parts of the body and nouns of relationship, it may be noted, are syllabically 'odd' in Berber as well as Arabic.

25 In conformity with them, it may be remarked, are the interesting facts of phonaesthetic association between certain features or sequences of features and some fairly clearly recognizable semantic fields, like that by which (voice+velarity+plosion), variously accompanied by back versus front vowel quality and emphasis versus non-emphasis, relates to actions of cutting, breaking,

chopping, slicing, etc (*cf* 'guTɑ9' (he cut), 'guTɑf' (he cut or plucked [flower]), 'guSɑf' (he snapped off [twig from tree], plucked [pigeon]), 'guTɑʃ' (he cut off [tips of donkey's ears, for good luck]), 'gɑSS' (he cut [with any instrument along the length of an object, as cloth with scissors]), 'gɑbb' (he sliced through [sharp incisive action, as cutting through snake's head]), 'ginad' (he cut or chopped in two [*eg* piece of wood or pencil, across its length; also he cut across (wadi)]), 'gaddad' (he chopped up [meat]), 'gulɑ9' (he extracted [tooth], uprooted [plant]), 'Tugɑr' (the chipped [cup or glass]), 'fugɑʃ' (he split open [*eg* melon or pumpkin with instrument or by short sharp blow with the hand]), 'fugɑS' (he cracked [egg], sliced [tomato]), 'fallɑg' (he cleaved [wood or trunk of tree with axe or pick])). The membership of such groups cannot, of course, be closely defined – should we, for example, include with the foregoing 'gubɑS' (he picked out [delicately with tips of fingers, as thorn from flesh]), 'gubɑÐ' (he grasped), 'kɑmmɑÐ' (he enclosed in his palm), etc? – but, however fugitive, phonaesthesia of this and other kinds is interesting in Arabic, not least for historical and dialectological study. What match is there, one wonders, between Cyrenaican Bedouin and other dialects in those verbs that, characterized by varying forms of gutturality, relate to digging, scraping, scratching, perforating, etc (*cf* 'ħafɑr' (he dug [with spade, pick, etc]), 'ħafan' (he scooped up [in cupped hands, *eg* cereals, sugar, water]), 'juħɑr' (he scooped up [earth with hands; also used of cats and dogs digging up earth]), 'juxɑr' (he dug out [*eg* the dough of a loaf, leaving the crust; also used of rodent gnawing into object]), 'gu9ɑr' (he perforated), 'harɑd' (it pierced [as of nail entering flesh]), 'biħaθ' (he scratched [aimlessly on ground with stick, nail, etc]), 'ħakk' (he scraped, scratched [with fingernails], groomed [horse with coarse brush]), 'xɑtaʃ' (he scratched lightly), 'xɑbaʃ' (it clawed [of cat scratching violently and deeply]), 'xɑrɑT' (he scraped [*eg* with knife to remove dirt or paint])?

Three

Prominence and syllabication in Arabic

The incidence of tonicity in Classical Arabic words as pronounced by Egyptian 'ɡulama' *varies regularly according to the syllable structure of the whole form. Rules of accentuation given in the available grammars are mistaken and fail principally because they take no account of the influence of colloquial Arabic in a particular area, which leads to considerable accentual differences between the several parts of the Arab world. The Egyptian 'high Classical' pronunciation of the* 'ɡulama' *seems to be unique to the extent that there are no grammatical conditions affecting tonic incidence; in other forms of Arabic, Classical and colloquial, tonicity must be considered to some extent within a grammatical framework, although for a given grammatical class, syllable structure is again the determining factor. Tonicity is thus part of the syllable pattern of an individual form, but in order to establish a system of patterns in a given style of pronunciation, it is also interestingly necessary to recognize differences between short vowels less as to their quality in response to different consonantal environments than to such features as their stability or instability in related forms. Distinction is drawn below between* 'V' *and* 'v' *as categories of sonant in relation mainly to the elision or non-elision of short vowels in paradigms of related forms; vowel quality must be considered quite separately from sonant status. Once again, different forms of Arabic vary as to their behaviour in these respects and, with tonicity also varying in relation to difference of short vowel sequences in adjacent syllables, questions of syllable patterning as a whole are probably more important to Arabic phonological studies than the usual run of accounts of consonantal differences between the manifold forms of the language. At all events, Arabic is interestingly* sui generis *in respect of the features described below.*[1]

Faced with the fact that in many varieties of Arabic, including Bedouin dialects of the kind to which Sibawayhi was wont to turn, polysyllabic words and certain other unitary complexes are characterized in pronunciation by the prominence which makes one syllable stand out to the ear above the others,[2] the linguist is understandably puzzled by the failure of the Arab grammarians to mention the subject of accentuation. Bewilderment increases with the realization not only that *rules* of prominence are statable for a given colloquial but also that correspondence between colloquials or between a colloquial and a given 'Classical' pronunciation is equally regular. Confusion is complete when the 'rules' given in all reference grammars of Classical Arabic are found to take no cognizance of regional differences of pronunciation and, what is worse, to bear little or no resemblance to the facts in any one region.

There is doubtless much truth in the generally accepted view that the form or forms of Arabic familiar to the grammarians were not characterized by prominence, but one may also with some justification believe that these scholars lacked the interest to devise techniques and categories of the kind necessary for rigorous observation and analysis. They were in large measure orthoepists, concerned to describe the phonetic powers of Arabic letters and to use these more or less traditional letter-powers as their framework of reference and description in response to spoken utterance. For many practical linguistic purposes this is not necessarily bad procedure, provided, for instance, that the frequently heard comment on the nature of the first consonant in such an Egyptian word as 'dɑrb' (path) (*cf* 'dars' (lesson) and 'Dɑrb' (hitting)), *viz* 'It is really "daal"[3] but sounds like "Dɑɑd"',[3] is recognized as a claim on the part of the speaker to no more knowledge than that of how to spell the word; or again, provided that such a statement as 'In . . . they pronounce "qɑɑf" like "jiim"' is seen to imply an erroneous belief that Arabic letters have absolute values, values doubtless not as ineffable as that associated in ancient times with 'Dɑɑd' but none the less immutable and inviolate. It is such concentration on written form that has led in Arabic phonology to an obsessive concern with consonants[4] and a consequent failure to appreciate the vital importance of the syllable and, more especially, of the total pattern provided by syllables in combination. Prominence in a given word of Classical Arabic as pronounced by teachers at Al-Azhar Mosque and University in Cairo and at Dār al-'Ulūm, the teachers' training college of Cairo University, is part of and inseparable from such total syllable patterns, but the fact does not appear to be recognized by the teachers themselves. In other kinds of Arabic, as we shall see later, vowel quality, too, is often a reflex of whole syllabic complexes; let us first, however, consider the facts of prominence in the pronunciation of Classical Arabic as taught in the Egyptian centres that have been mentioned, a form of Arabic which, for convenience, may be labelled CA(E).[5]

CA(E) syllables, each of which must *ex hypothesi* begin with a consonant, exhibit the following structures in terms of consonant and vowel: CV, CVV, CVC, CVVC, CVCC, CVVCC.[6] In the process of research, material was collected in such a way as to exhaust the possible combinations of these structures up to a permitted maximum of seven syllables. The forms analysed included those containing the pronominal suffixes, but it was found that, with two exceptions which are given below, inclusion or exclusion of suffixes is irrelevant to the facts of prominence; apart from the two exceptions, there is structural parallelism between suffixed and unsuffixed forms. It was also found that particle prefixes, including the article, which are fused with the word in Arabic writing are without interest for prominence as far as CA(E) is concerned.[7] The following is a representative selection of forms, all unsuffixed; the prominent syllable is indicated by an acute accent over the appropriate vowel. The word-isolate may be pronounced in two forms, pause- and non-pause, for example in the context of teaching, and examples of both are included:[8]

> Dɑrɑ́bt, ˡaɡmáal, ħaajjáat, yuSɑllúun, yursiláan, muʃtaaqɑ́ɑt, ħaaqqɑtáan, yataħaddáwn; ˡáħad, qúmtum, ʃáadda, katábtum, mustáʃfaa, haaðáani, ʃaabbáatun, yataqɑɑtalúuna, mutaħakkimúuna, muʃtɑqqɑtáani; qɑttála, qɑttálat, kaatába, kaatábaa, ħaaqqɑ́tun, muɡallímun, katabtúmaa, mustɑqbílun, muħmɑɑrrɑ́tun; kátaba, ˡinkásɑrɑ, kaatábataa, waaqífatun, bulahníyatun, muqɑɑtílatun, mutajanníbatun; faɡalátun, katabátaa, murtabiTɑ́tun.[9]

A first indication of the connection between prominence and total syllable pattern is provided by a comparison between pause- and non-pause forms. Thus, for example, different specific syllables of the same word are prominent in the forms 'muɡállim' (pause) and 'muɡallímun' (non-pause), though both are paroxytones. On the hypothesis that prominence is a function of total syllable pattern, 'muɡállim' may be seen to resemble, not 'muɡallímun', but, let us say, 'mustáʃfaa'; there is no 'shift' of stress, except metaphorically, between the forms. Similarly, the first syllable of pausal 'kátab' and non-pausal 'kátaba' is not to be regarded as 'inherently' prominent; as we shall see, the two forms are classificatorily different, 'kátab' belongs with *eg* 'ˡáħad', and 'kátaba' has more in common with 'ˡinkásɑrɑ'.

The first fact that strikes the investigator is that all forms containing a final long syllable of structure CVVC or CVCC,[10] *ie* 'Dɑrɑ́bt, ˡaɡmáal, yuSɑllúun', etc, are oxytonic and, conversely, that all forms with final syllable of structure CV, CVV, or CVC are either paroxytonic or proparoxytonic. The first major division of the material, therefore, is into forms with long (L) ultimate and those with not-long (L̲) ultimate, and it will be seen that, as far as disyllabic forms are concerned, such a division is definitive: once the ultimate syllable has been identified as L or L̲, no more need be known in order to place the prominent syllable; the penultimate syllable may be of structure CV, CVV, CVC, or CVVC, *eg* 'ráˈaa, qɑ́ɑlat, qúmtum, ʃáadda', but no purpose is served by subdividing these structures. To turn to longer forms and to pre-ultimate syllables, comparison between such forms as 'kátaba', on the one hand, and 'katábta, kitáabah, mumáaddah', on the other, suggests that it is necessary to distinguish in pre-ultimate position between CV and CVC/CVV/CVVC. Operative contrasts in pre-ultimate position are in fact never more than twofold between short CV (S) and not-short CVC/CVV/CVVC (S̲). There might appear *prima facie* to be a case for recognizing a system of three terms, short CV, medium CVV/CVC, and long CVVC/CVCC, but such a system would be inappropriate and over-all, without reference either to the place of the syllable in the total structure or to the structural pattern as a whole. It is the latter and the establishment of a system of such patterns that are of paramount interest for the statement of prominence. The primary and fundamentally interesting linguistic fact about prominence in CA(E) is not that it is necessary to handle it in terms of such abstractions as C and V, L and L̲, S and S̲, but that it is part of the total syllable pattern of the form.

So far only one definitive division of the material has been made, into ultimate L and L̲. Further analysis of ultimate-L̲ forms shows that if the penultimate syllable is S̲, then the form is always paroxytonic, *eg* 'mustáʃfaa, mu9állim, muqɑ́ɑtil, taqɑ́ɑSSɑ, ʃaabbáatun, muʃtɑqqɑtáani, yataqɑɑtalúuna', but that if this syllable is S, then both paroxytones and proparoxytones are found, *eg* 'kaatába, qɑttálat, maktábah, ħaaqqɑ́tun, ʃajɑrɑ́tun, katabátaa, murtabiTɑ́tun', but 'kátaba, ˈinkásɑrɑ, bulahníyatun'. Examination of these –/S/L̲ forms reveals that if the antepenultimate syllable is S̲, then paroxytones are the rule, *eg* 'kaatába, qɑttálat, maktábah, ħaaqqɑ́tun', but that if it is S, then again both paroxytones and proparoxytones are found, *eg* 'ʃajɑrɑ́tun, katabátaa, murtabiTɑ́tun', on the one hand, 'kátaba, ˈinkásɑrɑ, bulahníyatun', on the other. Finally, forms of which the three final syllables are –/S/S/L̲ are found to be regularly proparoxytonic when either there is no pre-antepenultimate syllable (*eg* 'kátaba') or that syllable is S̲ (*eg* 'ˈinkásɑrɑ, bulahníyatun') but equally regularly paroxytonic when the pre-antepenultimate is S (*eg* 'ʃajɑrɑ́tun, katabátaa, murtabiTɑ́tun').

It will be clear from analysis so far that sequences of short syllables are of particular interest in the matter of prominence, and it is to be anticipated that pre-ultimate sequences of four and five such syllables will require special notice. These sequences are exhibited only by suffixed forms and may be illustrated by forms containing the 3rd person singular masculine suffix '–hu' and the 3rd person dual suffix '–humaa'. Thus we find, for example,

(i) 'ʃajɑrɑ́tuhu', *ie* S/S/S/S/$\underline{L}$, regularly proparoxytonic and thus contrasting with paroxytonic 'ˈadwiyatúhu', *ie* $\underline{S}$/S/S/S/$\underline{L}$, and
(ii) 'ʃajɑrɑtuhúmaa',[11] *ie* S/S/S/S/S/$\underline{L}$, paroxytonic and thus contrasting with proparoxytonic 'ˈadwiyatúhumaa', *ie* $\underline{S}$/S/S/S/S/$\underline{L}$.

These patterns do not contradict but simply extend earlier analysis. The facts of prominence in CA(E) can be exhaustively stated within the framework of a 7-term system of patterns, which, with reference to 6 places of final syllables, may be displayed as below. It is possible to regard pause (#) as equivalent to $\underline{S}$ in certain pre-ultimate places and to achieve thereby a unified exposition, which avoids the need to subdivide forms in accordance with the number of their constituent syllables; for example, 'maktábah' ($\underline{S}$/S/$\underline{L}$) and 'ˈáħad' (#/S/$\underline{L}$), 'ˈinkásɑrɑ' ($\underline{S}$/S/S/$\underline{L}$) and 'kátaba' (#/S/S/$\underline{L}$), 'murtabiTɑ́tun' ($\underline{S}$/S/S/S/$\underline{L}$) and 'ʃajɑrɑ́tun' (#/S/S/S/$\underline{L}$), etc, may be looked upon as structurally equivalent. The notation /. . . / below in respect of pre-ultimate syllables means that the quantity of the syllable so represented is immaterial:

	Prominence	*Examples*
1. /. . ./. . ./. . ./. . ./. . ./ L	Oxytonic	Dɑrɑ́bt, ˈa9máal, yuSɑllúun, yataħaddáwn, etc
2. /. . ./. . ./. . ./. . ./ $\underline{S}$ / $\underline{L}$	Paroxytonic	mustáʃfaa, mu9állim, muqɑ́atil, ʃaab-báatun, etc
3. /. . ./. . ./. . ./ $\underline{S}$ or # / S / $\underline{L}$	Paroxytonic	kaatába, qɑttálat, maktábah, ħaaq-qɑ́tun, etc rɑ́ˈaa, kátab, híya, etc
4. /. . ./. . ./ $\underline{S}$ or # / S / S / $\underline{L}$	Proparoxytonic	ˈinkásɑrɑ, ˈiDTɑ́rɑba, bulahníyatun, etc kátaba, ʃájɑrah, etc
5. /. . ./ $\underline{S}$ or # / S / S / S / $\underline{L}$	Paroxytonic	ˈadwiyatúhu, ma9rifatúhu, murtabiTɑ́tun, etc ʃajɑrɑ́tun, katabátaa, etc

6. / S̲ / S / S / S / S / L̲ or #	Proparoxytonic	ˈadwiyatúhumaa, ma9rifatúhumaa, etc ʃajarɑ́tuhu, baqɑrɑ́-tuhu, etc
7. / S / S / S / S / S / L̲	Paroxytonic	ʃajarɑtuhúmaa, baqɑrɑtuhúmaa, etc

The fact of similarity of function between S̲ and # is interesting. Paroxytonic prominence in trisyllabic 'maktábah, qɑttálat', etc, is recognized throughout the Arab world as characteristically Egyptian. That the prominence in such cases is felt to be striking is doubtless due to the statistical frequency of such trisyllabic forms but it can now be seen that a good deal more is involved than isolated trisyllables and the simple comparison of, say, Egyptian 'maktábah' with Cyrenaican 'máktibih'.

Classical, and for that matter also so-called Modern or Contemporary Arabic, is a *Schriftsprache* capable of as much difference of phonetic interpretation between countries as was ecclesiastical Latin in the Mass. In the matter of prominence, the form 'katabataa', for example, is, within a comparatively restricted geographical area, regularly and variously pronounced as (1) an oxytone (Lebanon),[12] (2) a paroxytone (CA(E)), (3) a proparoxytone (Nablus in Palestine),[13] (4) a prototone (see below) (Upper Egypt). It is perhaps hardly surprising that the reference grammars should be so much at sea. The similarity in respect of prominence between the Classical and colloquial Arabic of a given area is well known but has yet to be investigated thoroughly. The two Egyptian informants who supplied the material for the above analysis came from regions of their country between which differences of colloquial Arabic are most marked; A was from Tanta in the Delta and D from Qena in Upper Egypt. In view of this difference of origin it was remarkable that they agreed completely in their renderings of the word-isolates, but, after all, they had been trained over a period of nine years. They did not always agree, however, in their renderings of two patterns in connected texts, and the fact that D from Qena modified his forms in the context of isolation is to be taken as another indication of the fact that, for Classical as well as colloquial Arabic, standards are set in Egypt by the Delta and particularly by Cairo. The two patterns concerned are –/S/S/S/L̲ and –/S̲/S/L̲ and both are illustrated by 'wajadataa' and 'qiT9ata' in the first line of the well known fable which begins 'hirrɑtaani wajadataa qiT9ata jubn' (Two cats found a piece of cheese). A's rendering was the expected 'hirratáani wajadátaa qiT9áta júbn' but D gave 'hirratáani wájadataa qíT9ata júbn', *ie* with prototonic 'wajadataa' and proparoxytonic 'qiT9ata'; it is not, therefore, surprising to find in D's dialect such forms as '9ágalatak' (your bicycle) and 'mírwaħa' (fan) with the first syllables similarly prominent.[14] Let us turn now to consider forms of colloquial Arabic more closely.

In typical accounts of colloquial Arabic,[15] the facts of prominence are framed in the form of 'rules' which tend to gloss over certain important features. Typical 'rules' for Cairene Colloquial (CC) might be formulated as follows:

> All words, suffixed or unsuffixed, are paroxytones, except
> (a) those containing an ultimate syllable of structure CVV,[16] CVVC, or CVCC, which are oxytones, *eg* 'maskáa' (holding [fem sing] him), 'gatóo' (cake), 'fanagíin' (cups), 'ˈiʃtaɣált' (I/you [masc sing] worked);
> (b) the vast majority of those containing an ultimate syllable of structure either CV or CVC, penultimate and antepenultimate both CV, and pre-antepenultimate either CVC or nil, which are proparoxytonic, *eg* 'ˈinkásarit' (it [fem] was broken), 'kátaba' (clerks), etc.

Such a formulation, defensible on pedagogical grounds, says nothing about total pattern, fails to make such interesting contrasts as that between CVC–CVCVCV(C) and CV–CVCVCV(C), *eg* 'ˈinkásarit' and 'Darabítu(h)' (*cf* similar patterns in the analysis of CA(E) above), and, in the words 'the vast majority', conceals some truly interesting facts. It is to these 'exceptions' to (b) that we shall now turn.

Harrell dismissed such CC forms as 'subú9a, Dubú9a, ħiSína, libísa, ɣiríba', as a 'handful of lexical items'.[17] In the manner of most 'exceptions', however, these forms are highly significant. It is found in CC and confirmed in other forms of colloquial Egyptian Arabic that difference of prominence is relatable not only to difference of total syllable pattern in terms of C and V but also, for example in the favourite pattern CVCVCV, to difference of total vowel-sequence. Thus, in the CC pattern CVCVCa, a sequence of close vowels in the first two syllables is associated with paroxytonic prominence for the form and other sequences with proparoxytonic prominence; thus, 'subú9a' and 'libísa', but 'búxala', '9ínaba', and 'kátaba'. In the Egyptian dialect of Ṭahwēh (otherwise Ṭahwāy) (TD)[18] the noun plural pattern CuCuCa, *eg* 'fuħúla' (bulls), 'kubúʃa' (rams), etc, is extremely common and regularly associated with paroxytonic prominence.[19]

In contrast with CC, the TD pattern CiCiCa, *eg* 'kíniza' (narrow), 'míziga' (touchy), 'wíriʃa' (crafty), 'míħika' (lazy), 'ríSiSɑ' (heavy), '9íʃiʃa' (nasty), '9ídila' (straight), etc, is characteristic not of noun plurals but of feminine singular adjectives. Moreover, the sequence i-i-a, unlike u-u-a above, is regularly associated with proparoxytonic prominence. An analysis omitting reference to the grammatical categories partially characterized by the phonological patterns of which prominence is a part would be arbitrary and disintegrated. The facts of prominence, which have been exhaustively stated above for CA(E) in wholly phonological terms, are not statable for colloquial Arabic without some reference to linguistic categories other than phonological ones. Nevertheless, when, for example, TD '9ídila' and '9udúla' or '9udúla' and '9úrujit' (she became lame) have been separated grammatically, there still remains to be considered within a given grammatical category, and in terms of total vowel-sequence, such wholly phonological difference as that between, say, '9udúla' and '9úgala' (wise men). In passing it may be observed that the difference between TD '9ídila' (no variant form) and 'libísa' (freely variant with 'ilbísa') might well be considered 'crucial' by the phonemically inclined, but the contrast is extremely rare and that between '9ídila' and '9udúla' is every bit as crucial and much more frequent.

Analytical categories of whatever order are established by considering the similarities and differences which obtain not only between forms but also between relationships. Description of structural elements comprising 'absolute' forms is a comparatively straightforward matter, but to state relationship between forms and between sets of forms in suitably objective terms is not always easy. It is necessary, for example, in the absence of any more suitable term, to redefine 'elision' as a term of relationship between forms, before using it in the description of an extremely important feature of Arabic phonology; it is, moreover, in general unlikely that the term can be suitably employed unless specific contrast is made between relations of elision and 'non-elision'. Without such terms it is very difficult indeed to describe the relation between, say, CC 'fíhim' (he understood) and 'fíhmit (fihim+it)' (she understood) as well as the very important difference between the 'fíhim:fíhmit' relation and that obtaining between, say, 'Dɑ́rɑb' (he hit) and 'Dɑ́rɑbit (Dɑrɑb+it)' (she hit). A relation of 'elision of unstressed i' is illustrated by 'fíhim:fíhmit' and one of 'non-elision of unstressed ɑ' by 'Dɑ́rɑbit'. Further CC examples of varied structures are as follows; it will be seen from them that unstressed 'u' behaves like 'i', and unlike 'a' or 'ɑ': 'yáaxud:yáxdu (yaaxud+u)' (he takes:they take), 'ˡáabil:ˡáblu (ˡaabil+u)' (he met:

they met), 'yitwígid: yitwígdu (yitwigid+u)' (it is found: they are found), 'ˈitwágad: ˈitwágadu (ˈitwagad+u)' (it was found: they were found), 'fihímt: ˈana fhímt (ˈana+fihimt)' (I/you [masc sing] understood: I understood), 'katábt: ˈana katábt (ˈana+katabt)' (I/you [masc sing] wrote: I wrote), 'hudúumak: ˈiddíini hdúumak (ˈiddiini+huduumak)' (your clothes: give me your clothes), 'ʃɑrɑ́ɑbak: ˈiddíini ʃɑrɑ́ɑbak (ˈiddiini+ʃɑrɑɑbak)' (your socks: give me your socks), 'ħuséen: ˈabu ħséen' (Husein: Husein's father), 'faríid: ˈabu faríid' (Fareed: Fareed's father).[20] The conclusion is therefore inescapable that the structural status of short unstressed *close* vowels is unlike that of similar *open* vowels. As word-classes are established and then used in the designation and description of colligations,[21] so classes of vowel and consonant may be established and then similarly used in the statement of phonological structures. The difference between CC close and open short vowels as syllable-markers or what may be called *sonants* requires recognition in any structural notation, and a distinction between V (=a, ɑ) and v (=i, u) would seem to meet the needs of the case, so that the earlier 'fíhim' and 'Dɑ́rɑb' might be said to illustrate CVCvC and CVCVC respectively. It is to these and other features of syllabication and syllable pattern rather than to prominence as such that the remainder of this paper is mostly devoted.[22] It will be seen subsequently that, at least as far as Cyrenaican Arabic is concerned, no satisfactory exposition of the facts of prominence is feasible without prior examination of somewhat similar but rather more complex features of syllabication than those just considered.

In the varieties of Arabic examined so far the relation between phonetic form and phonological structure has been comparatively clear-cut and there has been little difficulty in deciding on the structure of a given form, simple or suffixed, in terms of consonants and vowels, though it was found necessary for colloquial Egyptian Arabic to distinguish between two sonants, V and v. For other varieties, however, and notably for Bedouin dialects, the structural elements comprising a given form are not so easily identified, since relations between forms are *prima facie* less straightforward than those encountered hitherto. The remainder of this paper is concerned with a Bedouin dialect of the Cyrenaican Jebel (CyD).[23] It is beyond the scope of the paper to examine the whole range of CyD syllable patterns, but the purpose of analysis is sufficiently served by a series of comparisons between simple forms and those containing pronominal suffixes, verbal tense suffixes, and the feminine-singulative suffix.

A first comparison of CC and CyD forms, as for instance,

CC :: CyD
kátab : kátabit : katabítu(h) :: kitáb : iktíbat : iktibíetih[24]
máktab : maktábu(h) :: máktab : máktibih[25]
yíktib : yiktíbu :: yíktib : yíkitbu[26]
yíf ham : yif hámu :: yáf ham : yáf hamɑw[27]

shows that CC short vowels are more 'stable' as to (i) quality and (ii) position in relation to the consonants of the root. It will be clear that a Classical framework of reference, all too often employed, is totally inadequate for the purpose of description; it is utterly misleading, for example, to ask whether the second vowel of CyD 'máktibih' (*cf* 'máktab') is 'kasrah' (Classical i) or 'fatħah' (Classical a). These terms, together with 'Dammah' (Classical u), function for Classical Arabic in a three-term system of commutable vowels and corresponding written diacritica; in CyD, however, a threefold alternance of short vowels is extremely rare, and can only conceivably be established for a few structures in which the consonantal features of trill or voiced velar plosion also regularly figure.[28] A quasi-Classical approach to CyD would, furthermore, necessitate the recognition for certain structures involving a voiceless velar consonant an alternance of two short *open* vowels, front and back, but for the description of this distinction no traditional Arabic terms are available.[29]

The transcribed difference between the vowels of the first syllable of, say, 'ħaʃíiʃ' (grass), 'Turíig' (road), and 'kibíir' (big [masc sing]), should not be taken to imply the recognition of a three-term vowel system for the syllable. The differences of vowel quality to which the transcription corresponds are, in fact, regularly relatable to differences of the initial consonant, so that vowel quality is a property of the syllable and not of an individual vowel-unit.[30] The openness of the vowel in 'ħaʃíiʃ' is regularly associated with initial *gutturality*;[31] central vowel quality in 'Turíig' relates to initial *emphasis*; half-close frontness in 'kibíir' to an initial articulatory complex which contains neither gutturality nor emphasis. No vowel alternance of the usual kind can be established for short open syllables in CyD; it is only with reference to closed syllables and to V in a structure CVCəC, where ə is an anaptyctic vowel (see below), that such alternances operate; moreover, since allowance has to be made for difference of vocalic form in association with difference of other features in total syntagms, no such vowel-alternance is ever more than twofold.

A twofold alternance operates at many points in the dialect: for example, in the distinction between perfect tense, on the one hand, and imperfect tense and imperative, on the other, in certain of the 'derived forms' of the verb, *eg* 'ɣɑ́yyɑr' (he changed) : 'ɣɑ́yyir' (change! [imp masc sing]), 'kɑ́SSɑr' (he broke) : 'kássir' (break!), 'sáamaħ' (he forgave): 'síemiħ' (forgive!), or again in the distinction between active voice, *eg* 'gitál' (he killed), and the passive, *eg* 'igtíl' (he was killed), or yet again, and with purely phonological relevance, between such pairs as 'kábiʃ' (ram) and 'líbis' (clothes).[32] Comparison of simple and suffixed forms introduces features recalling what was termed 'a relation of elision' in regard to Egyptian varieties of colloquial Arabic considered earlier. Thus, for example,

gássam : gássimih (gassam + ih) : gassámha (gassam + ha)
≠ gássim : gássmih (gassim + ih) : gassímha (gassim + ha)[33]
and sáamaħ : síemiħih (saamaħ + ih) : sa(a)máħha (saamaħ + ha)
≠ síemiħ : síemħih (siemiħ + ih) : sa(a)míħha (siemiħ + ha)[34]

It will be seen that a relation of elision obtains between 'gássim' and 'gássmih' (also 'síemiħ' and 'síemħih') but not between 'gássam' and 'gássimih' (also 'sáamaħ' and 'síemiħih') nor 'gássim' and 'gassímha' (also 'síemiħ' and 'sa(a)míħha'). It is reasonable to recognize again two sonant units of different syllabic function; V, which may stand in a short open syllable, and, v, which may not. Vowel quality is irrelevant to the establishment of sonants; the vowels of the second syllables of 'gássimih, síemiħih, máktibih (maktab + ih)' (his office), etc, belong to the sonant category V, although qualitatively they are the equivalent of 'i' (= sonant v) in 'gássim' and 'síemiħ';[35] nor should it be thought that it is only in atonic syllables, as in 'gássam : gássimih', that the qualitative relation 'a, ɑ : i, u' obtains between exponents of V, *cf* 'ilfáf : ilfífih (ilfaf + ih)' (his bundles). Qualitative difference in the form of V in short open syllables relates to accompanying consonantal features as in the earlier examples of 'ħaʃiiʃ', 'Turíig', and 'kibíir'; without preceding gutturality or emphasis, the vowel of the second syllable of 'yálbisɑw (yalbas + ɑw)' (they [masc] dress) differs in the manner indicated by the transcription from the corresponding vowels in 'yáfhamɑw (yafham + ɑw)' (they understand) and 'yáʃrubɑw (yaʃrab + ɑw)' (they drink), but again all three vowels are classifiable as sonant V, not v. This variation in the form of V in open and closed syllables correlates with a twofold division of pronominal suffixes into consonant-beginning and vowel-beginning suffixes, as the following paradigms show:

		Suffix	máktab	ilfáf
Sing	1st pers	–i	máktibi	ilfífi
	2nd pers masc	–ɑk	máktibɑk	ilfífɑk
	2nd pers fem	–ik	máktibik	ilfífik
	3rd pers masc	–ih, –ɑh[36]	máktibih	ilfífih
	3rd pers fem	–ha, –hɑ	maktábha	ilfáffa[37]

Pl	1st pers	–na	maktábna	ilfáfna
	2nd pers masc	–kɑm	maktábkɑm	ilfɑ́fkɑm
	2nd pers fem	–kan	maktábkan	ilfáfkan
	3rd pers masc	–hum	maktábhum	ilfɑ́ffum
	3rd pers fem	–hin	maktábhin	ilfáffin

Such qualitative difference in the exponents of V is in marked contrast with Cairene, wherein sonant category and vowel quality are more closely associated. Contrast, for example, CyD 'huu kibiir' and CC 'huwwa kbiir'; as far as the structure of the initial syllable is concerned, the form 'kibiir' is CyD CV– and CC Cv–. The CyD distinction V : v corresponds without exception to Classical a : i/u; *cf*, for example, CyD 'kibíir, iktíeb, ukbɑ́ɑr' : CA 'kabíir, kitáab, kubɑ́ɑr'. CA contains many examples of straightforward threefold vowel alternance, but a typical CyD set of contrasts is provided by, say, '9agɑ́ɑb' (cigarette-end, butt), 'i9gíeb' (mountain roads, passes), and 'u9gɑ́ɑb' (hawk); in passing we may observe that it would be feasible to transliterate the Arabic written form and to write 'i9gaab' for 'i9gieb', since the key to pronunciation would be provided by initial 'i' in contrast with the 'u' of 'u9gɑɑb', but the transcription adopted is considered more likely to evoke an appropriate response from the reader; whatever the merits or demerits of the transcription, however, the interesting fact is that the features of frontness and backness belong, as indeed they do in almost every variety of living Arabic, to at least two syllables and as often as not to whole forms. It is not, however, within the scope of this paper to examine further these and similar phonological features, which have been discussed earlier.

An apparent exception to the otherwise generally true statement that an alternance of short vowels in CyD is referable only to closed syllables is provided by such pairs as 'kitábit' (I/you [masc sing] wrote) and 'ismí9it' (I/you [masc sing] heard). The vowel of the final syllable of these forms, however, is structurally neither V nor v, but an anaptyctic vowel (ə). Initial and final clusters of two consonants and medial clusters of three consonants are inadmissible in the dialect, and accordingly three contexts of anaptyxis are recognized. Any unstressed vowel of half-close front or of central quality[38] which is either (i) initial and preceding two consonants, or (ii) medial, preceding two consonants and in a syllable following a short open syllable, or (iii) in a final syllable following a short open stressed syllable, is anaptyctic. ə does not function in any system of commutable vowel-terms, and it is only in syllables immediately preceding anaptyxis that an alternance of short vowels in *open* syllables is permitted, as in the case of 'kitábit' (CVCVCəC) and 'ismí9it' (əCCvCəC) above. It is feasible to regard pause (#) as phonologically equipollent with C, as in the following formulation of the three contexts of anaptyxis:

Context			
Initial	#	ə	CC *eg* 'ismí9' (he heard), 'iktíbat' (she wrote), 'iʃtáa' (winter), 'iktíb' (books)
Medial	C	ə	CC *eg* 'lí9ibtih' (his toy), 'yíkitbu' (they write), 'fáridtih' (his loaf), 'inigtílat' (she was killed)
Final	C	ə	C# *eg* 'kitábit', 'ismí9it', 'kábiʃ' (ram), 'kúbur' (size)

Anaptyctic vowels might have been omitted from the reading transcription but their inclusion more satisfactorily serves the purpose of reading, and, moreover, transcribed forms as 'yiktbu, smi9t', etc, are better reserved for those forms of Arabic (Cyrenaican and other) in which anaptyxis is not associated with such sequences.[39]

Comparison of such pairs as 'gá9imzu (ga9miz+u)' (sit down! [imp masc pl]) and 'gássmu (gassim+u)' (divide up! [ditto]), 'lí9ibtih (li9bih+ih)'[40] (his toy) and 'ħísstih (ħissih+ih)' (his voice), shows that medial $C_1C_1C_2$ (where C_1C_1 = gemination) ('gássmu, ħísstih') is not to be equated with $C_1C_2C_3$ ('gá9imzu, lí9ibtih') as far as anaptyxis is concerned. Clusters in which C_1 = 'y' or 'w' are similarly not associated with anaptyxis, *cf* 'báytta' (her tent), 'jáwzha' (her husband). From the following paradigm, included by way of exemplification, it will be seen that (i) the relation of elision or non-elision of v of the feminine-singulative suffix –vh as between simple and suffixed forms, as well as (ii) the presence or absence of an anaptyctic vowel medially, are once again relatable to the twofold division of vowel- and consonant-beginning suffixes; both 'elision' and anaptyxis are associated with the vowel-beginning suffixes:

		Suffix	lí9bih	(CVCCvC)
Sing	1st pers	–i	lí9ibti	(CVCəCCV)
	2nd pers masc	–ɑk	lí9ibtɑk	(CVCəCCVC)
	2nd pers fem	–ik	lí9ibtik	(CVCəCCVC)
	3rd pers masc	–ih, –ɑh[41]	lí9ibtih	(CVCəCCVC)
	3rd pers fem	–ha, –hɑ	li9bítta	(CVCCvCCV)
Pl	1st pers	–na	li9bítna	(CVCCvCCV)
	2nd pers masc	–kɑm	li9bítkɑm	(CVCCvCCVC)
	2nd pers fem	–kan	li9bítkan	(CVCCvCCVC)
	3rd pers masc	–hum	li9bíttum	(CVCCvCCVC)
	3rd pers fem	–hin	li9bíttin	(CVCCvCCVC)

In regard to anaptyxis generally, CyD resembles CC but differs from most Maghribi dialects; nevertheless patterning differs radically as between Cyrenaica and Egypt: for example, medially in CC, but not in CyD, anaptyxis is associated with $C_1C_1C_2$ as well as $C_1C_2C_3$, and, again in contrast with CyD, the anaptyctic vowel, which may be open and stressed, precedes the last consonant of the cluster, *cf* CC 'ħaǁáha (ħaǁ+ha)' (her right): CyD 'hɑ́ggha', CC 'bintúhum (bint+hum)' (their daughter): CyD 'bínittum', etc. The qualitative association of the anaptyctic vowel and the vowel of the pronominal suffix is characteristic of CC, and to some extent also of Classical Arabic, but not of CyD.

It will be seen that the stressed vocalic element in *eg* 'li9bítna' above relates to a sequence of 4 medial consonants ('–9bitn–'). In this context incremental consonant-length (gemination) behaves as C, *cf* 'li9bítna' and 'guSSútna (guSSɑh+na)' (our story), and the same is true of incremental vowel-length, *cf* 'fa(a)kíhtih (fíekhih+ih)' (his fruit).[42] In addition, the relation exhibited, for example, by 'iktíb: kítbih (iktib+ih)' (his books) suggests that pause (#) and C may again be recognized as structurally equipollent and the new facts formulated in the following manner:

Medial

$$\left.\begin{matrix}CC\\(V)VC\\\#C\end{matrix}\right\}\ v\ \left\{\begin{matrix}CC\\CC\\CC\end{matrix}\right.$$

The vowel is assignable to v, not ə, since it is associated with (i) stress and (ii) commutability, *cf* 'kítbih' (his books)/'kábʃih' (his ram), 'li9bítta' (her toy)/'li9bátta' (she played it [fem]), and also as v, not V, since it is 'elided' in relation to other comparable forms, *eg* 'kítbih' (CvCCVC): 'iktíb' (əCCvC). On the basis of non-elision in related forms, there is no justification for regarding, say, the stressed vowels of 'íktib' (VCCvC) (write!) [imp masc sing], 'íjrɑ(ɑ)' (VCCV(V)) (hire),[43] 'kílmih' (CVCCvC) (word), etc, as other than exponents of V. The exceptional circumstance of V-elision remains now to be specified.

The complete perfect tense paradigms from which the earlier examples of 'kitábit' and 'ismí9it' were drawn are as follows, and include the forms 'sím9at', 'sím9u', and 'sím9an' which are structurally parallel to the nominal 'kítbih' of the preceding paragraph:

		Suffix	(kitáb)		(ismí9)	
Sing	1st pers	–t	kitábit	(CVCVCəC)	ismí9it	(əCCvCəC)
	2nd pers masc	–t	kitábit	(CVCVCəC)	ismí9it	(əCCvCəC)
	2nd pers fem	–ti	kitábti	(CVCVCCV)	ismí9ti	(əCCvCCV)
	3rd pers masc	zero	kitáb	(CVCVC)	ismí9	(əCCvC)
	3rd pers fem	–at	iktíbat	(əCCVCVC)	sím9at	(CvCCVC)

Pl	1st pers	–na	kitábna	(CVCVCCV)	ismíʕna	(əCCvCCV)
	2nd pers masc	–tu	kitábtu	(CVCVCCV)	ismíʕtu	(əCCvCCV)
	2nd pers fem	–tan	kitábtan	(CVCVCCVC)	ismíʕtan	(əCCvCCVC)
	3rd pers masc	–ɑw, –u	iktíbɑw	(əCCVCVC)	símʕu	(CvCCV)
	3rd pers fem	–an	iktíban	(əCCVCVC)	símʕan	(CvCCVC)

It emerges from considering the zero-form 'kitáb' in relation to the forms containing vowel-beginning suffixes ('iktíbat, iktíbɑw, iktíban') that a sequence of two short open syllables is inadmissible, a fact which concerns nominal as well as verbal forms, *cf* 'dibáʃ: idbíʃih (dibaʃ+ih)' (his kit, luggage). This feature is in marked contrast with Egyptian Arabic, *cf* CC 'kátabit (katab+it)': CyD 'iktíbat (kitab+at)', and the form 'iktíbat' also contrasts with general Maghribi (including Benghasi) 'kitbat' or 'kitbit'.[44] Inadmissibility relates not only to initial syllable sequences as in the examples of 'iktíbat' and 'idbíʃih' but also to medial sequences. Compare, for example, with 'kitáb: iktíbat', 'íngital (in+gital)' (he was killed): 'inigtílat (ingital+at)' (VCəCCVCVC). The relation between such a form as 'kitáb' and its suffixed relatum 'iktíbih (kitab+ih)' (he wrote it/his name) should be compared with 'íktib: íkitbih' (write it/his name!) and 'iktíb: kítbih' (his books). It is likely that the phonemicist would set up, on the basis of the contrast 'íktib: iktíb', a phoneme of stress, but the form 'iktíb' could be written unambiguously as 'ktib' and in any event the contrast is trivial in comparison with the relational one of 'kitáb' (CVCVC): 'iktíbih' (əCCVCVC) ≠ 'íktib' (VCCvC): 'íkitbih' (VCəCCVC) ≠ 'iktíb' (əCCvC): 'kítbih' (CvCCVC).

The medial context illustrated above by 'íngital: inigtílat' introduces the new and interesting feature of difference of relation between simple and suffixed form in proportion to the difference of sonant sequence V–V and V–v in the simple form. The imperfect forms corresponding to 'íngital' (VCCV̲CV̲C): 'inigtílɑw' (they were killed) are 'yíngitil' (he can *or* will be killed) (CVCCV̲Cv̲C): 'yingítlu' (not *'yingátlu') (they [masc] etc) (CVCCvCCV). Between 'yíngitil' and 'yingítlu' there obtains the 'elision' of the total sequence V–v, whereas the first V only is 'elided' of the sequence V–V; the stressed vowel of 'yingítlu' is regarded as v of the earlier 4-consonant medial context. Strong support for this view of the relation between 'yíngitil' and 'yingítlu' as exemplifying that between –CVCvC and –CvCC is provided by the correspondence between simple and suffixed forms of the numerous feminine-singulative nouns of the structure CVCCVCvh. From the facts that (i) the only positive *prima facie* link between vowel quality and sonant category is that openness = V, (ii) the vowel of the feminine-singulative suffix belongs to the sonant category v, (iii) in such comparable sets of forms as 'máktab: máktibih: maktábha' the sonant V in closed syllables correlates with open vowel quality, from these facts it might have been expected that '*karhábtih, *maSxártih, *ma9ráktih, *muħrámtih, *maħlábtih' would constitute the 'ih'-suffixed forms corresponding to the unsuffixed 'kárhabah' (car), 'máSxarah' (joke), 'má9rukah' (quarrel), 'múħrumah' (headkerchief), 'máħlibih' (milk-pail); in fact, however, the relevant suffixed forms are 'karhúbtih, maSxúrtih, ma9rúktih, muħrúmtih, maħlíbtih'.[45]

The inadmissibility of sequences of short open syllables appears at yet other places in the dialect. For example, a structure CVCVCVCVC relating to, say, 'ʃVjVr (*trees*)+Vt (*one*)+Vh (*his*)' is admissible in Classical Arabic (*cf* 'ʃajaratuh') but is purely hypothetical as far as CyD is concerned. v in CyD 'ʃújurtih' (CvCəCCVC) (his tree) and 'ʃujurtáyn' (CvCəCCVCC) (two trees) (*cf* 'ʃujár' (trees) [collective], 'iʃjúrah' (tree), 'iʃjurútta' (her tree)) is considered to relate to a 4-consonant context ('ʃjrt–') which, unlike the earlier one, is initial, not medial. Commutation between v and V operates in this context as elsewhere, *cf* 'ʃújurtih' (CvCəCCVC), 'bádiltih' (CVCəCCVC) (his suit), etc. In passing, the contrast may be noticed between 'u9wurútta (u9wúrah+ha)' (əCCVCvCCV) (her blind eye) and 'u9wurátta (u9wúrat+ha)' (əCCVCVCCV) (she blinded her in one eye); both v and V (underlined) contrast with, but do not commute with, ə in, say, 'ismí9itta (ismí9it+ha)' (əCCvCəCCV) (I/you [masc sing] heard her).

Suffixed forms containing the verbal 3rd pers pl fem suffix '–an' provide yet other examples of the inadmissibility of successive short (open) syllables; notice the gemination of the suffix consonant in the second form of the following pairs: 'yáfhaman' (they [fem] understand): 'yafhamánnih' (they understand him), 'iktíban' (they [fem] wrote): 'iktibánnih' (they wrote it/his name). Parallel to this use of gemination is the increment of vowel-length in the 3rd pers sing fem perfect tense suffix '–at', *cf* 'iktíbat: iktibíetih (iktibat+ih)' (she wrote it/his name).[46]

In conclusion, we may return to the topic of prominence. Dissociated from the structural features which this paper has attempted to handle in terms of sonants, anaptyxis, and the inadmissibility of successive short open syllables, the formulation of CyD rules of prominence would mean little. The facts are as follows:

(i) patterns with ultimate syllable –CVVC, –CVCC (where –CC= gemination), or –CVVCC (ditto) are *oxytonic*; *eg* 'kilíem' (speech), 'iʃwáal' (sack), 'fina(a)jíil'[47] (cups), 'uSɣayyríet' (very small) [fem pl diminutive], 'mugáSS' (shears, scissors), 'amgáaSS' (pairs of shears, scissors), etc;

(ii) disyllabic patterns of structure CVCVV, CVCVC, əCCVV, əCCVC, əCCvC are also *oxytonic*, with the exception of nouns and adjectives of colour and physical defect (structure CVCVV or CVCVC, where C_1 = guttural); *eg* 'simáa' (sky), '9aʃáa' (dinner), 'gulám' (pen, pencil), 'kitáb' (he wrote), 'ilħáa' (beards), 'ubTám' (buttons), 'iktíb' (books; it was written),[48] 'ħabáʃ' (Abyssinian), but 'ħámar' (red [masc sing]), 'hábal' (foolish [masc sing]);
(iii) patterns in which the ultimate syllable is not long (see (i)), the penultimate is CV, and the antepenultimate is variously CVC, VC, CVV, and VV, are *proparoxytonic*; *eg* 'márħabah' (welcome), 'ráhwinih' (ambling), 'márfugak' (your [masc] elbow), 'máktibak' (your [masc] office), 'gá9mizat' (she sat down), 'yínsilib' (he can *or* will be robbed), 'ínsilab' (he was robbed), 'yíbtidi' (he begins), 'íbtida' (he began), 'íjjibal'[49] (the Jebel) 'ílɣada' (the lunch), '(tu)ráafugan' (they [fem] accompanied), 'áamurat' (she ordered), etc;
(iv) patterns in which the ultimate syllable is again not long, the penultimate is CəC, and the antepenultimate variously CV and V (initial only) are also *proparoxytonic*; *eg* 'mí9irfih' (knowledge, acquaintance), 'ismí9itta' (I/you [masc sing] heard her), 'kitábitta' (I/you [masc sing] wrote it [fem]/her name), 'dawwárilna (dáwwar+ ilnáa)' (he looked on our behalf), 'mintisíbilna (míntisib+ilnáa)' (he is related to us by marriage), 'ásimha' (her name), 'íliktib' (the books), etc;[50]
(v) all other patterns are *paroxytonic*: *eg* 'bállaɣ' (CVCCVC) (he forwarded), 'ráwʃan' (CVCCVC) (window), 'íktib' (VCCVC) (write [imp masc sing]), 'íjra(a)' (VCCV(V)) (hire), 'árja(a)' (VCCV(V)) (wait [imp masc sing]), 'marfágha' (CVCCVCCV) (her elbow), 'kitábit' (CVCVCəC) (I/you [masc sing] wrote), 'iktíbat' (əCCVCVC) (she wrote), 'inihzímat' (VCəCCVCVC) (she escaped), 'ilbárid' (vCCVCəC) (the cold), 'ma9rúktih' (CVCCvCCVC) (his quarrel), 'ma9rukútta' (CVCCVCvCCV) (her quarrel), etc.

As in other forms of colloquial Arabic, there is often close association between prominence and grammatical category in CyD. For example, in contrast with other prefixed particles, the article is regularly characterized by prominence when associated with a disyllabic noun of structure CVCVV, CVCVC, əCCVV, əCCVC, əCCvC, *eg* 'íssima (is+simáa)' (the sky), 'ílbuɣal' (the mule), 'íʃʃta (iʃ+iʃtáa)' (the winter), 'íllfaf[51] (il+ilfáf)' (the bundles), 'ílubTam (il+ubTám)' (the buttons), 'íliktib (il+iktíb)' (the books), etc. Again, the vocative particle 'yaa', like the article, is the mark of a grammatical category 'definite' in Arabic, and it is a fact of Arabic grammar that more than one such mark, *ie* different marks, are generally inadmissible in a 'definite' grammatical complex. A category of 'proper noun', by nature 'definite' since it is regularly associated with definite concord patterns only, may be established by several criteria, and one of these is a difference of behaviour in comparison with other nominal categories when colligated with 'yaa'. In the manner of the article, 'yaa' is prominent when it precedes nouns of structure CVCVV or CVCVC, *eg* 'yáɑ wilad' (Boy!), but if the noun is a proper noun, then its final syllable is the prominent syllable of the total complex, *eg* 'ya furáj' (Faraj!), 'ya 9alíi' (Ali!). Yet again, and finally, the difference in prominence between, on the one hand 'ħajál' (partridges) [collective], 'ħabáʃ' (Abyssinian), etc, and, on the other, 'ħájal' ((horse) having white hair on forelegs), 'ħámɑr' (red [masc sing]), etc, relates to the fact that the last two examples belong to the category of so-called noun or adjective of colour and physical defect. The scatter of forms belonging to this category is quite distinctive, as, for example,

masc sing	*fem sing*	*pl*
ħájal	ħájla	ħíjil
ħámɑr	ħámrɑ	ħúmur[52]

Classical forms corresponding to 'ħájal' and 'ħámɑr' are of the pattern ˡaCCaC, *ie* 'ˡáħjal', 'ˡáħmɑr', and it will be seen that, notwithstanding other differences, paroxytonic prominence is common to both the Classical and Cyrenaican forms.

Appendix

Guttural consonants and syllabication in CyD

Classical nouns of structure $C_1aC_2C_3$, where C_2='x', 'ɣ', 'ħ', '9', *or* 'h', and C_3 usually='l', 'r' *or* 'm', regularly correspond to a CyD structure which is disyllabic and oxytonic, CVCV́C; if, however, the Classical vowel-unit concerned is i or u, then the CA:CyD correspondence is Ci/uCC:CV́CəC. Examples are:

CA : CyD			CA : CyD	
nɑxl : nuxɑ́l	palm-trees	*but*	ʃuɣl : ʃúɣul	work
rɑxm : ruxɑ́m	vultures		luɣm : lúɣum	mine (explosive)
bɑɣl : buɣɑ́l	mule		kuħl : kíħil	antimony
naħl : niħál	bees		siħr : síħir	magic
faħl : fiħál	stud-camel		si9r : sí9ir	price
bɑħr : buħɑ́r	sea		ʃi9r : ʃí9ir	poetry
laħm : liħám	meat		Tu9m : Tú9um	bait, poison
ʃɑ9r : ʃu9ɑ́r	hair		muhr : múhur	colt, foal
ʃɑhr : ʃuhɑ́r	month			

A system of two short vowels (symbols α and ι) may be set up elsewhere to account in part for such CyD differences as those between, say, 'kábiʃ' (CαCəC) and 'líbis' (CιCəC), 'bɑ́Tun' (CαCəC) (stomach) and 'kúbur' (CιCəC),[53] but alternance in the 'guttural' examples above is between total structures $C_1VC_2\acute{\alpha}C_3$ and $C_1\acute{\iota}C_2əC_3$, where C_2=guttural and C_3=liquid. The above forms behave, of course, exactly as others which are of parallel structure but which do not contain a guttural consonant; thus, for example,

niħál : inħálih : niħálha :: dibáʃ : idbíʃih : dibáʃʃa
and síħir : síħrih : síħirha :: líbis : líbsih : líbissa

The special implications of gutturality may be seen also in relation to other structures. For example, the structure $C_1VC_2C_3VC_4$ ('máktab') is inadmissible when C_2 is guttural; equally inadmissible, as we have seen, is a succession of short open syllables: thus, we find, unlike 'máktab', neither *'mɑɣrɑf' nor *'mɑɣɑrɑf' but 'umɣɑ́rɑf' (ladle), and similarly 'umxɑ́lɑb' (claws, talons), 'umɡɑ́Tɑn' (well), 'iθɡálab' (fox),[54] '(i)yɡɑ́Ti' (he gives), etc. In comparison with Classical forms, correspondence is regularly between CA CVC– and CyD əCCV–. From an historical and comparative standpoint, it would be reasonable to postulate between Classical and Cyrenaican forms an intermediate *CVCV–. Inadmissibility of C_1VC_2– (where C_2 is guttural) does not, however, apply to structures in which the following non-final syllable is of structure CV, *eg* 'máħlibih' (milk-pail); *'imħalibih' is just as impossible a CyD form as *'dibaʃih' and *'mɑɣɑrɑf', and for the same reason of inadmissibility of short syllable sequences.

We have devoted fairly considerable space to exemplifying the syntagmatic aspects of phonology that Firth wished to see subsumed under 'prosodic analysis', and it is time now to turn to other pillars of Firthianism. Before doing so, however, we can at least appreciate the justice of Firth's reminder of Whitney's dictum that 'articulation consists not in the mode of production of individual sounds, but in the mode of their combination for the purposes of speech' and the fact that a great deal more than 'articulation' is involved.

Notes

1 The varieties of Arabic that are considered are Egyptian (Classical and colloquial) and Cyrenaican (Jebel Bedouin). Preliminary research indicates the possibility of substantially similar statement for Kuwaiti Arabic. Some years ago at the then Institut des Hautes Etudes Marocaines in Rabat, Professor Louis Brunot kindly gave me his assistance and guidance in using the services of the Institute's two 'répétiteurs', Si Kouta from Marrakesh and Si Seddiq

from Fez. The results were interesting but it is not feasible to include them in the present paper. The Moroccan facts are materially different from those presented here; moreover, in the opinion of the writer, it is not very profitable to study prominence and syllabication in any form of Moroccan Arabic without parallel study of associated Berber dialects.

2 The chief phonetic features distinguishing the prominent syllable are (i) the greater stress or force with which it is uttered in comparison with other syllables of the form, (ii) the higher pitch of at least its initial phase in relation to adjoining syllables, (iii) the kinetic or moving (falling) tone on which it is pronounced in contrast with the static or level tones of the remaining non-prominent syllables. The typical pitch-pattern of, say, the Classical paroxytone 'katabataa', as pronounced in Egypt as a word-isolate in unemphatic style, may be represented - - \ _ .

3 Arabic letter-name.

4 This is not intended as a criticism of the Arabic (consonantal) system of writing, which serves exceedingly well the orthographic purpose for which it is intended.

5 The research on which subsequent analysis of CA(E) material is based was conducted many years ago with two postgraduate students, A and D, of the Department of Phonetics and Linguistics at the School of Oriental and African Studies, both of whom were approximately 30 years of age and had spent eight or nine years at Al-Azhar.

6 CVCC and CVVCC are distributionally restricted to final position. CVVCC is, in fact, rare and almost wholly associated with monosyllables.

7 The only 'exceptions' found concern the so-called '"wa" of accompanying circumstance' followed by either of the two pronominal forms 'huwa' and 'hiya'; 'wáhwa' and 'wáhya' are regularly heard. This is likely to be a reflex of colloquial usage, in which the comparable particle 'wi' is often similarly prominent. Since 'wahwa' and 'wahya' are not isolable in the manner of the rest of the material we are considering, they are not, strictly speaking, exceptional.

8 Pause-forms in relation to non-pause forms involve principally the 'omission' of final flectional 'a', 'i', 'u', 'un', and 'in', and the use of a common ending '–ah' to correspond variously to non-pausal '–atun/–atan/–atin'. Thus, quoting for purposes of illustration one example only from a range of possible non-pause forms, we have the same words: 'kátab (pause)-kátaba (non-pause)', 'yáɡrif (pause)-yaɡrífu (non-pause)', 'muɡállim (pause)-muɡallímun (non-pause)', 'muqɑɑtílah (pause)-muqɑɑtílatun (non-pause)'.

9 In the sample of forms, the semicolon has been used in anticipation of the clasification that will subsequently be made.

10 CVVCC has not been specifically illustrated but in the few disyllabic forms in which it occurs, it is quantitatively equipollent with CVCC.

11 In the single case of the pattern illustrated by 'ʃajɑrɑtuhúmaa', though the prominent syllable is distinguished by the same features as elsewhere, certain of the remaining syllables are also more prominent than others by virtue of the higher relative pitch with which they are associated. The total pitch pattern of 'ʃajɑrɑtuhúmaa' in typical unemphatic utterance may be shown ‾ _ –
– \ _ .

12 My Lebanese informant was Professor Anis Frayha of the American University in Beirut. Unlike the two Azhar-trained Egyptians, F did not distinguish between short and long vowels in post-tonic position; thus, F's 'rɑ́'a, háwwa, rɑqɑ́bati,' etc, correspond to A's and D's 'rɑ́'aa, háwwaa, rɑqɑbátii', etc.

The distinction observed by A and D between, say, 'kátaba' (3rd pers sing masc perfect) and 'kátabaa' (3rd pers dual masc perfect) corresponds to a difference of prominence and final vowel length in F's usage between 'kátaba' and 'katabáa'. Vowel-length and prominence here are concomitant and serve to mark the dual grammatical category in the verb (*cf*, too, F's corresponding feminine dual form 'katabatáa'). Other regular differences of prominence between F's Classical usage and that of A and D relate to the patterns –/S̲/S/L̲ and –/S/S/S/L̲, both proparoxytonic for F as in, say, 'ˈíSbɑ9ah, saˈálahu, rɑqɑ́bati, mufakkirɑ́tuhu'.

13 My informant in this case was Professor Walīd 'Arafāt, a colleague at SOAS, now at the University of Lancaster.

14 See 'The phonetics of Il-Karnak dialect (Upper Egypt)' by T. H. O. M. Dawood, thesis presented for the degree of Master of Arts in the University of London in April 1949.

15 See, for example, *The Phonology of Colloquial Egyptian Arabic*, by Richard S. Harrell, American Council of Learned Societies, New York, 1957, *pp* 15–16. For Harrell prominence in Cairene is 'phonemic', *ie* is 'significant' in some not very clearly defined manner, 'is not completely predictable in terms of other phonological elements'. The case for prominence as a phoneme seems to rest on such contrasting pairs as 'síkit' (he was silent) and 'sikít' (I/you [masc sing] was/were silent), or on, say, 'musta9íd' (ready) and 'mu9támid' (dependent). Harrell objects to the practice of writing double letters final in Cairene words, as, for example, 'sikítt' and 'musta9ídd', since 'a prepause geminate becomes definable only in terms of length' and 'Egyptian Arabic shows no organized use of prepausal consonant length'. Insufficiency is often thus encountered in phonemic analyses when important differential features are observable but do not lend themselves readily to representation in roman writing; as far as consonant length goes, Harrell's observation is accurate and timely, but he has not noticed other relevant differences of phonetic form. Firmer contact between the tongue and the denti-alveolar zone of the palate as well as greater muscular tension of the tongue are perceptible in the pronunciation of the final consonant of 'sikít' and 'musta9íd' as compared with that of 'síkit' and 'mu9támid'; difference of length in the vowels of the pretonic syllables is also observable. These differences cannot easily be rendered in roman form except by the device of doubling the letter for 'sikítt' and 'musta9ídd', and, provided that reading conventions are adequately stated, it is difficult to see any valid objection to a practice which *inter alia* does much to simplify the formulation of rules of prominence.

16 Vowel-length and prominence are concomitant in CC. Moreover, long vowels do not occur, in typical unemphatic style, in closed pre-ultimate syllables. The structures CVVC and CVCC are limited to ultimate position, and ultimate CVV, since always associated with prominence, is most satisfactorily classified with CVVC and CVCC as long. –CVV often appears as –CVVh.

17 Harrell, *op cit*, *p* 16.

18 A village and its surroundings approximately 20 km south-south-west of Menouf (French spelling) in Munufiyya province. The linguistic information concerning this dialect was provided by the late Dr Mohamed Abu Farag, a lecturer in Arabic at the University of Alexandria, a native of Ṭahwēh and former student at SOAS.

19 Other examples are 'Suħúna' (plates), 'dukúra' (males), 'wurúda' ([land] documents), 'numúra' (tigers), 'ku9úba' (counterfoils), 'durúba' (lanes), 'fuSúla' ([underhand] tricks), 'buɣúla' (mulish people), 'nu9úla' (heels), 'butúma' ([field-]boundaries), 'nusúra' (eagles), 'turúsa' (gear-wheels),

'furúɡa' (necklaces), 'rumúʃa' (eyelashes), 'wuħúʃa' (wild animals), 'fulúga' (cracks, splits), 'kurúta' (cards), 'kuʃúfa' (lists), '(iʃ)ʃurúɡa' ([the] members of the Shar' family), '(il)ɡudúla' ([the] members of the 'Adli family), '(il)ɡutúsa' ([the] members of the 'Abu 'Ats family), etc. Educated speakers in the village would tend to use 'Suħúun' for 'Suħúna', 'fuSúul' for 'fuSúla', 'rumúuʃ' (*or* 'ri–') for 'rumúʃa', 'wuħúuʃ' for 'wuħúʃa', etc, but no alternatives are available even in educated colloquial usage for 'dukúra, subúɡa, Dubúɡa', and some others.

20 It should be observed that elision of 'i' and 'u' does not obtain if the relevant syllable is also prominent, a good example of the close relation between prominence and syllabication; *cf* 'fɑ́DDɑ+ɡílabu=fɑ́DDɑ ɡílabu' (he emptied his boxes), ''ábu+ɡúmɑr='ábu ɡúmɑr' (Omar's father), etc.

21 See my 'Syntagmatic relations in linguistic analysis', *Transactions of the Philological Society*, 1958, and *p* 121 for more recent use.

22 Similar sonant behaviour, differently distributed, is observable in all Egyptian dialects and in most other colloquial forms of Eastern Arabic. The 'placing' of a form in relation to others within the total material to be analysed always involves consideration of a whole set or whole sets of forms to which it belongs. To take an example from TD, it might at first seem reasonable to be satisfied with a straightforward phonemic alternance in the first syllable of, say, 'ɡádla (ɡaadil+a)' (just [fem sing]), 'gírba' (goatskin), and 'ɡúgla' (section of sugar-cane or maize stalk). That such an alternance may be established for a structure CVCCV is unquestionable, but 'fɑ́rxa' (chicken), for example, would be better chosen than 'ɡádla' to illustrate CaCCV. Partly on the basis of the relation between 'ɡáadil' and 'ɡádla', there are good grounds for considering 'ɡádla' as 'ɡadζla', where ζ=zero, and for contrasting zero with the vowel of the second syllables of, say, 'kátaba, ɡínaba, ɡúgala', etc. Although the nominal and adjectival patterns CáCaCa, CíCaCa, CúCaCa, CuCúca, and CíCiCa are common, it is an interesting corroboration of the view of 'ɡádla' as CáCζCa that the only two forms exhibiting the pattern CáCiCa, *viz* 'sámiga' (antipathetic [fem sing]) and 'wɑ́qiħa' (rude [fem sing]), are 'learned' and used only by educated inhabitants of the village.

23 My chief informant over a period of 18 months, was Idris Abdalla, a Bedouin from Cyrene and the Ḥāsa tribe. Examples given are based on I's usage, subsequently checked in the field. See also *p* 198, *n* 1.

24 'he wrote: she wrote: she wrote it'.

25 'office: his office'.

26 'he writes: they write'.

27 'he understands: they understand'.

28 Examples are 'ħɑgg' (he looked; right): 'ħugg' (look [imp masc sing]): 'ħigg' (young camel; calf), 'rɑ́bbi' (God): 'rúbbi' (kind of jam): 'ríbbi' (rabbi), 'urkɑ́b' (stirrups): 'urkúb' (knees): 'irkíb' (he mounted). Even in these examples, phonetic differences which may in the phonemic manner be minimally localized in the vowel are never more than twofold; see *pp* 52–4.

29 An example of this difference is 'ʃakk' (he became angry; he doubted; doubt): 'ʃɑkk' (he scratched, struck a match). *Cf*, too, the 2nd pers pl pronominal suffixes '–kan [fem]' and '–kɑm [masc]'. See *p* 53.

30 The corresponding long vowel of, say 'gaadúum' (axe) may, in rapid style, be pronounced as short as in 'ħaʃíiʃ', but elsewhere it is pronounced slightly longer and may, unlike 'a' in 'ħaʃíiʃ', be fully long in poetry. These facts have been represented in the reading transcription by brackets as in 'ga(a)dúum'. In similar manner, the first vowel in, say, 'miizíen' (scales) may be pronounced short in rapid speech but, in addition to its greater length

elsewhere, it is always qualitatively closer than 'i' in 'kibíir'. In the same way, 'uu' in 'suuníyyih' (basin), whatever its length in the instance, is always close, back, and rounded, unlike 'u' in 'Turíig'.

31 Variously transcribed 'x', 'ɣ', 'ħ', '9', 'h'.

32 In the difference of verb-type or conjugation exemplified by 'yáfham', on the one hand, and 'yíktib', on the other, the alternance is better regarded as of both syllables considered as a whole rather than individually; features of openness and closeness characterize the whole forms, and this is even more strikingly so in the corresponding plural forms 'yáfhamɑw' and 'yíkitbu'. See *pp* 57–8.

33 'he divided up: he divided it [masc] up: he divided it [fem] up≠ divide up!: divide it [masc] up!: divide it [fem] up!'.

34 'he forgave: he forgave him: he forgave her≠forgive!: forgive him!: forgive her!'. For 'a(a)', see above, *n* 30.

35 The limit of close definition is represented by the statement that any open vowel is V, except in the case of the '–ɑh' variant of the feminine-singulative suffix, *eg* 'ʃɑ́nTɑh' (bag), 'iʃjúrɑh' (tree). The sonant v, once established, is found never to correlate with open quality, with the exception just quoted.

36 See below, *n* 40.

37 The implication of the junction of 'h–' with a preceding voiceless consonant is gemination of the consonant.

38 Quality varies in direct proportion to other differences in total forms; there are no subclasses of anaptyctic vowel based on qualitative differences.

39 An initial anaptyctic vowel may be very short, especially in rapid style, and may, in the presence of a voiceless first consonant, correlate not with vocalic form but with greater length of the consonant than in other contexts. The impression received from such a pronunciation of, say, 'ismí9' (contrast 'símɡat') is always of a disyllable, due partly no doubt to the length of the sibilant and other factors not relevant to our present concern. It may be noted that in order to write such forms in Arabic script an initial *alif* was invariably used by my informant and also invariably occurs in the Bedouin poems that appear in local newspapers.

40 There are in CyD two suffixes, grammatically distinct but similar as to phonetic form – completely so when final. 'Conditioned' variants of the suffixes are transcribed '–ih' and '–ɑh', the quality of the vowel belonging to syntagmatic categories of frontness and backness characteristic of total forms. One of these suffixes is that of the 3rd pers masc sing, which has already been extensively illustrated. The other is a mark of feminine gender and frequently also of singulative number. The term 'singulative' is needed to designate such a form as, say, 'iʃjúrɑh' ([one] tree) within a total scatter which includes 'ʃujɑ́r' (trees [collective]), 'iʃjúrɑh' (tree [singulative]), 'iʃjurɑ́ɑt' ([a few] trees ['counted' or little plural]), 'ʃujurtáyn' (two trees [dual]), 'aʃjɑ́ɑr' ([groups of or various kinds of] trees [plural or big plural]). The 3rd pers masc sing suffix only occurs final and there is no justification from comparison with related forms within the range of material we are considering for regarding its vowel component as other than sonant V. The feminine-singulative suffix, on the other hand, may occur both final and non-final; in the latter case, it is characterized by a consonant '–t–' and, in appropriate contexts, by a vowel which precedes '–t–' and varies in quality between half-close front (i) and central (u) as the total form varies between front and back. The behaviour of this vowel is an exact reflex of the vowel (italicized) in, say, 'gáss*i*m, yíkt*i*b', etc, *cf* 'ɣɑ́ɑbah' (wood, copse): 'ɣɑ́ɑbtih (ɣɑɑbah+ih)' (his, its wood), 'gúSSɑh' (story): 'gúSStih (guSSɑh+ih)', 'kílmih' (word):

'kílimtih (kilmih+ih)', etc, and it is therefore regarded as belonging to the sonant category v.

41 See preceding note.

42 See above, *n* 30.

43 *Cf* 'ijrɑ́ɑ' (puppies).

44 The CyD form is, in fact, reminiscent of that found in Bedouin dialects of Arabia, including Kuwait. See now T. M. Johnstone's 'Some characteristics of the Dōsiri dialect of Arabic as spoken in Kuwait', *BSOAS* 24/2 (1961), *pp* 249–97, and the same author's 'Aspects of syllabication in the spoken Arabic of 'Anaiza', *BSOAS* 30/1 (1967), *pp* 1–16; also his *Eastern Arabian Dialect Studies*, London, 1967. See, too, Haim Blanc, 'The Arabic dialect of the Negev Bedouins', *Proceedings of the Israel Academy of Sciences and Humanities*, 4/7 (1970).

45 The corresponding forms containing consonant-beginning suffixes are – with the suffix '–ha' used for illustration – as follows: 'kɑrhɑbútta, mɑSxɑrútta, mɑ9rukútta, muħrumútta, maħlibítta'.

46 In spite of the similarity of pattern, therefore, 'íe' in 'iktibíetih' is not to be equated with the 'íe' of the feminine plural nominal suffix (variously '–íet, –áat, –ɑ́ɑt') in, say, 'iħjilíetih' (his [few] partridges).

47 The vowel in the second syllable is longer than that in the first but not as long as that in the third.

48 The form 'ikta(a)bíet' occurs more frequently than 'iktíb' in the sense of 'books'.

49 The vowel of the article is regarded as belonging to the sonant category v, not V, since in certain structures it is regularly 'elided'.

50 '–əw–' and '–əy–' in such contexts are realized as a close back rounded vowel and close front spread vowel respectively, both short; examples are 'túSuwrih' (CVCəwCVC) (his photo), 'máʃiytih' (CVCəyCVC) (his going, gait). This would apply also to '–əw' and '–əy' final, *eg* 'fíluw' (CVCəw) (foal), 'máʃiy' (CVCəy) (going, gait), and to 'əy–' initial, *eg* 'iy9ɑ́Ti' (əyCVCəy) (he gives).

51 The structure vCCCV is restricted almost wholly to article-noun complexes of which the noun in its corresponding isolate form is characterized by an initial syllable əC– and the articulation of C of that syllable by denti-alveolarity.

52 It is only to plural forms of this category that the structure CVwəC relates; *cf* 'ħuwil [not *ħuul]' (one-eyed [pl]) and contrast the verbal form 'ħuul' (separate! [imp masc sing]).

53 Once again it can be seen that certain phonetic features, roughly generalizable as front and back, are not exclusively referable to phonematic vowel-units. Such differences as those obtaining between 'kábiʃ' and 'bɑ́Tun', 'líbis', and 'kúbur', would be best formulated in a complete phonological analysis in terms of syntagmatic categories of frontness and backness.

54 We may notice the parallelism between the forms 'θíɡilbih (iθ9álab+ih)', 'θiɡilbáyn (iθ9álab+ayn)', 'iθ9alábha (iθ9álab+ha)', and the earlier 'ʃújurtih, ʃujurtáyn, iʃjurútta'.

Four

Linguistic 'goings-on': collocations and other lexical matters arising on the syntagmatic record

An attempt is made in this paper to develop inter alia *the Firthian concept of 'collocation' and to define it somewhat more closely than hitherto.*[1] *In the process it is necessary to consider interrelated lexical categories of a syntagmatic kind as well as the status of 'word'. Concern is principally with 'forms of language', but it has seemed appropriate to locate this interest against the background of a total approach to meaning.*

Meaning

One may approve of the Mad Hatter's intellectual misgivings, if not of his manners, when he tells Alice at the Tea Party that saying what she means and meaning what she says are not the same thing a bit – and he might have added that there is a good deal more than that to 'saying' and 'meaning'. One sympathizes less with more modern linguists who separate the domains of their professional concern into phonology, lexicon, grammar, and semantics without always explaining at all adequately how the separation is made and in particular how we are to recognize the scope of *semantics*, as if somehow meaning is known in advance, is given. Nor should we feel any more satisfied with the common enough view of semantics as concerning either the meaning of lexical items taken singly or that of a text over and above the meaning of its lexical items. This essay, it is hoped, will show that it is as unsatisfactory to regard what for the moment we may call 'word-meanings' as discrete, finite, and localized in advance as it is to see 'further' meaning as a kind of 'expressive' topping or dressing. If a somewhat scandalous example may be permitted at the outset, such an addressive sentence in English as *silly old bastard* may indicate the speaker's appreciation of a favour rendered by a close friend and impugn neither the addressee's intelligence, his vigour, nor his antecedents; rather would it mark gratitude and affection, the latter in a society in which close friendship or intimacy is shown less demonstratively than in some other cultures, even western European ones close at hand. It is in fact the contravention of the linguistic taboo, the 'escape' from socio-linguistic constraints appropriate to other relationships between interlocutors, that marks the 'meliorative' meaning of affectionate gratitude in the circumstances. This is not to say, of course, that the same 'form of words' may not be used very differently elsewhere, 'pejoratively' by a student, let us say, in reference to his professor. And grammar is directly involved! Not only is *silly old* recognizably an example of a 'meliorative-pejorative' adjectival compound in English[2] but, more generally, the example has just been shown to be ambiguous and ambiguity is rightly much to the fore today as a mode of demonstrating important meaningful distinctions and relationships that might otherwise go unobserved. The fact, however, remains that the type of ambiguity just illustrated goes by default and fails to engage the attention of influential linguists of the times. They would be likely to recognize the *pejorative* form of the example given, primarily because it illustrates the referential use of language, language 'at a distance', as it were, from the objects, people, qualities, etc to which it may refer; from this standpoint, the example may plausibly be regarded as derivable from an amalgamation of such 'underlying' sentences as *he is silly, he is old, he is a bastard.* But such a derivation makes little or no sense for the *meliorative* employment of the sequence in the face-to-face and ear-to-ear circumstances to which it is apt. Such contrasts, therefore, tend to be ignored, and one is left to wonder both why and how. At all events, meaning is clearly involved at all times in the close study of language forms; if nothing more, one is constantly asking oneself whether this or that sentence or part-sentence is meaningfully the same or different, and the important word here is 'constantly', such is the complexity of language. One cannot reasonably, then, examine sentences, the lexical items within them, and their possibilities of phonetic form save at all times within a semantic framework or envelope. For a linguistic statement to have ultimate value, it must probably be a simultaneous statement of meaning and of form. It seems therefore appropriate to indicate as briefly and informally as possible important aspects of meaning that the observer and analyst may need to be aware of and take into account when studying language and perhaps especially spoken language. It might perhaps be said in passing that all linguists are at one in recognizing the primacy of speech over the essentially different manifestations of language in writing but far from all linguists adduce examples of recognizably spoken language in their work and the close study of conversation, for example – a functionally vital form of spoken language – has barely begun.

The English sentence *That'll do*, like an infinite number of other sentences in the language, is ambiguous in isolation and only disambiguated in extended discourse. With final rising intonation, say, it may be used homophonously for example by dad either to his erring small boy or to the shop assistant looking him out a tie, but a repetition of the form of words, this time with falling intonation, is adapted to the continued recalcitrance of the child but hardly to the requirements of the shop transaction. From such examples comes the recognition that language – and meaning with it – is not only contrastive but also on-going. Dependency between sentences and in particular between elements of a sentence, otherwise the *syntagmatic* relations obtaining between parts of discourse, will be a recurring theme in this paper. Also on-going are the extra-linguistic or situational circumstances of language use. It would be hard to better J. R. Firth's example – 'Now just take these. I'm sure they'll do you good. You'll feel much better in the morning. Good-night.' No doubt not all hospital sisters behave in this way, but some do, and the identification of the speaker as a night-sister, of the place as a hospital ward, of the activity as the distribution of medicine, is surely correct. In the way that one 'sees' the ward, its activity and the participants therein, so also one 'hears' the sister using rising intonation in more than one sentence-final place in order to reassure the patient. It is at once instructive and comic to ring impossible intonational changes on the sentence forms of such an example of living speech. Meaning therefore not only resides in contrastive relationships and in the on-going nature of language; appropriateness to the situation (also on-going) is a further inescapable condition of the meaningful use of language. This is not to say that the situation 'determines' the linguistic choices made or *vice versa*, but the proper rejection of the narrowly behaviourist view of us as creatures of purely conditioned linguistic reflexes should not entail the simultaneous rejection of 'situational context' as linguistically uninteresting.

It is, then, part of the nature of language to be on-going in on-going situations. What now is discernible of uses to which language is put? We might distinguish at least the functional, the emotive, the topical, the socio-cultural, the ostensive, the referential or denotational, and the mnemonic. There are doubtless others as well as other possibilities of classification, nor does the order of presentation carry implications as to any priority of importance among the categories, some of which may even overlap. It is not our concern, moreover, to consider, for example, such questions as the part played by language in the formation of concepts and *vice versa*. The difficult question of metaphor is also completely omitted. Deferring for the time being consideration of that aspect of language which is of paramount importance for the linguist, namely the forms of language, let us look at what may be covered by the seven named categories and at the same time remember that not only is the web of meaning made up of many strands but that more than one of them may meet at one node of the web, at a single place in discourse.

Functional meaning

Language, spoken or written, is used, for instance, to ask questions, make requests, promises, bids, to deceive, to silence an opponent, to give orders, testimony, advice, warnings, instructions, to count and calculate, to eulogize, mourn, recite, curse, compliment, congratulate, cajole, to greet and take leave of people, to celebrate, train and educate, tell stories, make jokes, gossip, play games, insult and quarrel, to pray, and the reader may add other functions of his own. The function can be specialized as to production and perception. Not only is baby-talk, say, necessarily spoken but radio or TV commentary, for example, is a form of spoken language in which the need to keep up with or to give the semblance of rapidity in the activity under commentary leads to the adoption of linguistic features, grammatical, lexical, and phonological, that are characteristic of this use of language. The circumstances of immediate confrontation in speech must also give rise to uses of language that are *sui generis*, as J. B. Pride has pointed out in the case of what has been termed 'reinforcement of the speaker', whom one seeks to encourage and reassure by a display of interest in and understanding of what he has to say; the use of appropriate interjections (including *mm* and *ah*), the exploitation of the intonational resources of the language, the occasional supply of a word or filling in of a gap, are among features that may give *prima facie* an impression of bare articulateness in a speaker who is in fact doing a competent job of keeping a conversation going. Elsewhere, of course, there are purely written forms of language use – say, on forms or public notices, in newspaper headlines or the preambles to insurance policies as well as in The Times Law Reports, and so on. French, if one may be permitted a minor digression, is full of eye-grammar; you may be asked in that language to fill in a form giving *vos nom, prénoms, âge, et qualité*, which contains interesting features of 'number concord' but which belongs to the written language only; in the same way, one should not call upon some imaginary feature of 'liaison' (nowadays, it appears, as much as anything a matter of the generation gap) to disambiguate *père et mère* and *pères et mères* occurring in the following two extracts from Articles 57 and 76 of the French *Code Civil*, relating to births and marriages: *Sur le registre . . . sont portés le jour, l'heure . . . de la naissance de l'enfant . . . et les prénoms des père et mère*, to be compared with *les prénoms . . . des pères et mères* from the *acte de mariage*. It is probably easier to distinguish in speech between *my uncle and aunt* and *my uncles and aunts* in English than between *mes oncle et tante* and *mes oncles et tantes* in French. It is not always a simple choice between written and spoken presentation, of course. Language may be read aloud, for instance, and although the implication of spoken utterance is less assured for some written functions than others, nevertheless rehearsals and performances of plays and similar entertainments, newsreading, lecturing and public address, though not 'colloquial' language, illustrate speech with the implication of writing and *vice versa*. In general, it should perhaps be said in conclusion, the linguist is ultimately interested in the relationship between forms of language and language functions.

Emotive meaning

This aspect of meaning is more or less self-explanatory and need not detain us long. Emotive language is indicative of mood, anger, excitement, affection, cordiality, and so on. It is remarkable, for instance, how people tend to lose their educated hats when they get excited; the 'lapse' of an educated Arab from 'Classical' into colloquial forms of speech is a typical example, and the fact is used often enough for comic purposes in English plays and elsewhere; the use of 'diminutive' and 'augmentative' forms of nouns, adjectives, etc in Spanish is more often a matter of 'affectiveness' than size. The 'affective' use of language is thus marked not only by such phonetic means as voice quality, for example, but also by the lexical and grammatical choices made by speakers.

Topical meaning

Choices of language vary greatly with the subject matter or topic. Technical jargons are an obvious example. Perhaps we can recognize individual words in Firth's *Tooth Ripple Losses in Unwound Pole Shoes* but that is about all, and most of us will be little wiser on being told that it is the title of an article in an electrical trade journal. Technical jargons, necessary as they are, are at one end of a scale of choice according to topic, which would include less strictly codified differences, as between, say, intellectual and common-or-garden uses of language. More generally, much that comes under the heading of 'topical' can possibly be regarded as a subdivision of referential meaning (see below).

Socio-cultural meaning

Here we are concerned, as we have already partly seen, with linguistic aspects of who says what to whom and in which circumstances. An individual presents himself to his interlocutor/s in a variety of guises, largely translatable into terms of the relative roles and statuses of language users. One 'places' one's interlocutor and adjusts one's speech in accordance with various biographical assumptions. It should perhaps be said again that the aspects of meaning we are distinguishing intermesh and often meet in one text, in one sentence, even in one word or syllable. Thus, not only, say, deference, equality, superiority, reverence, etc will enter into language seen from the standpoint of role relations but also such emotive categories as cordiality, affection, dislike, etc. Commands may be requests may be suggestions may be invitations, and, as J. B. Pride has said, can as easily involve advice as orders, entreaty as persuasion, tentativeness as positiveness, familiarity as unfamiliarity, and so on. As a simple illustration of language selected in response to the interrelationships of speakers, consider the vocative in English sentences and the case of the middle-class young Englishman, perhaps of public school background, addressing his mother. The often observable use of her Christian name may give offence to some but reflection shows that the options open to the young man are few. *Mum* has class connotations which he may not 'overcome', if at all, until he is a good deal older, *Mummy* became impossible for him to use from the age of 10 or 11 or thereabouts, and *Mother* might suggest to some a measure of old-maidishness, 'uppishness', or the status of bachelor living with his mother. There seem therefore in many cases to be few available choices other than the use of the Christian name or the adoption of a deliberately jocular form such as *Ma*. It is not only, then, the occurrence elsewhere of such phrases, whose putative semantic essence is frustratingly fugitive, as *Reverend Mother*, *Mother Mary*, *Mother India*, and *Old Mother Riley* that severely restricts the interest of the type of feature analysis by which *mother* will be analysed into semantic components corresponding to those of *bachelor*, whose meaning, we are told by some semanticists, comprises the features 'human', 'male', and 'unmarried'. Such analysis is explanatorily inadequate for one who wishes to come to grips with the fully meaningful use of language rather than simply with the 'ideal', logical implications of kin relations. Feature analysis has its place and the feature analyst is in any case hardly to be censured when the great majority of linguists to date have restricted their view of meaning to those aspects which follow, yet have not explained how this is done. These aspects relate to the symbolic nature of language and to language at a remove from speech, *grosso modo* to the use of language to explain, refer to and remember artefacts, people, abstract concepts, etc. In the literature, at least the following terms are applied to these facets of meaning: 'cognitive', 'notional', 'conceptual', 'denotative', 'referential', 'representational', 'designative', terminological usage which, even if no more is involved, is decidedly confusing.[3]

Ostensive meaning

'Specification' as a category of linguistic experience may encompass such varied grammatical classes as articles, ordinal numerals, and deictics (*eg* demonstrative *this/that*, *these/those*). It is perhaps particularly to the area of deixis that 'ostensiveness' belongs. In the world of the here and now with, say, flowers as objects of ostensive definition, we may point at a particular horticultural specimen and simultaneously say to our companion by way of explanation – 'That is a japonica'. We are thus at one remove from the subsequent referential, *in absentia* use of language.

Referential meaning

We may ostensively define, for instance, 'a table' and can go on from there to idealize the concept 'table', even if we are uncertain whether, say, 'dressing-table' should be included within the same conceptual domain. It is noteworthy that not only objects, events, persons, and qualities can be conceptualized; the whole of meaning may be so, including all aspects already considered. There is some risk, however, of confusing as data for analysis a metalanguage of explanation with the living language we encounter. Nor is there any compulsion to believe in the primacy of any subdivision of meaning, for instance in the referential 'table'-ness of 'table'. As will be shown subsequently, for example, an addressive sentence like *that's a good boy* in English cannot adequately be dealt with in the usual, word-bound referential terms.

The explanation – often in their absence – of what things are, of how things work, of how people act, and so on, draws on our capacity for abstract conceptualization among other things. For referential reasons we should no doubt wish to regard *book* as the same item in *the book*, *the French book*, and *the accounts book*. It is the linguist's task to justify this equivalence overtly by adducing similarities of linguistic behaviour in extended and comparable contexts, if he considers it of interest to do so. In the same way, at a more abstract level than that of *book*, 'continuous spatio-temporal movement' may be used mnemonically to label or gloss the various associations of *run* with *men, engines, taps, noses, plays, films, trains, buses,* etc, while 'loss of intensity' is an appropriate gloss for *wear off* in *the pain/paint/enthusiasm/*etc *wears off.* Be it said again that the linguist should be able to justify his acceptance of such similarity in terms of the analytical operations which he will subsequently be seen to perform – association with a similar range of adverbs, for example, may provide one criterion in the case of *wear off.* Intuitions as to the sameness or difference of items should always be capable of overt demonstration.

Mnemonic meaning

The mnemonic, perhaps better the 'naming' function of language should not be confused with that of ostensive definition. The human being seems endowed with a more or less discrete naming faculty, often sadly blurred by advancing years. The thesis is put forward later that words and word-classes are essentially names and classes of names serving at least two purposes: firstly, the mnemonic end of all abstraction, and secondly, the purpose of 'mention' or 'citation' for combinations of those abstract elements of linguistic structure which we shall subsequently call roots (or lexemes) and morphemes. Thus, for example, words 'figure forth' otherwise 'unmentionable' public notices, as *Please tender exact fare and state destination* in the British bus. Strictly, the root common to, *eg, tears* and *tore* is unpronounceable and so are the morphemes, *eg –s,* associated with it; associations, however, of roots and morphemes are utterable in speech or writing as 'words'. In a not wholly dissimilar way, the word *shall,* let us say initial in the sentence *shall we go?,* provides a means of referring en bloc to as well as separately identifying such greatly varied pronunciation forms as [ʃɪ, ʃə, ʃæ, ʃʷ, ʃl, ʃəl, ʃæl, etc], just as the two words *is that* act in relation to a greatly varied range of phonetic possibility initially in the sentence *is that all you've got?,* variety by no means accounted for by the phonetician's styles (slow colloquial, rapid colloquial, formal, etc). Such variation reveals that we do in fact resort to some tacit editing of our observations prior to presentation and that the contrasts we focus on are probably less often between single forms (uniforms, so to speak) than between potential ranges of form. This, however, in passing; more central to the present approach to language is the view that so-called 'definitions' or glosses in dictionaries are not seen as 'the meanings' of the entries to which they correspond but rather as a somewhat mixed bag of essentially mnemonic extensions of the word-entry, in which an attempt, usually less than conscious, is made at summing up the entry's distributional 'privileges of occurrence', to use the current jargon. 'felis leo' or 'large, strong, flesh-eating animal indigenous to Africa and Asia', possible glosses for the entry *lion*, may serve *inter alia* as summations of the contextual occurrences of *lion* that are listed or might be listed in the dictionary article or, in the case of 'felis leo', as a referential switching device from one English style to another. The fact remains that neither gloss is of much if any relevance to, say, *L for lion* or *The Red Lion* in British English.

Such, then, is a general background of awareness against which linguistic form may be seen and evaluated. Much has been omitted from this summary and doubtless inadequate sketch of meaningful aspects of language. Its gaps and inconsistencies must, however, remain, so that we may proceed to that aspect of meaning which most centrally concerns this paper – *formal meaning*, the patterns and interrelations of linguistic form we use and respond to.

Formal meaning

The patterned arrangements of linguistic form, variously phonological, lexical, and grammatical, is its own strand of meaning separable from all others yet intertwined with them. It will be with abstract arrangements of a lexico-grammatical kind that this paper will henceforth be concerned. The formal value of an item depends closely on (a) other items present in the text and the constraints and dependencies observable between them, (b) the 'permutability' of the text in terms of the analytical operations of substitution, expansion or contraction as the case may be, interpolation (a form of expansion), and transposition. (a) may be termed *intra*-textual dependence and (b) *inter*-textual dependence; (a) is almost certainly consequent upon (b). A textual item is recognizable largely on the grounds of what may or may not be present in the text, all within a framework of judgment as to what is or is not meaningfully equivalent. For equivalence, as C. E. Bazell has said, there seem to be no truly rigorous tests; the linguist offers rather facts for or against by the application of his analytical operations. It has already been said that a linguistic item or class of items is meaningful not because of inherent properties of its own but because of the contrastive or differential relationships it develops with other items and classes. In an attempt to solve the difficult problem of presentation posed by this proportional nature of meaning, we posit items and classes as poles between which contrast seems reasonably to obtain and we name these end-points more or less extensively by the use of words, word-classes, dictionary- and other glosses. Meaning, however, is much less in the name than in the network of relevant differential relationships. The presence of *off*, let us say, in *the milk has gone off* (expansion) marks a different *gone* from that in *the milk has gone* (contraction), just as a different *off* is almost certainly 'determined' by the presence (substitution) of *John* in place of *the milk*. Many other features of distinctive linguistic behaviour will relate to (*go* ± *off*) and, in turn, the lexicographer-grammarian must needs go on to consider (*go* + *off*) and to distinguish at least between *go off* (= *away*), *go off* (± *the field*), *go off* (*someone*), *go off* (± *bang*), *go off* (*one's head*), (*milk*) *go off*. It might be advantageous to illustrate the manner in which meaningfully distinct items are formally recognizable. Let us base our observations primarily on the ubiquitous spoken English category of 'particle' and, since we have started with it, let us stay mostly with the exemplar *off*, which – disregarding such occurrences as in the collocational frame *well/badly/comfortably*/etc . . . or in such composite items as *come off* (= succeed) – may perhaps be glossed as referring to 'separation, release, removal, departure (*eg* from a location, an expectation, a norm of acceptability, etc), unavailability'.

The term 'particle' is deliberately used since *off* is variously prepositional, adverbial, and adjectival. Moreover, it is sometimes difficult to distinguish between prepositional and adverbial (and even adjectival) *off* and all three grammatical subdivisions of particle demand considerable further subdivision themselves. Notice in passing the reference to *grammar* in connection with *general* class names (particle; preposition, adverb, adjective). Other particles (*eg: on, up, down*, etc) behave similarly to *off*, so that generalization is possible having regard to facts subsequently indicated. Grammar is first and foremost generality in relation to lexical particularity, but this does not imply any denial of the essential one-ness of grammar, lexis, and meaning. Syntax and, more generally, syntagmatic analysis is additionally concerned with textual dependencies and constraints.[4] But to resume with *off*.

The category of 'preposition' in contradistinction to 'adverb' is usually recognized by its association or potential association with following nominal and pronominal forms. Such forms frequently but not necessarily follow the preposition component of a 'prepositional phrase'. A noun follows, for example, in *he fell off his bike/rolled off the bed/ran off the field*, but not in *I saw him riding his bike but I didn't see him fall off/it's not the sort of bed to roll off*, although it is probably always possible to 'derive' the second type from the first. In certain circumstances the noun or pronoun may be optionally omitted and it may not be clear whether one is left with preposition or adverb. In cases where *away* may be substituted for *off* (*eg: he ran off*), most would regard *off* as 'adverbial' but there may be less certainty in response to the TV commentator's remark that *the players are running off*, to which *the field* may be optionally added; in the same way, when the restaurant waitress tells you that *the fish is off*, she is less likely to be saying that it is putrescent than that it is *off the menu*; again, is there any equivalence between the *off*'s of, say, *the wind blew the roof off the house* and *the wind blew the roof of the house off*? The omissibility of a following noun, moreover, is not limited to the 'intransitive' case, *cf: run someone off* (± *your land*). It might seem plausible to regard the case of, *eg he ran off the field* as a coalescence of 'prepositional' *off* and 'adverbial' *off* and thus derivable from *he ran off off the field*; it is also possible to consider *off* in *the wind blew the roof off the house* as a coalescence of *off* and *of*, which do occur together in regional speech (see also *p* 113).

The case of verb + particle is interesting in numerous ways. Some verbs, for example, do not occur without aspectival (inceptive *off*, continuative *on*) or directional (*up*, *down*, *across*, *on to*, etc) extension: *shamble*, for instance, requires the 'complementation' of *off*, *on*, *up*, *down*, *across*, etc, a fact to which its phonaesthetic overtones of *amble*, *shuffle*, and perhaps also *stumble* may or may not relate. Then again, there is the wider relevance of the fact of cognitive equivalence or difference of the verbal form in the context of particle extension. The inclusion of *off* simply provides 'adverbial' or 'prepositional' extension in the case of, say, *run off* (± *the field*); one *runs*, whether or not *off*, so to say. Similarly, with the directional particle *down*, the ball *rolled*, whether or not *down the road*. On the other hand, the verbal forms are greatly different in value as between *John tore down the poster* and *John tore down the road*. It is instructive to look at such examples a little more closely in order to demonstrate something of the complexity of intra- and inter-sentential dependency. The italicized portion of the sentence Noun + *tore down the poster* is ambiguous, 'interpretable' variously as 'ripped the poster violently from the surface to which it adhered' or 'rushed headlong down the poster'. In terms of 'the world of experience', the second interpretation relates perhaps to the activity of something mobile and smaller in size than the poster, for example an insect: on the first interpretation, *down* stands in similar relation to *tore* as the earlier example of *off* to *run* in *run off* (± *the field*) and the particle and second noun (*poster*) are transposable, *ie John tore the poster down*. Therefore the first noun, (*John*, *the centipede*, etc) not only disambiguates *tore* but also 'determines' the prepositional or adverbial classification of *down* and thus the type of relationship between verb and particle. Thus, *cf*

1 *John tore down the poster.*
2 *The centipede tore down the poster.*

But the second noun also, no less than the first, is relevant to the interpretation of both *tore* and *down*, severally and conjointly. *Cf*

3 *John tore down the poster.*

4 *John tore down the road.*

Relationships so far discerned might be indicated in general terms by using initial letters for the noun, verb, and particle classes and different kinds of brackets as follows:

$$((N_1 \{[V) [P)\} N_2]]$$

The conjunction of N_1 and N_2, taken as a discontinuous whole, permits or not the inclusion of post-verbal aspectival particles, notably *off* and *on*. When N_2=*road*, then concomitantly N_1=*eg*, *man* and ≠*eg*, *centipede* for *off* to be admissible; contrariwise, *off* is inadmissible where N_1=*man* and N_2=*poster*. This relationship is indicated by the horizontal braces in

5 (a) *The man tore off down the road.*

(b) *The centipede tore off down the poster.*

There must be added the relationship between verb and aspectival particle, indicated by the oblique stroke in the 'formula'

$$((\overbrace{N_1} /\{[V) \overbrace{P_1}/ [P_2)\} \overbrace{N_2}]]$$

Finally for the present, with certain other comparable particles (*eg*, *up*) substituted for *down*, the sentence

6 *John tore up the road.*

is ambiguous and may be glossed as (i) John brought a pickaxe to bear on the road surface or (ii) John rushed headlong up the road. In such cases, an aspectival particle (*eg*, *off*) disambiguates the sentence. *Cf*

7 *John tore off up the road.*

There obtains, therefore, a further relationship between the aspectival and the prepositional/adverbial particles. For the reader with the goodwill, time and inclination to resolve the brackets, the relationships we have distinguished may be expressed *in toto* as follows:

$$((\overbrace{N_1} /\{[V) /\overbrace{P_1}/ [P_2)\}/ \overbrace{N_2}]]$$

The complexity of things is clear enough, as is the multiplicity of relationships developed by a single item, which derives its value from such relationship at the same time as it contributes to the 'definition' of other items in the text. This analytical circularity need not deter us; the important thing is to describe circles of sufficient size to meet the needs of descriptive adequacy. It will have been noted that no justification has been offered for or against the view of *tore* in *John tore down the poster* and *John tore down the road* as belonging or not to the same lexical root or lexeme. The answer to the question would hinge on the further extensibility of the texts and judgments as to similarity or difference between extension. It is hoped, however, that the above exploitation of a small sample of comparable texts will suffice to reveal the arbitrariness and artificiality of attempts to separate, on the one hand, lexicon and grammar except in terms of generality, and, on the other, ultimately lexico-grammatical analysis and meaning.

The case of adjectival *off*, definable *qua* adjective on numerous grounds, among others by association with marks of comparison (*more, most, less, least*), with adverbial intensifiers (*eg, completely, very*), etc may serve to reveal further the need to subdivide classes distinguished in analysis. There is insufficient space to attempt a detailed subclassification of the uses of predicative *off* listed below but the reader might find it amusing and instructive to ask himself such questions as the following: (i) are there any constraints on the verbs which may precede *off*? (ii) what would be the corresponding 'transitive' verb or verbs in a given case (*eg, the tap be off* [intrans]: *turn off the tap* [trans])? (iii) does *off* in the example stand in antonymous relation to *on* (*cf*: *the match is off/on* but *the milk is off/*on*)? (iv) are there any limitations on the initial noun in terms, for example, of a distinction human/animate/inanimate (*cf: she looked decidedly off* versus **the cat/the garden looked decidedly off*)? (v) does *off* require 'completion' within the phrase, as by *a long way* in *it's a long way off* or by *to the right* in *the house is off to the right*? (vi) may *off* be replaced by *away*? (vii) where does ambiguity occur and how may it be resolved (*cf: he is off today* = either (a) *he is off-form today* or (b) *he is away from work today. Cf* the relatability of (b) with *he has today off, a day-off, he is off ill today*, etc). The reader will doubtless think of other questions to ask himself. Here are the examples – a random selection of what might be:

1 *The water/radiator/heating/*etc *is/feels/seems off.*
2 *The tap/radio/switch/light is/seems off.*
3 *The brakes are off.*
4 *The milk/meat/fish/*etc *is/smells/tastes/looks/seems/*etc *off.*
5 *She was/looked/seemed off* (*to us*).
6 *His coat was off.*
7 *The match is off.*
8 *He is off today.*
9 *The door-handle is off.*
10 *The town is miles off.*
11 *The entrance is/lies off to the right.*

It will be seen that the earlier gloss (*p* 108) was serving a genuine mnemonic purpose as an abstraction from such varied relationships.

By way of further illustration of the operations of formal linguistic analysis, let us stay with *off*, now variously associated with *take* in a 'transitive' verbal phrase. Consider the following examples:

1 *He took the money off John.*
2 *He took John off to tea.*
3 *He took off his coat.*
4 *He took John off to a T.*
5 *The wind took off the roof of the house.*

In (1) *off* is prepositional, the prepositional phrase is omissible, and the sentence is a 'transitive' counterpart of, *eg*, *he turned off the road.* In (2) *off* is the motive-inceptive particle already noted and is omissible without prejudice to the meaning of the remainder. Omission, however, is only possible if the following prepositional phrase is not omitted at the same time. That *off* belongs here to a system of aspectival particles is shown by the substitutability of continuative *on* in *he took John on to tea*, wherein for practical purposes the remainder of the sentence is meaningfully the same. Other points of contrast with the other examples include the interpolability before *off* of the 'adverbial' forms *straight* or *right*, the substitutability of *away* for *off*, the irreversibility of the object noun (*John*) and *off* (*ie*, **He took off John to tea*; *cf* (3), (4), and (5)), etc. In (3) *off* is inomissible and of a piece with *took*, is transposable with *his coat* (*ie*, *he took his coat off*). *He took his coat off* is ambiguous since the personal reference of the pronominal forms *he* and *his* may not be the same; if *his* refers to a different person from *he*, then the sentence may be substituted by *he took his coat off him* but not in the 'reflexive' case when *he* and *his* are of the same personal reference. As to (4), the criteria which set off (3) from the other types also set off (4) but *take off* in (4) is an idiom. *off* does not stand in antonymous relation to *on* as in (3) (*cf: he put on his coat*), nor can *took* be replaced by any other verbal form in the way that *took* in (3) may be replaced by *eg leave* without disturbing the cognitive equivalence of the remainder. *Took off* in (4), therefore, illustrates the characteristic non-productivity of the parts in relation to the idiomatic whole. Transposability of *John* and *off* is shared with (3) and so, too, is the stylistic substitutability of a single verbal form (*eg*, *imitate*, *mimic*) for idiomatic *take off*. Notice, as a further illustration of syntagmatic dependency, how the introduction of the participial/gerundial form (perhaps better the *–ing* form) following *off* involves ambiguity (*cf: he took John off lecturing*=(a) he imitated

John lecturing, (b) he took John away to lecture, (c) he relieved John from the duty of lecturing). In (5) the (verb+particle) complex is associated with a genitival phrase comprising two determined nouns separated by *of*, *ie*, *the roof of the house*. The sentence type differs in many respects from the others. Thus, any of the following three sentence forms are possible for (5):

the wind took off the roof of the house
the wind took the roof of the house off
the wind took the roof off the house

It is especially the third form that is interesting. **off of* is regional English and *the wind took the roof off of the house* is dialectal, but *cf* the case of *in* substituted for *off*, *ie*

the wind blew in the wall of the house
the wind blew the wall of the house in
the wind blew the wall in of the house

The genitival phrases in such sentences, *ie*, *the roof of the house*, *the handle of the door* (*cf: he took the handle off the door*) appear to exhibit a relationship of the part to the whole. Although *took off* may be stylistically substituted by *removed* at both (5) and (3), there are clearly important differences between the two sentence types concerned. It may also be observed in passing that some of the five sentences (1, 3, 5) exhibit certain similarities of behaviour not shared with the others (2, 4). No attempt is being made in this essay to provide a complete, far less an explicit, rule-ordered formulation.

In the foregoing illustrations the operations of analysis clearly suggest grammatical generalizations. The same operations, however, are performed in 'defining' in formal linguistic terms even very particular items. Take *come off* (=succeed), for instance, which seems plausibly relatable to a corresponding transitive form *bring off*, an equation supported by the similar *come: bring* relationship in association with other particles, *cf: come to* (=revive (intrans)):*bring to* (=revive (trans)), *come out:bring out*, etc. Supporting criteria include non-extensibility with a following noun or pronoun (contrast, *eg*, *come off it*), the inomissibility of *off* from *come off*, the non-transposability of *off* in contrast with adverbial *off* (=away) (*cf: off it comes*), and so on. In passing it may be noted that this transpositional front-shifting is an important criterion for the recognition of the inceptive-motive and directional categories of particle to which reference has already been made, *cf: off/on/away/up/down/in/out/over/*etc *he went; off came his coat and down he got to work.*

Grammar and lexicon; syntax and morphology

Having seen something of meaning in general and formal linguistic patterning in particular, let us turn to grammar and related topics, staying with intra- and intertextual constraint and dependency and with relationships of particularity and generality. Grammar is often divided into morphology and syntax, the former concerned with characteristics of words and their paradigms, the latter with patterned arrangements of words in larger stretches of language, typically sentences but also phrases and 'clauses'.[5] It is not the purpose of this paper to discuss arrangements within word-boundaries of infra-word elements – the reader will recognize the composite nature not only of, say, familiar compounds like *armchair* or *milk jug* but also of *unfashionable* and *disestablishmentarianism.* Nor shall we be much concerned with the grounds on which word-recognition may be based (for instance, transposability, uninterruptability, irreversibility, separability, criteria which are indeed employable on a broader linguistic front). The division between morphology and syntax is in fact a great deal less clear-cut than is often assumed and may even be otiose. Many of the roots and affixes, inflections and derivations of morphology have their implications as to choices made elsewhere in word+ domains, and *vice versa*; *good* (with zero suffix) is by no means the singular of *goods* and will not therefore appear in such associations as *consumer* – or – *and chattels,* while *goodness* not only does not occur indiscriminately with any kind of following verb (*cf* the impossibility of **goodness hates him*) but also excludes pronominal forms other than those of the first person singular from exclamations like (*my*) – and – *gracious* (*me*). The view has already been expressed that words are names (of lexical items) derived from the combination of roots (or lexemes) and affixes (or morphemes). In addition, the traditional belief is endorsed by which linguistic awareness is divisible into more particular (lexical) and more general (grammatical) levels. By the exploitation of the human phonatory and scribal capacity, both levels may be given phonological shape in speech and graphological shape in writing. An important tenet of this paper, then, is the interdependence of grammar and lexicon. Lexical particularities are considered to derive their formal meaning not only from contextual extension of a lexical kind but also from the generalized grammatical patterns within which they appear, and, conversely, the recognition of general patterns is seen as justifiable only in response to selected comparisons of lexical combinations. It behoves us now to attempt at least working definitions of important related concepts and terms that lexical analysis appears to require.

'Root' or 'lexeme', 'morpheme'; 'word', 'word-class'; 'collocation'

Rather as in the days of 'classical' phonemics much play was made of the 'minimal pair' in order to establish throughout a language such lexical differences as those between *pin*, *bin*, *tin*, *din*, *sin*, *thin*, etc, so today ambiguity informing sentences and sequences of words is greatly used as a presentational device and has already been sufficiently illustrated above. It should, however, be borne in mind, firstly, that – for reasons he does not explain but which derive from the on-going nature of speech – the analyst is apt to stuff his sentences to the tolerable limit with elements that more often than not in living discourse occur transsententially and, secondly, that if sentences are frequently ambiguous, then words and their parts are greatly more so. Consider a scatter of forms like the following, related to a lexical item *work:*

1 (I) *work* (he) *work*(*s*) (he is) *work*(*ing*) (he) *work*(*ed*)
2 (he is a/they are) *work*(*er/s*)
3 (it is hard) *work*
4 (good) *works*
5 (a) *work*(*/s*) (of art, genius, supererogation, etc)
6 (a) (cement) *works*

Presumably, *–s* in (2) and (5) may justifiably be regarded as 'same' but *cf* (1), (4) and (6), not to mention what one might find elsewhere in, say, *Marseilles*, *facilities*, or *linguistics*. Presumably, too, *work* at (3), (4), (5) and (6) is also the 'same' linguistic item, but at (3) it is not associable with the indefinite article nor with 'pluralizing' *–s*, at (4) there appears at first sight to be no corresponding singular form without *–s*, (5) suggests that the indefinite article may not precede *work* unless in turn the latter is followed by *of*+abstract noun, while (6) does not admit a corresponding form without *–s* yet is regularly preceded by the indefinite article. That *works* at (6) is not to be equated with *works* at (4) is in part justified by the various associability of (6) with a following singular or plural verbal form, *cf: the works is/are on the other side of the road*, with which the obligatory plural contrasts in *good works are hard work*. *Works* at (4) may be relatable to *work* at (5) in terms of a regular correspondence of (plural) *–s* to (singular) (*a*+[*of*)+Noun], but there is more to it than this and *–s* at (4) must be regarded as part of lexical patterning that will be dealt with below under 'collocability'.[6]

The 'ambiguity' of morphemic *–s* equally characterizes *–ing*, to name only one further flection. There has to be considered not only the *–ing*'s of *he is working* or *working long hours is bad for the health* but also those of *the working classes* and *hard-working*. Let us examine in turn the different questions posed by the last two examples. There are many kinds of adjectival or qualifying periphrases that follow nouns in English, *cf: men who work (for their living)*, *men in the professions*, *people with money*, *men and women of leisure*, etc. In cases where shortened forms of such periphrases precede the noun, the appropriate lexical item is associated with one of a given selection of morphemes, *cf: work + ing men*, *profession + al men*, *money + ed people*, *leisure + ed men and women*. Such examples serve to illustrate not only the uncertain basis of the usual division between morphology and syntax but also the play of lexical constraint as well as the recognizability of semantic fields. On the last topic, if in the common phrase structure of Adjective + Noun, the noun selected is *classes*, then *working* is to be seen in relation to *lower*, *middle*, *upper*, *professional*, *moneyed*, *leisured*, etc with subdivisions as appropriate. Within such a selection of phrases, *working* is definable as adjectival on the basis of the relationships it accretes paradigmatically (by substitution) with *lower/middle/* etc and syntagmatically (by transposition and expansion) with (*men*) *who work (for their living)* as well as by its association with the noun *classes* in an Adj + N phrase. It has already been implied more than once that the recognition of semantic fields too often involves putting the cognitive cart before the formal linguistic horse and that it is the linguist's job to justify the fitness of the cart to ride in. It is true that much has often to be taken for granted, but it is in the questioning of such assumptions that advances are made. The earlier scatter of *work* rests on such assumptions, namely that careful analysis would reveal a basis of similar linguistic distribution justifying the scatter. No reason has been advanced for including *working* of *working classes* in the scatter. Even, however, if a *working man* is seen not to work but to be on public assistance, let us make the probably justifiable assumption that *working* belongs within the scatter of forms we have grouped together as belonging to some single lexical item labelled *work*. In other cases, decisions might be more difficult to arrive at – one not only *works* but also *works pumps*, *mines*, *tricks*, and even *miracles* and it may not be at all clear whether all these *work*'s should be included in the same scatter. The problem has been posed if not answered, and will arise again – and again, for the linguist's job is never done. Such questions are, however, relevant to the understanding of the use made in this paper of the concepts and terms of 'root' (or lexeme) and 'morpheme'.

The questions raised by the earlier compound *hard-working* are of a different though related kind and concern the linguistic status of a composite element *hard work*. It will be seen that the inclusion of a single additional item serves to reduce in some measure the indeterminacy we have noted as attending the parts and the whole of words. Invoking the inescapable condition of cognitive equivalence and considering that the same complex element is present in *he works hard, a hard worker, hard-working*, and *hard work* – the ambiguity of the last association of forms is immaterial – we see, firstly, that such a composite element comprises simpler elements occurring elsewhere in other company, *ie, hard* and *work* considered separately, and, secondly, that the composite element can exhibit its own distribution *qua compositum*. Such an abstract composite element as *hard work* we shall term a 'collocation'. It is a particular member of a generalizable class of such associations, but we shall return to this aspect of collocability later. In the meantime we may notice that distribution is to be seen in both lexical and grammatical terms and that collocations are recognizable by their own extended 'distributional privileges of occurrence'. Thus, for example, men – specifically cement workers – work *in* cement works; others of different occupation work *on* works of art; others again, or both, *perform* good works. Not only are good works *performed* but cement works are *built* and works of art *produced*.

The concept and term of 'collocation' has to be seen partly in relation to that of 'root' or 'lexeme'. One may speak of the root √*work*, which exhibits the scatter, no doubt extensible, indicated earlier, and talk subsequently of the collocation of roots. 'Morphemes', typically flections but often words like *a, the, of, for*, etc and including such less overt features as sequential order, are fused with roots as a result of dependencies within extended texts. Amalgams of flectional morphemes, including zero, and roots are 'words'. There are thus three homophonous words in *good works, cement works*, and *works of art*, all belonging to √*work*, which would supply the relevant dictionary entry. Collocations, therefore, are of roots, not of words, which are essentially means of reference. Collocations are at the particular end of the scale of particularity/generality within which analysis proceeds at all times. The recognition of paradigms of morphemes, such as those underlying the subdivisions of the scatter of √*work* – for example, the verbal *zero/–s/–ing/–ed* associated with $\sqrt{\textit{work}_1}$ – also rests ultimately on collocability, but collocations are so infinitely numerous in such cases that observed regularities of association (*eg*, of verbal with adverbial forms) may be generalized in grammatical terms. The analyst is constantly taking decisions as to where to locate his abstractions on the aforementioned scale; in contrast with the final flectional difference in the case of *facility* and *facilities*, forms whose virtually total dissimilarity of collocability suggests a need to ascribe them to separate roots, unlike, too, the case of *–s* in (*cement*) *works*, no collocational statement seems called for in relation to the verbal flections *zero/–s/–ing/–ed* or those of adjectival comparison (*eg*, *zero/–er/–est* with *heavy*). A recognizably regular association of roots or a collocation nevertheless undergoes flectional variation which is accountable in terms of the extended context. For instance, the last two words of *he drinks heavily* severally contain marks of verbal agreement with a preceding third person singular subject (*–s* in *drinks*) and of an 'adverbial adjunct' (*–ly* in *heavily*); comparable word forms are *heavy* and *drinker* in *he is a heavy drinker*, *heavy* and *drinking* in *he is putting in some heavy drinking*, and *drinking* and *heavily* in *he is drinking pretty heavily*. Notwithstanding this variation – cutting across paradigmatic borders – there is clearly involved a regular association between *heavily* and *heavy*, on the one hand, and *drinks*, *drinker*, *drinking1* and *drinking2*, on the other. The common elements of each word form may be abstracted and labelled 'root' and associations of roots 'collocations'; the flectional accretions to roots, determined by the further context, form – in conjunction with roots – 'words'. The latter are pronounceable and enable us to give shape to particular texts and are in turn recognizable within them. In addition to flections, further morphemic accretions, as *a*, *the*, *of*, *as*, etc, or sequential order (*cf* postnominal *as white as snow* versus pre-nominal *snow-white*) enable us to pronounce collocations. Although neither root nor collocation is strictly pronounceable as such, it often happens in English that a root and a word are – as in the case of √*work* – formally similar, but if we assume that the root of the word *heavy*, say, includes in its scatter such forms as *heave*, not to mention *heft* and *hefty*, then a postulated root √*heav–* might clearly appear as the unpronounceable abstraction it is, without our turning to the wholly suppletive evidence offered by, for instance, *go* and *went* or *I* and *me*. For most practical purposes, the root may be identified as the HCF of *relata* within a scatter, so that odd-looking roots like √*educ–* and √*polit–* are recognizable as contributing to the collocations (√*educ–* ~ √*system*) (~ = 'transposable with') in *an educational system* and a *system of education* and (√*party* ~ √*polit–*) in *political party*, *party politics*, *party politician*, and *party political broadcast*. This is not, however, to say that there is no root recognizable on distributional grounds as common to *eg: I* and *me* (or probably, for that matter, to *eg: borrow* and *lend*).

Collocational analysis, then, has at least two important objects. Firstly, to provide palpable identity for abstract roots, whose putative central cores or features are forever so maddeningly elusive and which are so ill-defined by the application to them of vague aprioristic notions and glosses deriving in any case, however unconsciously, from the use of the root *in extenso*. To arrive at the meaning of any element of linguistic structure, it first behoves us to put it back where it came from and, unlike linguists, human beings do not speak in roots. To take the adjectival paradigm only of the root √*heav–*, there is clearly no other lexical item in English regularly associated *inter alia* with the roots of *cold/blow/dew/soil/damage/damages/sarcasm/sky/drinking/ breathing / make-up / hand / crop / rain / work / lorry / gun / accent / fall / heart/ features / top-spin / humour / hydrogen / meal / going /* etc. Roots themselves, however, are zero collocations and the second purpose of collocational study is to recognize the root+ elements which discourse further comprises. A collocation is a composite structural element in its own right. If the reader takes the trouble to sift the foregoing collocations containing adjectival √*heav–* through their several grammatical distributions, he will find very little matching from one collocation to the next. Take, for instance, the examples I have used elsewhere – (√*heav–* ~ √*drink–*) and (√*heav–* ~ √*damage–*); the first occurs in the grammatical patterns Adjective+Agentive Noun (*heavy drinker*), Verb (intransitive)+Adverb (=Adj+*–ly*) (*to drink heavily*), Adj+Gerund (*heavy drinking*), and in the compound adjectival form involving adjectival *–ing* ((*a*) *heavy drinking* (*man*)): the second example, on the other hand, is distributed among Adj+Non-agentive Noun (singular) (*heavy damage*), Verb (transitive)+Adverb (=Adj+*–ly*) (*damage heavily*), Adv+Passive Participle (*heavily damaged*). Any matching is clearly minimal. We may perhaps remind ourselves in passing that underlying all such present distinctions and those recognized in the subsequently extended frame of reference is the notion of contrast, by which a linguistic item or class of items derives its meaning from the place it occupies and the contrasts it develops within widely ramifying networks of differential relations, which it is unfortunately quite beyond the capacity of even the most sophisticated contemporary machinery to discern for us.

The term 'class' was used in the last sentence. Class-labels, 'noun', 'verb', 'adjective', etc have already been used and the so-called paradigms of √*work* were nameable in such terms. A great number of roots share the potentiality of association with the verbal set of morphemic flections, for example; others keep company regularly with such flections as *–ness*, *–ation*, *–er*, *–s*, etc as well as with preceding articles and article-like words (*a/the/my*/etc), preceding adjectival words, and so on. The latter class of words are termed 'nouns' for these and many other reasons of grammatical behaviour. A verb is not a 'doing' word, of course, or anything of the sort, for *work* in *hard work* or *good works* would equally merit such designation – it is a verb because for reasons of grammatical behaviour it is not a noun, an adjective, and so on. Such syntactically equivalent types of (root+morpheme) combinations are termed 'word-classes', which, like words but at the more abstract level of grammar, provide the means of giving shapes and names to generalized syntactic structures. As has already been said, both the word-name and the word-class name are further glossed as a rule, more or less memorably, in dictionaries and grammars but we should not make the mistake of looking upon the gloss or the label as *the meaning* rather than as a more or less extensive summation of the distributional facts glossed or labelled. This is not, of course, to say that there is not a great deal in a name, but it is to say that the great deal may be of confusion, especially as far as the word-name is concerned. Linguistic analysis has been bedevilled by the use of 'word' as both several kinds of linguistic unit and as the names for those units, but the point is becoming unduly laboured.

Further collocational exegesis; 'colligation'; types of collocations; multi-directional dependency

Consideration of our earlier sentence *he tore up the road* shows that collocations not only cut across such word-class boundaries as noun and verb but also across such sentence functions as subject and predicate. For that matter they cut across sentence boundaries and in doing so provide apt enough illustration of the essentially on-going nature of language; *cf* the collocation (√*job* ~ √*apply*) in, say, *He didn't want the job. I don't think he even applied.* (with or without a change of speaker between sentences). A collocation is not a mere juxtaposition or co-occurrence; *off* or *on*, for example, though developing their own collocational relationships with *tore* in *he tore off/on up the road* do not belong to the collocation (√*tVr* ~ √*up*) (*V*=vowel), between whose elements they are interposed. Moreover, as we have seen, more than one constraint is usually focused on a particular root; thus, in *he tore up the road, tore* will relate to other features of 'tense' in the context – *cf*, for instance, a narrative sequence of tenses as *The man rushed/rushes from the house. He stopped/stops for a moment, then tore/tears up the road.* Simultaneously, however, so to speak, much of the meaning of the form derives from its association with *up* and, as far as the collocation (√*tVr* ~ √*up*) is concerned, it is immaterial whether √*tVr* appears as *tore* or *tears*. We shall see that the concept of a collocation has also to be considered in relation not only to 'root', 'morpheme' and 'word' but also to 'idiom', of which more subsequently. A collocation is not an idiom. An idiom resembles rather a root; it is a bloc or assemblage of roots, non-productive in terms, let us say, of the substitutability of roots within it. The collocation (√*tVr* ~ √*up*) is not an idiom because there is no such fixity of association between √*tVr* and √*up*; √*lope*, √*amble*, √*shamble* √*race*, √*rVn*, etc may be substituted for √*tVr*, and √*down*, √*across*, √*on to*, √*into*, √*along*, etc for √*up*, *cf*: *he ambled up the road*, *he tore across the road*, etc. (√*tVr* ~ √*up*) is clearly a particular member of a generalizable class of collocations involving in this case a subclass of the word-classes 'verb' and 'particle', nameable perhaps as 'motive verbs' and 'directional particles'. Such a class of collocations may be termed a 'colligation'. As collocations are nameable by words, so colligations involve the use of word-classes to name the collocational class. Colligational labels underline the necessary admixture of 'functional' and 'formal' as in the case of ('motive' verb + 'directional' particle) – a fact indicated in the example by the use versus non-use of quotation marks. Again, as in the case of the individual collocations making up the class, the colligation is to be seen as an entity, and to this extent the measure of inescapable tautology involved between 'motive' and 'directional' is unfortunate and a better labelling might be ('motive' (verb + particle)). The collocability or compatibility of textual elements is perhaps our highest relevant order of abstraction and grammar attempts to capture as much of it as possible in its own network of generalized concepts and terms. Collocations are particular members of generalized classes of associations that we have labelled 'colligations'. The relationship between 'collocation' and 'colligation', then, is on a scale of *generality*. That between 'collocation' and 'root' is one of *size*, roots being included within a collocation, with or without morphemic 'infilling'. It will be seen that stress is being laid throughout this essay on the paramount importance of the *syntagmatic* relations obtaining between linguistic items in texts and differences of such relations between texts; 'syntagmatic' includes 'syntactic', a term usually reserved for the consideration of such relations at the general level of grammar. The unwarrantable artificiality of separating syntax from other pertinent aspects of syntagmatics has, I hope, been sufficiently demonstrated. At the same time, the descriptive categories recognized are available for the purpose of formulating structural statements and an attempt is being made to avoid the pitfalls involved – from the standpoint of meaning, the ultimate objective – in splitting unitary associations of various kinds and forcing fictitious parts of their meaning into word-size or word-class size 'jars of conceptual content'.

We have seen that the particular final noun in *he tore up the road* does not resolve the ambiguity of the sentence. If, say, *paper* is substituted for *road*, the latter can be seen to belong to at least two conceivable subdivisions of noun: 'reducible' or 'destructible' in *he tore up the road/paper/*etc and 'travellable' in *he tore up the road/path/ finishing straight/*etc. The ambiguity of *he tore up the road* is resolved rather by associability or not with 'inceptive' *off, ie, he tore off up the road, off he tore up the road,* wherein *up* is identifiable unmistakably as the prepositional particle of a phrase (Preposition+N). The case of variously classifiable *road* in *he tore up the road* is simply one instance of an infinite amount of overlapping between linguistic classes, which reflects in part the infinite distinctions recognizable within the total aggregate of our experience of the world. There is little interest in trying to account for all such facts of distribution; the occurrence of *road* with *paper* is of no major significance and it is very easy to demonstrate the difference of linguistic value or distribution of the nouns. The infinity of experience and the fact that it is reflected in language could be further shown by the substitution of *the spider* for *he* in *the spider tore up the paper,* when *tore* clearly belongs to the class 'motive' verb. Of more fundamental linguistic interest, however, is the establishment of such a class as well as the recognition of such abstractions as collocations and their classes and of the fact that they spread across sentence parts. The decision as to whether the recognition of a set of relations is linguistically interesting or not must lie with the linguist as a human being, prompted by his own awareness of language organization and usually by a natural desire to make statements of as high a degree of generality as facts permit, as well as by his assessment of the 'habitualness' of collocational associations. His analytical purpose is also relevant. Use was made above of the highly specific association *come off* (succeed) to illustrate quite general modes of analytical procedure; it could also be used for the general purpose of distinguishing between collocations and idioms. Again, at a lower level of structural generality than that to which the association of $\sqrt{}$*tVr* and $\sqrt{}$*up* belongs, there may well be justification for recognizing classes of 'occupational' noun and 'employment-terminating' verb, when one notices the collocational constraints operating in the cases of *barristers* who are *disbarred, doctors* who are *struck off, solicitors* who are *struck off the roll(s), officers* who are *cashiered, priests* who are *unfrocked, stockbrokers* who are *hammered, schoolboys* who are *expelled, students* who are *sent down, footballers* who are *suspended, working men* who are *sacked,* and *chairmen of regional gas boards* who are *sent on indefinite leave.* We are probably all aware of the operation of even weaker collocational constraints as we search for the 'right' choice among, say, *achieve, accomplish, effect, execute, implement, realize,* etc to associate with *plan* or *project* or *proposal* or *ambition* or *object* or *objective,* and a certain inescapable 'prescriptivism' informing language choices is perhaps worthy of note in passing.

It should not be believed that texts are constructed according to a kind of linear successivity, that meaning diminishes in terms of a left-to-right or earlier-to-later unidirectional progression. As in the case of *he tore (off) up the road*, linguistic dependencies look from right to left, so to speak, as often as from left to right, and often enough in both 'directions' at once. Cumulative choices on the part of speaker and hearer are almost certainly the rule rather than the exception. Consider the collocational association of √*green* and √*grass* in (*as*) *green as grass*, where (*as*)–*as*– is a discontinuous morpheme appropriate to the collocational class concerned and where the bracket encloses an optionally omissible element. In contrast with the case of (√*tVr* ~ √*up*), in which the interpretation of each element is dependent on relations developed with further textual elements, the association of √*grass* with √*green* does not 'modify' the meaning of √*green* any more than collocation with √*green* 'modifies' √*envy* in *green with envy*. The reversal of orientation in the dependencies observable in (*as*) *green as grass* and *green with envy* might perhaps be indicated by the use of arrows, thus (√*green* → √*grass*) and (√*green* ← √*envy*). (. . . → √*grass*) is an intensifying extension of √*green* and is one of a class of over a hundred of what might be termed 'similative intensifiers' in English. It has nothing to do with herbiage as such but (within the predicative adjectival phrase) is to be seen rather in relation to *very green, extremely green, greener than, as green as* (*that is*), etc. The further 'proof' of the rightness of this interpretation is provided by the existence of such comparable intensifying elements as *a doornail/mutton* (*as dead as a doornail/mutton*) or *a post* (*as deaf as a post*), which bear no cognitive resemblance to homophonous linguistic items employed elsewhere. There are numerous similar examples elsewhere in the language. For example, as √*grass* is to √*green* in *as green as grass* or √*green* to √*envy* in *green with envy*, so is 'intensifying' √*up* to √*tVr* in *he tore up the paper* (*cf: he tore the paper*). *Tear up* is not to be considered an idiom any more than *as green as grass*, since *tore* may be recognized as equivalent in both *he tore the paper* and *he tore up the paper* and, in contrast with idiomatic immutability, we may substitute *across, down*, etc for *up* and *ripped, bundled*, etc for *tore*. *Up* in *he tore up the paper* is one of a system of particles of aspect involving concepts of timing and continuity in time; the others are importantly *off* and *on* and all three may be illustrated by *he started off* (inceptive) *running, carried on* (continuative) *walking, and finished up* (completive) *crawling*.[7] *Tore up* in *he tore up the paper* and *tore off* in *he tore off up the road* both belong to the same generalized class of (verb + particle of aspect). We have already noticed that in *he tore off up the road*, 'he', 'off', 'up', and 'the road' all enter into their several grammatical relationships with *tore*; such is the intricacy of language organization.

A further example of 'fore and aft', cumulate linguistic dependency and one in which the usual word-based referential approach to semantics is clearly not very helpful, is the sentence *that's a good boy* – commonly said to a small boy or perhaps a pet animal as a sign of approval of what he has just done or, with appropriate phonological adjustment, as a means of encouraging him to do what one wants. Now it is commonly believed that the difference between *this* and *that* is 'fully grammatical',[8] words which would be unobjectionable if based on different theoretical assumptions but which seem to imply a belief that one can always substitute *this* for *that* and *vice versa* without 'modifying' the textual remainder and while remaining presumably within a generally agreed world of deixis or ostensive definition. But outside the schoolroom and the somewhat lifeless examples of the kind *this/that is a book* or *that/this is a pencil*, one has to account not only for the moderately 'odd' American use of *this* in *who is this?* to one's interlocutor at the other end of the telephone line or for the non-substitutability of *that* for *this* in story-telling (*cf: now this man I'm telling you about* . . .) but also, conversely, for the inadmissibility of *this* but admissibility of *there* in the addressive sentence *that's a good boy*. Now we may also substitute *naughty* for *good* in this sentence and say *that's a naughty boy* to a child or pet taken in misdemeanour, and we may label the language function involved 'approval/disapproval', but this is not the general linguistic point being made, which is rather that, apart from phonological features of intonation, voice quality, rhythm, etc, the language function in question is grounded in the choices that may be made *at one and the same time* in the ultimate nominal and penultimate adjectival positions as well as in the initial option between *that* and *there*. To see that one is not at all concerned with deixis and the facts of linguistic structuring that go with it, one need only substitute, say, *piano* for *boy*, whereafter we can point as well as substitute *this* for *that* and adjectives like *new* for *good*. Once again, then, it will be seen that a linguistic item derives its meaning from the total syntagm and the contrasts obtaining between it and other syntagms within our linguistic organization, so that we might metaphorically speak of the use of *good/naughty* versus *good/new* and of *boy/girl* versus *piano/book* 'determining' the use of *that/there* in *that's a good boy*, all within a semantic framework that is built on more than just 'reference' as that term is commonly understood.

'Idiom'

We have now indicated what we mean by root, morpheme, word, word-class, collocation, and colligation. There remain to be noticed idiomatic and compounded types of composite element. For ease of reference we shall henceforth cite examples in the form of words, except where attention is specifically drawn to roots or morphemes. First, the idiom. Idioms (subsequently enclosed in square brackets) can occur as part of collocations (*eg*, [*the nose on your face*] in *as plain as* [*the nose on your face*]) or combine to form a collocation (*eg* [*take off*] (= imitate) + [*to a T*] (= perfectly) in [*to take* (*someone*) *off to a T*]). Some readers may have been accustomed to regarding as idioms certain of the collocations that have been specified earlier but the idiom belongs to a different order of abstraction. It is a *particular* cumulate association, as a rule inoperable in the sense that its parts are unproductive in relation to the whole in terms of the normal operational processes, that of substitution above all. This is presumably what is implied by the usual notional definition of an idiom as an entity whose meaning cannot be deduced from its parts – a definition, it should be said, that does not indicate how the parts are to be recognized. Thus, (√*put* + √*down*) in *he put down the book* is a collocation like (√*tVr* ~ √*up*) in *he tore up the paper* but the comparable forms in *he* [*put down*] *the rebellion* constitute an idiom, the parts of which are, so to say, both separable (*cf*: *he put the rebellion down*) and inseparable (*cf*, for example, the inomissibility of *down* in contrast with the case of *he put down the book* (*on the table*)). In regard to this important type of association between verb and particle, it may be said in passing that the whole often corresponds to a cognitively similar single form which may replace it either optionally or obligatorily in certain (stylistic) contexts (*cf* [*make up*] = *compose*, [*make it up*] = (*be*) *reconcile*(*d*), [*make up to*] = *flatter*, [*make it up to*] = *compensate*, etc), but although such correspondences are usually suggestive they are apparently not a necessary condition of idiomaticity and collocations are sometimes similarly replaceable (*cf*, *put down* (the book) = *deposit* (on the table), *come down* = *descend*, etc), while other idiomatic types may not be so substitutable (*cf* [*take* (someone) *for*] (someone else), [*take it out on*] (someone), etc).

Parts of idioms are subject to similar morphemic modifications as occur elsewhere, *cf* the verbal flectional possibilities in *he* [*kick*/*s*/*ed the bucket*], which serve both to 'isolate' *kick* and to separate it from *the*, as well as the insertability of expletives to precede immediately the strongly stressed nuclear or tonic syllable (*ie*, *he has kicked the* –'*Pygmalion*'– *bucket*), which not only serves to separate *the* and *bucket* but is also in parallel with the treatment in this respect of non-idiomatic lexical items (*cf*: *abso*–'*Pygmalion*'–*lutely*). Thus, separability and morphemic modification serve to identify the several roots comprising the idiom, notwithstanding its essential linguistic unity. Further support for the recognition of idioms is generally forthcoming from homophonous contrasts (much beloved of the punster), so that idiomatic (*he*) *kick*(*ed*) *the bucket* may be compared and contrasted with non-idiomatic (*he*) *kick*(*ed*) *the bucket* (*with his foot*), (*was that*) *the bucket* (*he*) *kick*(*ed*)*?*, etc. Again, the component parts of idiomatic [*may as well*] in *he may as well go* are recognizable on such grounds as the optional insertion of *just* (*ie*, *he may just as well go*) and the extensibility of the text to include a further infinitive before which *as* appears again but *well* is excluded (*eg*, *he may as well go as stay*).

It should not be thought that an idiom bears no resemblance to any other idiom. Idioms are often members of highly productive grammatical classes. [*kick the bucket*], for example, together with [*sow wild oats*], [*see the light*], etc, belongs to a type of verb-article/adjective-noun association commonly characterizing idioms, and [*go to the wall*], [*go by the board*], etc belong to another such type. It will be seen therefore that collocations and idioms are similar to the extent that both are generally relatable to grammatical generalizations and that both cut across syntactic classes (*eg* verb and so-called object complement in *kick the bucket*, verb and adverbial complement in *put off*=postpone, etc). The principal difference has been sufficiently emphasized, namely, that in contrast with the collocation, the idiom, if sometimes *eg* transposable (*cf: pull* s.o.'s *leg*/*leg-pull*), is certainly indissoluble. The semantic unity of the idiom corresponds generally to a 'tighter', often more immediately apparent collocability than in the case of the collocation. ($\surd$*smoke*+$\surd$*chimney*) in *to smoke like a chimney*, ($\surd$*swVr*+$\surd$*trooper*) in *to swear like a trooper*, ($\surd$*blue*+$\surd$*cold*) in *blue with cold*, etc are not idioms but collocations; in the same way as *as green as grass* is 'intensified' *green*, so *swearing like a trooper* is 'intensified' *swearing*, and *smoking like a chimney* 'intensified' *smoking*. Again, the fact that any movement of (manual) rotation is often no longer necessary to the turning off of a light (in contrast with a tap or car-engine) does not prevent the identification as collocation rather than idiom of *turn off* in *turn off the light*/*tap*/*engine*/etc; whatever the referential meaning of *turn*, *off* remains constant, formal evidence being provided *inter alia* by the uniformity of predicative transforms (*sc: the light*/*tap*/*engine is off*). *Turn off* thus contrasts with idiomatic [*take off*] (=imitate). The idiomatic type comprising verb+adverbial particle nevertheless behaves in a substantially similar manner to its non-idiomatic counterpart (*turn off* (the light)) and both of them differently from the comparable structure comprising verb+prepositional phrase (*cf: turn*+*off* (the road)).

Thus:

	A	B
non-idiom:	*he turned off the tap* *he turned the tap off*	*he turned off the road* (not **he turned the road off*)
idiom:	*he took off the P.M.* *he took the P.M. off*	
non-idiom:	*he turned it off*	*he turned off* (*it*)
idiom:	*he took him off*	
non-idiom:	**he turned suddenly off the tap*	*he turned suddenly off the road*
idiom:	**he took suddenly off the P.M.*	

Somewhat similar idioms are recognizable which comprise verbs and prepositional (as opposed to adverbial) particles, *eg* [*take to*] (=like) (someone), [*take* (someone) *for*] (someone else), others which involve more than one particle (*eg* [*do away with*] (someone/something)), others again which contain particles and the apparently pronominal form *it* (*eg* [*make it up*] (with someone), [*make it up to*] (someone)), others yet again which include nominal forms (*eg* [*put foot down*] in *they should put their foot* (**feet*) *down* – for the case of a morphemically variable noun form where the verb either is or is not part of the idiom, *cf* [*eat heart/s out*] in *they are eating their hearts out* and (*eat*) [*heads/ off*] in *they are eating their heads off*), etc. Some idioms of this general verbal type further resemble collocations in exhibiting specifiable patterns of grammatical distribution, *cf* [*make up*] (*sc* with cosmetics or greasepaint) (verb) and [*make-up*] (noun), [*let down*] (verb) and [*let-down*] (noun), examples whose multi-componential character as idioms is partly revealed by the difference of tonicity or accentuation corresponding to the grammatical distinction indicated. It must not, however, be thought that the recognition of idioms is any more straightforward than that of other linguistic categories; every supposed case must be considered on its own merits and will undoubtedly depend for its recognition on the type of relationship it accretes with other sentential features (*cf*, for example, the relevance of the 'reflexive' pronominal forms in, *eg*, *they are eating their hearts out/heads off*).

There occur also what might perhaps be termed 'functional' idioms (in the sense that 'language function' has been used in this paper), for example the entreating *do you think you could . . .* in *do you think you could* (*possibly*) *do this* (*for me*)*?*, the exclamatory *for* (*heaven's*) *sake!*, the military challenge *who goes there?*, aphoristic or proverbial comments like *waste not*, *want not* or *too many cooks spoil the broth*, and so on. It is noteworthy that such examples often cover whole sentences to the exclusion of all else. They have been termed 'ready-made expressions' but the label is not self-explanatory and this area of language remains to be explored effectively by the linguist. Part of the explanation for such 'pieces' of language may derive from the fact that we make use of a comparatively limited number of morphemes and morphemic patterns, of phonatory potentialities, and indeed of generalized formal patterns of grammar, even of sentential type, for the manifold functions of language. Thus, for instance, interrogative form considered in the abstract is as multivalent as the flection *-s* and is variously used, in addition to the challenging *who goes there?* above, for suggestions (*what about having something to eat?/wouldn't it be better if . . . ?*), exclamations (*what did I tell you!/is it as late as all that?/isn't it nice!*), threats (*will you* (or *are you going to*) *do as you're told!*), gestures of politeness (*may I give you some water?/* (the shop assistant's) *can I help you?*), requests for instructions (*shall I phone them or what?*), requests for advice and help (*do you think . . . ?/could you possibly . . . ?*), retorts (B's *can't I?!* in reply to A's *you can't prove it*), and so on. Conversely, the myriad functional uses to which language is put day by day may confidently be expected to correspond to extensive appearance of idioms and collocations of the kinds illustrated. *Do you think you could do this for me?* is apparently an expansion of *do this for me* and we should be even more unwise than elsewhere to rely in cases like this on word-based, referential meaning, applied here especially to *think* and *could*. The sentence form *do you think you could do that?* (pronounced with identical voice quality, rhythm, and intonation – let us say with an intonational rise from penultimate *do*) is wholly ambiguous. There is the interpretation we have just been considering, in which *do you think you could . . .* is an idiomatic formula of polite entreaty, and that in which an inquiry is being made as to the addressee's belief in his own capacity to perform whatever is in question. The ambiguity is easily resolved by transformational means, *cf: do you think you could* (*possibly*) *do that* (*for me*)*?*, where the inclusion of *possibly* and *for me* are inappropriate to the second interpretation.[9]

'Compound'

So much – undoubtedly far too sketchily – for idioms. To turn – it is feared more sketchily still – to compounds, composite elements of texts neither idioms nor collocations. Emphasis is placed on compounds (subsequently doubly hyphenated) as part of sentential patterning within the scatter of a collocation (*eg*, *bull=fight/-er/-ing*, which belong to (√*fVght* ~ √*bull*)) or even, though more rarely, of an idiom (*cf* verbal [*make* (oneself) *up*] and its cognate nominal compound [*make=up*]). The same collocation occurs three times in *a bullfighter fights bulls at a bullfight*, twice in compound form and, of course, in verbal and nominal forms appropriate to the syntactic conditions of occurrence. The individual compound is essentially bipartite and uninterruptable, except by *and* in the special case of coordinate compounds (*eg*, *knife=and=fork*, *brush=and=comb*, etc).

(*A*) *high=chair* (*sc* for the baby) is a chair and is high but is not to be equated with (*a*) *high chair* (*sc* any sort of chair that is high). The proof of this particular pudding lies not only in the different phonetic potentialities of the two sequences (in matters of tempo and vowel quality, for example) but also in their contrastive 'operability'. The baby's *high=chair* is not only uninterruptable, it is also adjectivally 'incomparable' and 'unintensifiable'; thus, neither (*a*) *higher chair* nor (*a*) *very high chair* refers to the artefact in question and, having regard to the rule by which, other things being equal, colour adjectives occur in closer proximity to the noun than *high* in the Adj+N phrase, we find that (*a*) *high red chair* (in contrast with (*a*) *red high=chair*) is again not specifically for the baby. Similarly, *New=York* is a compound within a collocationally productive pattern of place names. Although the compound here refers to a particular city and its parts are unproductive in relation to the particular linguistic whole, nevertheless they are productive in relation to other directly comparable wholes (*York*, *London*, *New=London*, *New=Guinea*, etc). *New=York* cannot therefore be regarded as an idiom (as it sometimes has been) and we should once again beware of the possibility of confusing the facts of reference with those of linguistic structuring.

Although *high=chair* and *New=York* do not enter into the same network of relations, they may perhaps both be reasonably seen as exemplifying a formative process of 'fusion' or 'welding'. This is not the only process of compounding in English and indeed other types of fused compound are recognizable. *Black=bird*, for example, noticeably differs from *high=chair* and *New=York* in respect of the placing of the tonic accent (a feature which is of considerable significance in English and which the reader will probably be familiar with from reference to it in the common run of grammar book in connection with such verbal/nominal distinctions as *convíct* (verb): *cónvict* (noun). Examples given of this tonic difference may also include compounds, *cf: make úp* (verb):*máke=up* (noun), *run abóut:rún=about*, *black óut:bláck=out*, etc). *Black=bird* is identifiable with more certainty as a compound than, say, *blackboard*, not only on the grounds of contrast with uncompounded *black bird* but also of relatability to *humming=bird*, etc; a blackboard may not be black or even a board, so that *blackboard* is less obviously relatable to *black board* than *blackbird* is to *black bird*. Perhaps, however, the relationship of synonymy between *blackboard* and *board* provides some justification of the view of *blackboard* as compound. We must not, however, allow etymology and orthographic conventions to confuse us. How do we justify the recognition of *ice-cream* as compound? *Public housing* is certainly a compound, but why should *public house* be? Once again, every text must be considered on its own merits in terms of plausible relations discernible within the contemporary language.

An earlier 'structuralist' linguistics tended to take compounds (as it took *meaning*) as effectively given in advance and to restrict its interest to the fused type of compound illustrated by *blackbird*. It rather ignored therefore the linguistic relations of many kinds surrounding compounds and in particular the highly productive processes of transposition (*cf: snow=white* (*hair*) versus (*hair*) *as white as snow*, *bull=fight/-er/-ing* versus *fight bulls*, etc). Morphemic modification in the case of transposed compounds takes many forms; *cf*, for example, the presence and absence of *-s* in *a game of billiards* versus *billiard=balls*, that of *as-as-* in *as white as snow* versus *snow=white*, that of *the-of-* in *the hunting of big game* versus *big game=hunting*, etc; *cf*, too, the use of the flection *-al* in (*a*) *professional woman* versus (*a*) *woman in the professions*. Sometimes particular collocational constraints may impose their somewhat frustrating limitations on generality, at least until further knowledge is acquired of regular processes that may be at work. Thus, *cf: medical book* (not **medicine book*) versus *book on medicine* versus *law book* (not **legal book*) versus *medicine chest* (not **medical chest*). While making these all too brief references to transpositional relationships, perhaps we should observe that the earlier non-compound *black bird* will be classified as 'phrase' and that its single form *black* is relatable to the relative periphrasis in, say, (*a*(*ny*) *bird*) *that is black*. As a corollary, relatives may not occur within compounds but the Adj + N phrase is nevertheless 'derivable' by formative process in a similar way to, say, *billiard=balls* and innumerable other examples of transposed compounding. The fact that *black bird* is labelled phrasally reflects, it seems, a combination of conventional practice, analytical convenience, and the ascribing of special significance to this particular type of structural relationship.

Nominal compounds have usually come in for the lion's share of attention, but, among other types, adjectival compounds are extremely common, *eg* (*a*) *fine=big* (*boy*) (adj=adj), *pearl=grey* (n=adj), *long legged* (adj=n), etc, and again illustrate the two main processes of compound formation, fused (*fine=big*) and transposed (*snow=white*) in addition to contributing their own patterns of morphemic modification.[10] Verbal compounds rarely comprise two verbal forms (*cf: make do* (*with*)) but the compounded association of verb and particle, for instance, is of correspondingly high frequency. *Over=produce* and *over=production*, for example, are verbal and nominal transposed compounds belonging to the scatter of the collocation also illustrated in (*to*) *produce over* (*what is required*), and the particle component in this case is markedly productive (*cf: over=estimate, over=value, over=rate, under=estimate, under=value, under=rate*, etc). On the other hand, verbal forms like *overcome, understand, undergo*, etc resist efforts to divide them in any plausible way and are almost certainly unrecognizable as compounds on any but descriptively inadequate etymological grounds.

The individual compound, we have said, is characterized by uninterruptability but the compounding process may be of compounds themselves. Thus, if *ivory=balls* is regarded as the compound transposed form of *balls made of ivory, ivory billiard balls* comprises two compounds, one of which is discontinuous. Perhaps in this case simplification might be achieved by regarding *ivory* as separable and adjectival (like *black* in *black bird* above) but other incontrovertible examples of discontinuous compounds are given below. The different feature of the coalescence of compounds is also very common. Thus, say, (*the*) *Roman Catholic Church* may be plausibly regarded as compounded by coalescence from *Roman Catholic* and (*the*) *Catholic Church*, with *Catholic* looking both ways at once, so to say. Similarly, in the attested example of (*a*) *young professional woman decorator*, the compounds *professional woman* and *woman decorator* have coalesced, while *professional* is also compounded with *decorator* (*cf* (*the*) *decorating profession*, (*the*) *profession of decorating/-or*) in the manner of *ivory* with *balls* in the earlier *ivory billiard balls*. Moreover, there are good reasons for considering *young* as compounded with *woman* (notice, for example, the fixed adjectival order in *a tall* (*promising*, etc) *young woman/man*, not **a young tall* (*promising*, etc) *woman/man*, and the fact that in the compound *young* is not associable with, say, the marks of adjectival comparison). Thus, the whole *young professional woman decorator* can be regarded as the coalescent form of *young woman, professional woman, professional decorator*, and *woman decorator*, with *young* and *woman, professional* and *decorator* discontinuously associated. What has not yet been completely explained in the absence of further research are the factors governing sequential order in such cases. We may note in passing that the whole phrase may be enlarged to include a prepositional extension, as in *a young professional woman decorator of* (or *with*) *charm* (*and discernment*) and that such prepositional phrases are, as we have seen in other cases, inadmissible for pre-nominal transposition, *cf: a charming* (, *discerning*) *young professional woman decorator*. The earlier example of *billiard balls* may be expanded to illustrate further the coalescence resulting from the compounding of compounds. Thus, balls used for billiards are *billiard =balls*, the supply of billiard balls is *billiard=ball=supply*, and a company which supplies billiard balls is a *billiard=ball=supply= company*. Diagrammatically, coalescence here might be shown as follows:

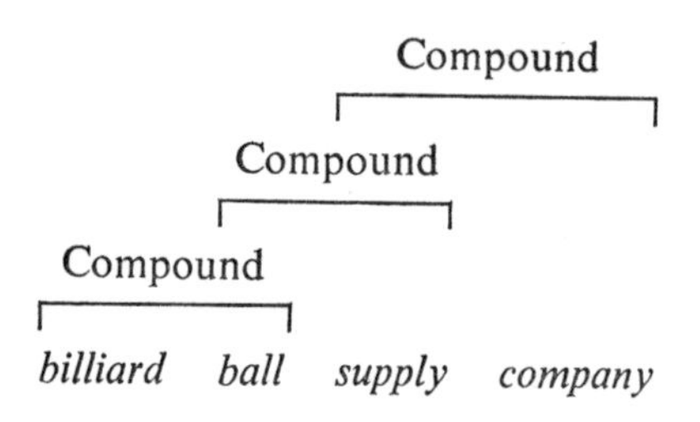

Discontinuity would require other means of diagrammatic representation, as, say,

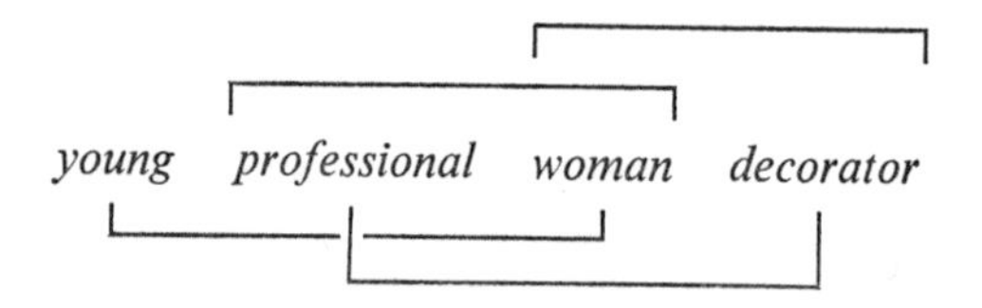

The compounding process is not an additive one, it seems, as in the case of, say, attributive adjectives of colour (*eg*, *white* in *white* (*billiard balls*)), which permit 'modifications' of other kinds, *eg* adjectival comparison (*white/–er/–est*) or 'adverbial' intensification (*very white*, etc). One may talk of some billiard balls as *whiter* than others but not of **whiter wine* in relation to the compound *white=wine*. It is presumably considerations such as these and also those of sequential order (*cf: Spanish+red=wine* but *red+Spanish+soil*) that underlie the recognition of *white* in *white billiard balls* and *charming* in *a charming young professional woman decorator* as essentially additions or extensions rather than as components of any particular type of compounded association.

Obviously, little has been said here on the complex subject of compounding. Some may indeed hold that, in view of the complexity of the topic, it would have been better to omit all reference to it than give it so summary a treatment. It has, however, seemed necessary to give the reader some idea of how compounds relate to the contrastive syntagmatic concepts of collocation and idiom. Even if cut and dried aprioristic solutions for all cases have not been provided, perhaps at least some theoretical means has been suggested of enabling the reader to sort out relevant linguistic complexes as he meets them or at any rate to ask questions about them. One of the principal objectives of scholarship is to inculcate the ability to recognize interesting particularities, from which, it may be hoped, valid general conclusions will follow.

It should perhaps be said here that this essay has confined itself mostly to lexical matters and that in any extended treatment morpheme, root, collocation, idiom, and compound would have to be seen in relation to such other commonly recognized elements of texts as phrase, 'clause', 'complement', etc. Interest has centred mainly on what transformational-generative grammarians and others would probably term 'surface structure' categories, but one clearly needs an ordered set of descriptive terms in which to talk about elements of linguistic structure and must explain the use one makes of them, even when firmly adhering to the view that meaning is the ultimate objective. The descriptive categories and terms that have been recognized may relate in some way to our linguistic 'competence', that is, presumably, to our neuro-psychological organization in respect of language, but roots, collocations, compounds, etc are not categories of meaning in the same way as, say, 'melioration/pejoration', and the ultimate contribution of the linguist is to the definition in his own terms of such functional categories as the latter. At the same time, language patterns as such are in some sense meaningful; one can, for instance, listen and inwardly respond – however rudely or however entranced – to the manner of a man's sounding without paying the slightest attention to what (else) he is saying. Similarly, as we have seen, the interrogative form of, say, an English sentence is a pattern which English speakers recognize but employ variously for threats, suggestions, entreaties, polite requests, exclamations, etc as well as for questions. Form seems to be organized in its own special ways and even reveals its different degrees of 'depth'; in the terms of this paper, words and compounds are 'nearer the surface' than roots, morphemes, collocations, and idioms, while the contrasts on which all depends and which are expressed in terms of operational relationships, seem to be at a deeper level still. There is at present disagreement among linguists over what is to be understood by 'deep structure'. Perhaps this could even ultimately turn out to be another name for 'meaning' and to comprise unitary language functions-cum-language forms, such as that distinguished above as 'approval/disapproval' as well as those of a referential kind ('time', 'instrumentality', etc), which at present figure more prominently in the literature. At all events, debate will continue – and continue to continue. At present all we can say with certainty is, with the Latin poet, that *Grammatici certant, et adhuc sub judice lis est* 'The grammarians are at variance, and the matter is still undecided'. And this is no bad thing.

Notes

1 It was in 'Modes of meaning', *Essays and Studies* (The English Association), 1951 (reprinted in *Papers in Linguistics 1934–1951*; Oxford, 1957 and subsequently) that J. R. Firth proposed 'to bring forward as a technical term, meaning by "collocation", and to apply the test of "collocability"'. The term was not originally Firth's and he may well have been influenced in its selection by H. E. Palmer, who from Tokyo wrote a monograph on the subject in the nineteen-thirties. The term appears in Palmer and Blandford's *Grammar of Spoken English* and Palmer doubtless did much to shape the *Second Interim Report on English Collocations* (Department of Education, Tokyo), mentioned in J. E. Mansion's edition of Harrap's *Standard French and English Dictionary* and in R. P. L. Ledésert's recent up-dating of Mansion in the introductory bibliography of works consulted. But the more or less technical employment of the term antedates Palmer, too, by upwards of 325 years according to the N.E.D., although the application of the concept and term to features of linguistic structure seems to be comparatively recent. Palmer appeared quite properly to see collocation as a highly abstract order of compatibility between linguistic elements but did not define the term with any degree of precision. Firth, for his part, appropriately thought of it as primarily lexical, as a means of restricting the 'vagrancy of words' and of providing 'stylistic' delineation of his 'restricted languages'. The lexical emphasis has been taken further by the neo-Firthians, and notably by M. A. K. Halliday and J. McH. Sinclair, to the point of regarding collocational study as independent of grammar (see, for example, M. A. K. Halliday, 'Lexis as a linguistic level' and J. McH. Sinclair, 'Beginning the study of lexis', respectively at *p* 148 *ff* and *p* 410 *ff* of *In Memory of J. R. Firth*, Longman, 1966). The contrary view is taken in this paper but Firth himself seemed to have no opinions in this matter. He tended to use the term somewhat generally for (restrictive) 'associability' and did not consider at all closely the relationship between collocation, colligation, idiom, compound, phrase, etc. Moreover, he saw collocation – like many who follow him – as of *words*, but it seems useful to distinguish between *word* and *root* and a collocation is seen here as of roots. *Collocation*, too, has often been used as a variant of *collocability*; in the present paper, *collocability* is reserved for the general compatibility of linguistic elements, while *collocation* is an element of linguistic structure. But, as will be seen, this is only one among numerous consequences that a syntagmatic view of language structure imposes.

2 See *p* 15, *n* 13.

3 I have myself, moreover, tended in this volume to use 'denotational' and 'referential' more or less interchangeably, probably to the chagrin of the philosopher among others.

4 Reference to grammar is necessary since lexical and grammatical study are here seen as closely related. Grammatical exemplification is required not only

for the purpose of illustrating formal linguistic analysis but also in order to 'place' the collocations and other lexical categories that are the main concern of this paper.

5 It may be that the concept and term *clause*, variously used by linguists or not used at all, is superfluous, since it is defined in terms equally applicable to *sentence*.

6 It should not be thought that what appears here is anything like an analysis or even a fully representative 'scatter' of *work* in English. The writer is also aware of the use of 'mass' and 'count' as terms relatable to distinction between, say, *marvellous work* and *a marvellous work/marvellous works* but finds more interesting the fact that the meaning of *work* derives from the several kinds of extension to which it is necessarily subject in the syntagmatic process. Adjectival extension, *eg* with *marvellous*, is one type, another is that of *of*+N; one can predicate of a work of art that *it is a marvellous work* or that *it is a work of art* but not that **it is a work*. The evident syntactical function of *a* and *of* in *a work of art* (pl *works of art*) has led some linguists to take the view that the lexicon is divisible into 'full' words (*eg*, *work*) and 'empty' (*eg a*, *of*, *the*, *for*, etc), a view of relatively small merit. It is true that *a*, *of*, etc do often act in the manner of morphemic flections elsewhere but any recognizable lexical item is capable of more particular meaningful employment in a language. Who is to say that the inclusion of *a* in, *eg*, *what sort of a dog is that?* may not warrantably be related to 'disparagement' in contrast with the case of the 'enquiry' after the canine species embodied in *what sort of dog is that?* In pre-ecumenical days, no Catholic would have regarded *the* as by implication meaningless in association with *faith*, just as the meaning of the French definite article *le* in combination with *Chambertin* is that you find the wine in question towards the bottom of the merchant's list of burgundies and pay significantly more for it than in most other cases.

7 *Be1* (continuative) in the English infinitival verbal periphrasis of maximal size (*eg*, *to be being asked*) is to be seen in relation to other aspectival auxiliaries that may be substituted for it, *eg*, *keep* ((on) *-ing*), *start* ((off) *-ing*), *finish* ((up) *-ing*), *leave* ((off) *-ing*), etc. In conjunction with the aspectival particles *off/on/up*, one needs to consider the associated behaviour of auxiliaries of aspect with the infinitival and *-ing* form of the main verb. *He started off laughing* is an example of (*laugh*+'inceptive' aspect) in both of the possible interpretations (i) he started to laugh (but stopped himself) and (ii) he started off laughing but finished up crying. In the second case *to laugh* may not be freely substituted for *laughing* and the contrast is therefore in parallel with *eg*, *he stopped to smoke* and *he stopped smoking*, but *cf* elsewhere, *eg*, *to laugh* (or *laughing*) *is good for you*. Aspectival meaning is rarely if ever attributable solely to the particle, which is to be considered rather, for example, from the standpoint of its omissibility or otherwise. Thus, the same particle *up* appears in the antonymous *he gave up running* and *he took up running*, and the elsewhere antonymous *up* and *down* occur in the synonymous sentences *why doesn't he slow up?* and *why doesn't he slow down?* It may fairly be said that the verb is of greater relevance to aspect and that it is *start-finish* that provides the antonymous contrast in *he started off laughing and finished up crying*, whence – provided that intonational form, notably in respect of *finished*, is appropriate – both *off* and *up* are omissible. Again, 'inceptive'–'iterative'/'continuative'–'completive' belongs rather to *start–keep–finish* than to *off–on–up* in *he started off running, kept on running, and finished up crawling*, whence – with appropriate safeguards as to intonation – all the particles are omissible. The particles serve mainly, it seems, to 'reinforce' the auxiliary of aspect, to

disambiguate otherwise ambiguous sentences, and to 'complement' certain verbal forms, *eg*, *set*, *cf*: *he set off walking* (not **he set walking*). As an example of the disambiguating part played by particles, *he finished crying* is variously interpretable as 'he was crying as he finished' and 'he completed his crying'; *off* unambiguously marks the latter 'completive' aspect in the more realistic example *he finished off painting the house* (notice in passing the superficially antonymous use of the same particle for 'inceptive' aspect in *he started off laughing*). It is, however, also important to distinguish between *-ing* forms, for example between the verbal act of participial *-ing* and the verbal activity of gerundial *-ing*, as another instance of the complexity of dependencies within sentences. A clearer example of the contrast is *he left off lecturing* versus *he left lecturing*; in the former case the lecturer stopped in mid-lecture, in the latter he renounced his career as a lecturer. Similarly, *he gave up running*, in which *up* is an inomissible element of the composite *give up*, variously relates to the race he was in the act of running or to his athletic career; in such a case disambiguation will rest on appeal to other criteria, *eg* difference as to transposability (*cf: he gave running up*). One final illustration in this brief *exposé* is capable of threefold interpretation: *he went off playing football* = (i) he was playing as he went, (ii) he went off (in order) to play football, (iii) he no longer liked playing football. Space is limited but the inomissibility of *off* in (iii) only, the substitutability of *to play* for *playing* in (ii) only, are among the means by which such 'homologous' forms can be interpreted.

8 See, for example, M. A. K. Halliday, Angus McIntosh, Peter Strevens, *The Linguistic Sciences and Language Teaching* (Longman, 1964), *pp* 32–3.

9 Within a discernible area of 'commands and requests', such a sentence as *leave your hat on the table* (with or without pre- or postposed *do/will you/please* . . .) may be spoken at the opposite ends of a scale 'polite-to-brusque'. Is such 'antonymy' not akin to ambiguity? To term, say, the politely preposed *would you care to* (*leave your hat* . . .) a 'ready-made expression' is to beg the question and the relegation of such matters to what some call 'expressiveness' might well seem defeatist.

10 For some of these, see perhaps 'Some English phrasal types', in *In Memory of J. R. Firth*, *p* 343 *ff*.

Five

Aspects of gender revisited, with special reference to Cairene Arabic

As with, say, reduplication, so with agreement, languages make greater or less use of such available devices of so-called 'surface structure' for various purposes, and it is not only inappropriate to base one's expectancies solely on the facts of English but it is also to say the least premature to regard gender as universally expendable, for instance in response to a postulated stabilization of word-order relative to grammatical function. A more sensitive and certainly no more arbitrary view of language meaning than those currently in vogue must often envisage grammatical gender otherwise than as 'redundant' or 'meaningless', since there is more to the semantic relevance of gender than any 'referential' implications it may have. On another topic, although nouns are always involved – actually or potentially – in the concordial processes of gender, the latter is not a noun-inherent feature, and the typical conception of gender as limited to nouns, which are thereafter regarded as 'determining' or 'controlling' the forms of accompanying articles, adjectives, verbs, etc takes in a word-class cart but fails to notice much if anything of the prior syntagmatic horse; Arabic, and in particular the colloquial Egyptian Arabic of Cairo, imposes a different view. Inappropriate preconceptions have led all linguists to date, including myself, to recognize distinctions of grammatical gender in Cairene Arabic; it is now proposed that such distinctions should be abandoned.[1]

It was one of Greenberg's grammatical universals that 'if a language has gender categories in the noun, it has gender categories in the pronoun'.[2] In a different context, with different emphasis but perhaps not from wholly dissimilar beliefs, Lyons affirms that 'it is clearly the pronominal function of gender which is of primary importance in communication'.[3] These and subsequent quotations from important recent or quite recent publications by well-known linguists of different orientations are not chosen in any polemical spirit but rather as representative of widely held opinions on certain fundamental and related aspects of gender. There is more than a hint in much of today's linguistic writing of the rehabilitation of natural at the expense of grammatical gender, especially in the light of statements as to the 'redundancy' of the latter.[4] Gleason had it that 'the gender of an English noun is defined solely in terms of the pronoun substitute *he*, *she*, or *it*, which may be used in its place',[5] but he is clear that he is writing about English and one cannot be sure how, on a broader front, Gleason's or any similar if more general view would accommodate the case of, say, Urdu. In that language, notwithstanding gender categories of a familiar Indo-European kind in the noun, a single 3rd person pronominal form *voh* translates English 'he, she, it, they', corresponding distinctions being incorporated in accompanying verbal forms, *eg* 'voh aayaa thaa/aa(y)ii thii/aa(y)ee thee/aa(y)ii thĩi' (he/she/they [masc]/they [fem] had come). Gender is not in any sense an inherent feature of nouns but a matter of 'surface structure' agreement, used meaningfully in greatly different ways among the world's languages. It is consequently confusing to speak if only by implication of both semantic gender and syntactic gender, nor is there any justification for the belief that gender is 'linguistically relevant sex specification'. In a recent very useful book on grammar, F. R. Palmer limits the derivation of grammatical gender from biological reference to an Indo-European and (? more questionably) Semitic tradition, but uses 'information' in a similar sense to 'communication' elsewhere and answers his own question about the amount of information provided by such categories as gender with the avowal that gender is irrelevant to any kind of meaning.[6] Yet not only may one experience misgivings over an implied truncation of meaning but in addition one may not share the opinion – by no means Palmer's alone – that comparative fixity of word-order relative to grammatical function is the condition *par excellence* for the supposed superfluity of gender distinctions.[7] In the important Indo-Pakistan area, there is a 'fairly fixed' order of words and grammatical functions in such representative languages as Hindi, Panjabi, Urdu, Sindhi, etc, wherein different concordial patterns involving gender and covering subject and object nouns together with following participles provide an indispensable means of recognizing and maintaining not only the aforementioned sentence functions but also such sentential distinctions as perfective/imperfective and transitive/intransitive.[8] Again, and on quite another point, if gender has virtually (? completely) disappeared from English, why has it not also disappeared from German? It does not seem that word-order is much more fixed in one of these languages than the other, and should not emotive and sociolinguistic factors be taken into account among others in any search to explain the elimination of gender distinctions? The greatly different sociolinguistic conditions surrounding the development of nations and their languages must surely be directly relevant to the question. Grammar, after all, as Firth used to say, is conformity, and the social and 'stylistic' conformity inherent in the grammar of speech is too pervasive to ignore. In the Indo-Pakistan sub-continent before partition – and perhaps even today among the 20,000,000 or so Urdu speakers of India – Delhi and Lucknow were recognized as the places where 'they spoke the best Urdu'. It happened, however, that the language differed markedly between them, not least in the matter of gender. If these differences were observable in the conversation of two speakers from each of the two cities, then local linguistic loyalties were being maintained, with all the implications of the fact for the total form of the dialogue; if, however, as might happen, one speaker adapted his habits to the norms of his interlocutor, then the chances were that he stood in some 'inferior' relation to him or was in fact suffering from an inferiority complex. One could at any rate be sure that the speakers were not friends. This is not the place to broach the question of the linguistically as well as socially complex but nevertheless codified interrelationships of Urdu interlocutors in terms of role and status, but it would be unwarrantable to dismiss such matters as other than meaningful, for they are deeply so. There seems little reason to disagree with Graff, who forty years ago said with specific reference to semantic aspects of gender that 'it seldom happens that linguistic signs are pure referential symbols. Their referential, emotive, and socially promotive functions are continually blended, and the categorizing in language follows the entwined zigzag lines traced by this mixture of functions.'[9]

The Firthian view of gender, then, is of a noun-centred, 'surface structure' device of grammatical concord with no meaning attaching to it *a priori* save the very important one of 'getting things right'. Belief in the redundancy of gender rests on the narrower semantics criticized throughout this book. Its adherents would, I think, consider that the very large number of concordial genders that run through the sentences of a Bantu language, say, could be reduced to simple morphological distinctions of the English 'count-countess' type or, more appropriately from a semantic point of view, of the south-east Asian type, where different classifiers respond to semantic distinctions of shape, clusters of things, means of transport, etc. In the same way, it does not really seem to matter if one makes mistakes with adjectives, pronouns, or articles, say – the native speaker will 'understand'. The Romance languages, for instance, make interesting use of articles for such semantic distinctions as the following in French:

le bourgogne (the burgundy one drinks): *la Bourgogne* (where it is made)
le gloria (the 'Gloria' of the Mass): *la Gloria* (of the night-club)
le France (the liner, a hotel, perhaps a cinema): *la France* (the country)
La Reine Elisabeth (Queen Elizabeth): *Le Reine Elisabeth* (the liner or a Montreal hotel)

It is usually said that, for example, *le bourgogne* is 'really' *le vin de bourgogne*, that *la Bourgogne* is *la région de Bourgogne*, that *le Portugal* is to be interpreted as *le pays de Portugal*. But what transformationally deleted forms can be claimed as underlying an elliptical *la France* or, for that matter, (*le*) *Paris*, (*capitale de la France et ville des lumières*,) which occurs with article and adjective in the words of the popular song *Sous les ponts du vieux Paris*. (*Le*) *Paris* is thus noticeably ambiguous, although with the article and otherwise in isolation, ambiguity is probably reduced to that between, say, cinema and hotel. The correct pronominal form in relation to the city is, of course, *il*, as in the following exchange between characters in a Simenon novel: *A. Paris ne vous a pas effrayée, au début?* (Didn't Paris frighten you at first?) *B. Il m'effraie encore.* (It still does.)[10] No doubt to get these things wrong would not impair native 'understanding', but the native speaker himself seems regularly to get things right and could in any case probably understand sign 'language'. The foreigner will, in fact, be understood to be such, and his interlocutor's speech behaviour adapted accordingly. If 'redundancy' is seen as 'stripping a language down to its bare essentials', then in the last analysis is this not the advocacy of getting things wrong, implying an unnecessary 'engineering' reminiscent of such palpably unconvincing 'languages' as Basic English? One does not have to be a prescriptivist to think that there is something in the old view that grammar is in fact about getting things *right* within statable limits of tolerance, about speakers of a given language or dialect sounding and wanting to sound like speakers of that language or dialect. Does the 'redundancy' view not logically entail the rejection or at least the re-definition of standards and standard forms of language? For example, in the 'surface' forms of the Cairene Arabic we are about to look at, quite apart from the evidence provided in justification of such semantic notions as 'collective', 'human', 'origin', etc, the facts of grammatical agreement are uniquely characteristic of that particular *prestigious* form of Egyptian speech, and therefore quite closely guarded by its speakers. Linguistic meaning involves a good deal more than the drawing of valid inferences from sentences in the honourable and time-honoured manner of logic.

Nouns have often been seen as the focus for differences of gender agreement less for justifiable syntactic reasons than because of a supposed property of 'inherent' gender with which to 'control' agreement. Thus, Gleason, for example, defines gender as 'a set of syntactic subclasses of nouns primarily controlling concord'[11] and says elsewhere that 'no adjective has an inherent gender, but may be inflected to provide a form for each gender'.[12] It is true that of all grammatical classes nouns alone are always present or potentially present within any syntactic domain to which features of agreement are referable, but the syntagmatic concept of *domain* is prior to that of *word-* or *form-class*, since the latter is first and foremost a means of giving shape and quotability to the former. The example of Cairene Arabic that follows shows quite clearly the misconceptions that can arise from putting things the other way round.

The noun phrase in Cairene Arabic

In describing relevant facts of the colloquial Arabic of Cairo, the noun-oriented, noun-inherent view of gender has led to serious illogicalities in the description of this language. The noun phrase in CA reveals a clear need for syntagmatic systematization in preference to a narrower starting point of words and word-classes conceivably stemming from classical traditions of language learning and teaching in western Europe. Since the study of any concordial category must transcend the boundaries of a single word-class, it is open to us to state necessary distinctions within appropriate wider domains. Subsequently to classify the narrow class into genders and to derive accompanying forms from rather dubious 'inherent' characteristics of nouns would be superfluous in description and at most justifiable as a formalistic device of rule-writing and ordering. All that one can say, as has already *been* said, is that in those syntagms within which gender distinctions seem to be appropriately made, nouns are either present or potentially so. Rather as collocational study[13] serves to define not only particular roots but also associations thereof, so the analysis of grammatical concord serves not only to isolate morphemes characteristic of this or that class of forms appropriate to given syntactic conditions of occurrence, but also to distinguish generalized types of syntagm. This is a different view from that by which nouns 'control concord' or gender is a 'linguistic classification of nouns into arbitrary groups for syntactic purposes'. It is the latter view that has led to serious distortion in accounting for CA facts.

Let us first consider the following possibilities within the CA noun phrase:

Noun	*Adj*	*Noun*	*Adj*
'beet' (house)	'kibiir' (big)	'gineena' (garden)	'kibiira' (big)
'ˡamiiS' (shirt)	'wisix' (dirty)	'ma9laˡa' (spoon)	'wisxa' (dirty)[14]
'rɑɑgil' (man)	'Tɑwiil' (tall)	'sitt' (woman)	'Tɑwiila' (tall)

These examples illustrate a frequent contrast of concordial type, difference relating to the presence or absence of a final open vowel, particularly in adjectival forms but often enough also in nouns. On the basis of such examples, we might well wish to regard the noun as having an 'inherent' gender and 'controlling' the form of the adjective. We would sort out two categories of noun on the basis of exclusive association with the different though related forms 'kibiir' and 'kibiira', 'wisix' and 'wisxa', 'Tɑwiil' and 'Tɑwiila', and thereafter label them masculine (without -a and including 'rɑɑgil' (man)) and feminine (with -a and including 'sitt' (woman)). But the foregoing examples are far from providing the whole story. 'siggaada' (carpet) '9ɑriiDɑ' (wide) is according to expectation and 'sitt 9agamiyya' (a Persian lady) is also 'regular' but so, too, is 'siggaada 9agami' (a Persian carpet). Clearly, this does not tally with the concordial patterns of familiar European languages and, in order to get things right, it is as necessary to know the subclass of adjective as of noun. The examples impose the recognition not only of *human* and *non-human* nouns (*eg*, 'sitt' versus 'siggaada') but also of adjectives of *origin* and others (*eg*, '9agami' versus '9ɑriiD'). There are, of course, other examples available in support. How, then, do these facts accord with the earlier quotation from Gleason that 'no adjective has an inherent gender, but may be inflected to produce a form for each gender'?[15]

Let us now take things a little further by considering the plural counterparts of the foregoing singular phrases. Subsequent bracketed adjectival forms are acceptable, though in some cases rare (*eg*, 'Tɑwiila' in association with 'riggaala' and 'sittaat'); unbracketed forms may be taken as the rule:

Noun	*Adj*	*Noun*	*Adj*
biyuut	kibiira (kubɑɑr)	ganaayin	kibiira (kubɑɑr)
(houses)	(big)	(gardens)	(big)
ˡumSɑɑn	wisxa (wisxiin)	ma9aaliˡ	wisxa (wisxiin)
(shirts)	(dirty)	(spoons)	(dirty)
riggaala	Tuwɑɑl (Tɑwiila)	sittaat	Tuwɑɑl (Tɑwiila)
(men)	(tall)	(women)	(tall)

Again an important distinction must be made between 'human' and 'non-human' nouns; adjectival -a forms, *eg* 'kibiira', 'wisxa', are preferred if the noun is 'non-human', while corresponding plurals ('kubɑɑr', 'wisxiin') are strongly favoured with 'human' nouns. In addition, certain morphological features of the noun and adjective have to be taken into account. Thus, the -a form of the adjective occurs, albeit rarely, with plural 'human' nouns ending in -a or -aat, as in the cases of 'riggaala' and 'sittaat' in the preceding table; 'Tuwɑɑl', not 'Tɑwiila', however, is *de rigueur* with a noun like 'ˡawlaad' (boys, young men), which does not include either of the terminations in question. The -a form of the adjective is admissible, however, though again rare, with whatever form or class of 'human' noun, *ie* with 'ˡawlaad' as with 'riggaala' and 'sittaat', when the adjective itself is of the type illustrated by 'kuwayyisiin' in 'ˡawlaad kuwayyisiin (kuwayyisa)' (nice young men). This type is that of the so-called 'sound' plural, which is differentiated *suffixally* from the singular by the addition of -iin (*eg* 'wisxiin' from 'wisix'), and contrasts with the type of 'broken' plural, which for its part is distinguished *infixally* from corresponding singular forms (as 'kubɑɑr' from 'kibiir').[16] Notwithstanding the facts of variation indicated as far as we have gone, the following associations may be taken as the norm:

Noun	*Adj*
biyuut ganaayin ˡumSɑɑn ma9aaliˡ	kibiira/wisxa
riggaala sittaat	Tuwɑɑl/wisxiin

A fundamental question arising is whether, *eg* 'kibiira' in, say, 'biyuut kibiira' (big houses) is to be identified with 'kibiira' in the singular phrase 'gineena kibiira' (a large garden) or whether this is a trivial case of homophony. In fact, there can be no doubt from overwhelming evidence elsewhere in the language that the adjectival form *is* one and the same in both examples. Thus, for instance, the plural noun 'malaabis' (clothes) is regularly associated not only with the -a adjectival form 'ˡurubbiyya' (European) but also with the 3rd pers sing pronominal suffix -ha in 'ʃuftu laabis malaabis ˡurubbiyya diik innɑhɑɑr. 9adatan ma byilbis*haaʃ*, muʃ kida?'[17] (I saw him wearing European clothes the other day. He doesn't wear *them* normally, does he?); again, plural 'ħagaat' (things) is accompanied by the sing fem demonstrative 'di', not plural 'dool', and the pronominal '-ha' (not plural '-hum') in 'ˡilħagaat di kullaha' (all these things); finally for the present purpose, the 3rd pers sing fem verbal form 'xilSit' (not plural 'xilSu') is required in agreement with the plural noun 'fawaakih' (fruits, (kinds of) fruit) in 'ma baˡaaʃ fawaakih fissuuˡ. xilSit xɑɑliS' (There's no more fruit in the market. It's all finished). It is, therefore, abundantly justifiable to regard 'kibiira' in 'gineena kibiira' and 'biyuut kibiira' as the same item. What are the consequences?

Clearly, differences of plural concord are not in parallel with corresponding distinctions in the singular.[18] The difference between, for example, 'Tɑwiila' and 'Tuwɑɑl' is relevant to plural concord but not to the difference between, say, 'riggaala' (men) and 'sittaat' (women) in the way that the difference between 'Tɑwiil' and 'Tɑwiila' is relevant to that between 'rɑɑgil' (man) and 'sitt' (woman). This is unlike anything we may be familiar with in, let us say, French, Latin or, for that matter, Sindhi. If we take the example 'ˡamiiS wisix' (a dirty shirt) versus the corresponding plural 'ˡumSɑɑn wisxa' and start from the premiss that a noun-stem has an inherent gender, then we are led to make the odd statement – one indeed that has so far been regularly made by scholars of Arabic – that a noun like 'ˡamiiS' is masculine in the singular but feminine in the plural. In fact, since 'wisxa' in 'ˡumSɑɑn wisxa' is the *same* form as that appearing in singular patterns elsewhere, we could go oddly further and say that CA 'ˡamiiS' is masculine in the singular but feminine singular in the plural, the absurdity of which is at once apparent. Moreover, the illogicality of such assertions is compounded by the fact that gender distinction cannot be attributed to individual CA plural forms. Thus, the so-called 'common' plural 'dool' (these/those) corresponds to singular 'da [masc]/di [fem]', 'yiktibu' (they write) to 'yiktib' (he writes)/'tiktib' (she writes), 'hum' (they) to 'huwwa' (he)/'hiyya' (she), and so on. In response to such facts it is nonsensical to speak of plural 'ˡumSɑɑn' as 'feminine', *ie* in terms appropriate to gender. Different concordial patterns require recognition in both plural and singular syntagms but the fact is that they are not aptly spoken of as *gender* distinctions at all, although we should recognize for the 'human' nominal class male and female subclasses for sex-reference.

As in the singular phrase, so in its plural counterpart, adjectives of 'origin' behave differently from others, *cf* 'sagagiid ϑagami' (Persian carpets), 'xoxaat Sɑbħiin (Sɑbħɑ)/kubɑɑr (kibiira)' (fresh/large peaches) but 'xoxaat Tulyaani (not *Tɑlɑyna)' (Italian peaches).

It will be seen from what has gone before that it is less confusing to refer to adjectival forms as 1, 2, or 3 in accordance with the following table than to speak of them as singular and plural, masculine and feminine:

1	2	3
kibiir	kibiira	kubɑɑr 'big'
wisix	wisxa	wisxiin 'dirty'
Tulyaani	Tulyaniyya	Tɑlɑyna 'Italian'

It is also clear that categories of number must be given priority in drawing up rules of concord for CA; once a noun is identified as to number, it is a comparatively simple matter to select the appropriate adjectival form from the threefold scatter of forms above. Singular nouns will involve selection between 1 and 2, and plural nouns, including the 'paucal' or 'little plural' form of collectives (see below), between 2 and 3, unless the noun is 'non-human' and the adjective 'origin', when the plural noun is accompanied by 'Adjl'. In order to account for distinctions within such a set as 'siggaada 9agami' (a Persian carpet), 'raagil 9agami' (a Persian man), 'sitt 9agamiyya' (a Persian lady), 'beet gidiid' (a new house), 'gineena gidiida' (a new garden), it is sufficient to classify nouns as 'human' versus 'non-human' ('sitt' versus 'siggaada'), 'male' versus 'female' ('raagil' versus 'sitt'), '*a*-ending' versus 'non-*a*-ending' ('siggaada' versus 'beet') and adjectives as 'origin' versus 'non-origin' ('9agami' versus 'gidiid'). Thereafter it would be unnecessary as well as mistaken to talk of masculine and feminine nouns. This is not, of course, to confuse grammatical (concordial) gender with sex-reference but rather to avoid the confusion.

Although the essentials of our concern have now been stated, concord in the CA noun phrase is more complex than has been indicated and is worth examining further for the conclusions that may be drawn from such examination. 'Countability' is perhaps an inherent feature of the noun[19] and it is necessary to consider the facts of enumeration within the noun phrase both for its own sake and for its implications as to the form of adjectives and nouns in the syntagm. 'Unity', 'duality', 'paucity' ('3–10'), and 'multiplicity' ('10^{+}') are features not of nouns but of enumerative syntagms, as much of numerals as of nouns in word-class terms. The facts are as follows:

(1) For the present purpose the adjectival and pronominal form 'waaħid' (one) can be ignored and the singular form of the noun quite properly considered as expressive of 'unity' in the absence of a preceding numeral. Patterns of accompaniment between singular nouns and adjectives have already been considered.

(2) It is necessary at this point to recognize a class of 'collective' nouns (mostly referring to edible things), exemplified by, say, the 'agglomerate' or 'mass' form 'xoox' (peaches), its corresponding 'singulative' 'xooxa' and 'little plural' or 'paucal' form 'xoxaat' (a few peaches), the singulative and paucal being formed by the addition of -a and -aat to the agglomerate. The latter is accompanied by Adj1, *eg* 'xoox Saabiħ' (fresh peaches); the singulative behaves as to adjectival accompaniment in the manner of non-collective singulars in -a (*eg* 'siggaada'); and the paucal, unlike comparable non-collective forms,

is normally accompanied by Adj3, less often by Adj2. Once again, adjectives of origin appear in form 1 with both singulative and paucal collective forms; thus, for example, notwithstanding *eg* 'xoxaat kubɑɑr (kibiira)', we have 'xoxaat Tulyaani' (a few Italian peaches). The form 'xoxaat' normally requires a preceding numeral of the appropriate class.

(3) The category 'dual' involves the complementarity of a nominal suffix '-een' and the numeral 'ˡitneen'. As a rule only human nouns, in plural form, follow the latter, *eg* 'ˡitneen mu9allimiin' (two teachers); *cf* 'beteen' (two houses). A few 'mensurative' loanwords like 'gineeh' (£) optionally occur with either '-een' or 'ˡitneen'. Duals, as well as co-ordinates like 'sikkiina wi ʃooka' (a knife and fork), must be accompanied by Adj3, *eg* 'beteen gudaad' (two new houses), 'ˡitneen mu9allimiin ʃɑTriin/mɑSriyyiin' (two clever/Egyptian teachers), 'rɑɑgil wi sitt mɑSriyyiin' (an Egyptian man and woman).[20]

(4) 'Paucal' ('3–10') numerals have two forms, the first of which is almost invariably used in enumerations; thus, 'talaata' (3) occurs in isolation and in certain specifiable contexts but – with one exception – 'talat' is the regular form of the numeral before a noun, *eg* 'talat biyuut/riggaala/sittaat' (three houses/men/women). The exceptional case is of the 'mensurative' loan as in 'talaata gineeh' (£3). This is also the exception to the rule that a noun following a paucal numeral is in the plural form. As to the form of an accompanying adjective, it is again interdependent with the noun, and indeed also with the numeral. A mensurative noun is accompanied by Adj3 if Adj is non-origin and by Adj1 if origin, *eg* 'talaata gineeh gudaad/ˡingiliizi' (three new/English pounds); if the noun is collective, then adjectival form is 3 (less often 2) if non-origin, 1 if origin, *eg* 'talat xoxaat Sɑbħiin (Sɑbħɑ)/Tulyaani' (three fresh/Italian peaches); otherwise – and this is the commonest case – if the noun is non-human, non-mensurative, and non-collective, then adjectival form is 2 (less often 3) if non-origin, 1 again if origin, *eg* 'talat sagagiid 9ɑriiDɑ (9urɑɑD)/9agami' (three large/Persian carpets); finally, if the noun is human, then Adj3 is obligatory whatever the form of noun. The last case should be contrasted with the non-numeral context, where in the case of *eg* 'riggaala', 'sittaat', and 'ˡawlaad', the adjectival form 'kuwayyisa' was admissible in addition to the more usual 'kuwayyisiin'; with *eg* 'talat', only 'kuwayyisiin' is tolerated in 'talat riggaala/sittaat/ˡawlaad kuwayyisiin' (three nice men/women/young men). So much again for nouns controlling the form of adjectives.

(5) 'Big plural' ('10⁺') numerals have one form only and the following noun is in its singular form. By comparison with the contrasting

facts of (4) it will be seen that the numeral and noun are also formally interdependent. Examples are '9iʃriin beet/raagil' (twenty houses/men). If N is human and male, a following adjective is in form 3 (rarely 1), obligatorily 1 if origin, *eg* '9iʃriin mu9allim gudaad (gidiid)/maSri' (twenty new/Egyptian teachers); if N is human and female, the adjective is of form 3 (less often 2), 2 if origin, *eg* '9iʃriin sitt kuwayyisiin (kuwayyisa)/maSriyya' (twenty pleasant/Egyptian ladies). These facts are in contrast with the obligatory Adj3 requirement of the 'dual' and 'paucal' contexts, so that once again it can be seen that it would be erroneous to claim that nouns control adjectival form in the CA noun phrase. If N is non-human and ends in -a (non-collective or collective), an adjective is in form 2 (less often 3) but in form 1 if origin; if N is non-human and does not include the termination -a, Adj1 (less often 3) is the rule and is again obligatory if Adj is origin. Examples are '9iʃriin siggaada 9ariiDa (9uraaD)/Tulyaani' (twenty large/Italian carpets), '9iʃriin beet kibiir (kubaar)/9agami' (twenty large/Persian houses).[21]

The above facts – summarized diagrammatically and tabularly as follows – are also clearly contrary to the conception of concord outlined at the beginning of this paper. Not only are the forms of numeral and noun mutually interacting but adjectival form varies with the presence or absence of a numeral, though the noun may remain unchanged. Dependencies clearly look many ways in the phrase and it is fallacious to look upon one class as controlling the form of another when all are mutually expectant. Some form of syntagmatic presentation is preferable to the usual formulation in terms of a hierarchy of word-classes. Nevertheless, following Wise[22] and subject to the omission of the distributional complementarity of the suffix '-een' and the numeral 'ˡitneen' – since this has no implications as to adjectival form – it is possible to summarize earlier findings in the form of a branching diagram. Adjectival form at the foot of the figure overleaf is derived from the contextual constraints that have been indicated and which are displayed in downward progression from N(oun). Yet the figure is in no sense a statement of inherent features of the noun. Since expectancies are mutual between the several components of the syntagm, the diagram could have been drawn in several ways; it is such facts as the larger membership of the class N in comparison with Nu and A and its more numerous morphological distinctions (as between singular and plural) that suggest the greatest suitability of N as the initiating node of the figure.

Perhaps some form of presentation along the lines of the subsequent table might suggest the syntagmatic interdependency of elements and categories more clearly than the diagram. The word-class inventory

Adjectival form in numeral-noun-adjective syntagms

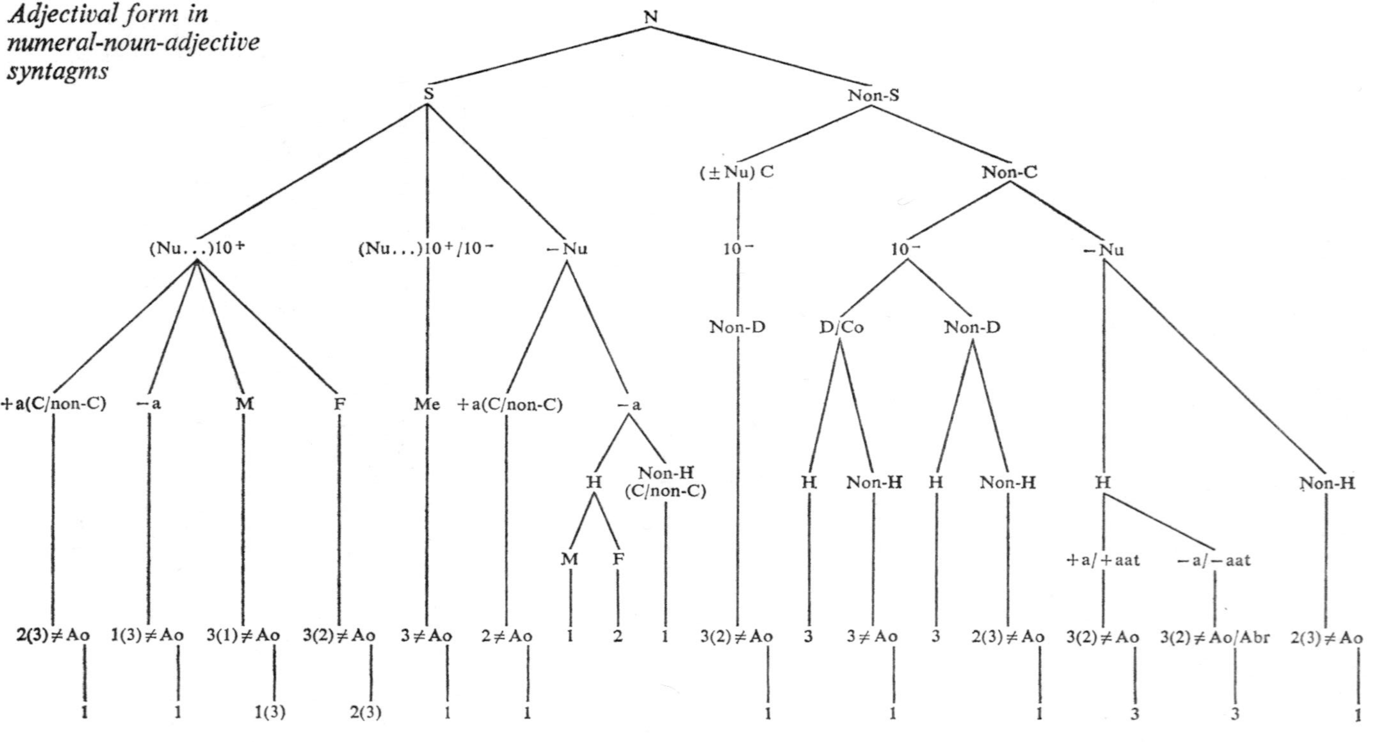

Legend: N noun; Nu numeral; Nu . . . N following a numeral; S singular form of noun; non-S collective and plural form of noun; C collective; + with; − without; 10^+ more than ten; 10^- more than one but less than ten; D dual; Co co-ordinate; H human; M male; F female; Me mensurative; / either . . . or; a suffix -a; aat suffix -aat; 1,2,3 adjectival forms 1,2,3; ( ) less often;

(I) at the head of the table is in terms of the three word-classes Numeral, Noun and Adjective (A, B, C) and is subdivided into as many subclasses as seem appropriate (A1–4, B1–7, C1–3). Classes and subclasses are displayed vertically. Sets of related forms containing the same root appear horizontally ((a)–(d)). The abbreviations and other symbols are those of the preceding figure with the addition of U = uncounted and su = 'sound' plural. The bracketed forms 'rɑgleen', 'waladeen', and 'gineheen' do occur in the language but do not in any way invalidate conclusions and have not been considered in the tabulation. A bracketed letter under column C of FORM OF SYNTAGM indicates the less favoured adjectival form in cases where more than one such form is acceptable. Under RELEVANT FEATURES, those of a syntactico-morphological kind are indicated by the use of lower-case letters.

I

WORD-CLASSES (Numeral, Noun, Adjective), SUBCLASSES, and SETS

A. *Numeral*

	(a)	(b)
1.	zero	
2.	ˈitneen	
3.	talat	talaata
	ˈɑrbɑ9	ˈɑrbɑ9a
	xamas	xamsa
	sitt	sitta
	saba9	sab9a
	taman	tamanya
	tisa9	tis9a
	9aʃɑr	9aʃɑrɑ
4.	ħiDɑɑʃɑr/ˈiTnɑɑʃɑr/etc	

B. *Noun*

	(a)	(b)	(c)	(d)
1.	beet	beteen	biyuut	
2.	siggaada	siggadteen	sagagiid	
3.	sitt		sittaat	
4.	rɑɑgil	(rɑgleen)	riggaala	
5.	walad	(waladeen)	ˈawlaad	
6.	gineeh	(gineheen)	ginehaat	
7.	xooxa	xoxteen	xoxaat	xoox

C. *Adjective*

	(a)	(b)	(c)
1.	kibiir	kibiira	kubɑɑr
2.	wisix	wisxa	wisxiin
3.	Tulyaani (mɑSri)	Tulyaniyya (mɑSriyya)	Tɑlɑyna (mɑSriyyiin)

II RELEVANT FEATURES (semantic, syntactic, morphological)			III FORM OF SYNTAGM (selected from I)			
Numerative	Nominal	Adjectival	A	B	C	Examples
+1	−a −H −Me	+br/su/O	1–	1a	– 1/2/3a	beet kibiir/wisix/Tulyaani (a lar dirty/Italian house)
+1	+a −H −Me ±C	+br/su	1–	2/7a	– 1/2b	gineena/xooxa kibiira/ kuwayyisa (a large/nice garde peach)
+1	+a −H −Me ±C	+O	1–	2/7a	– 3a	gineena/xooxa Tulyaani (an Italian garden/peach)
+1	+H +F	+br/su/O	1–	3a	– 1/2/3b	sitt kibiira/ʃɑTrɑ/Tulyaniyya (a old/intelligent/Italian lady)
+1	+H +M	+br/su/O	1–	4/5a	– 1/2/3a	rɑɑgil/walad kibiir/ʃɑɑTir/ Tulyaani (a big/clever/Italian man/boy)
$+1^{+}$ +U	−H −C	+br/su	1–	1/2c	– 1/2b(c)	biyuut/ganaayin kibiira (kubɑɑ wisxa (wisxiin) (large/dirty houses/gardens)
$+1^{+}$ +U	−H −C	+O	1–	1/2c	– 3a	biyuut/sagagiid Tulyaani (Italia houses/carpets)
$+1^{+}$ +U	−H +C	+br/su/O	1–	7d	– 1/2/3a	xoox kibiir/Sɑɑbih/Tulyaani (large/fresh/Italian peaches)
$+1^{+}$ +U	+H +a/aat	+br	1–	3/4c	– 1c(b)	riggaala/sittaat Tuwɑɑl (Tawiila (tall men/women)
$+1^{+}$ +U	+H −a/aat	+su	1–	5c	– 2c(b)	ˈawlaad ʃɑTriin (ʃɑTrɑ) (clever boys)
$+1^{+}$ +U	+H −a/aat	+br	1–	5c	– 1c	ˈawlaad Tuwɑɑl (tall boys)
$+1^{+}$ +U	+H ±a/aat	+O	1–	3/4/5c	– 3c	riggaala/sittaat/ˈawlaad Tɑlayna (Italian men/women/boys)
+2	−H −Me ±C	+br/su	1–	1/2/7b	– 1/2c	beteen/siggadteen/xoxteen kubɑ /wisxiin (two large/dirty hous carpets/peaches)
+2	−H −Me ±C	+O	1–	1/2/7b	– 3a	beteen/siggadteen/xoxteen Tulyaani (two Italian houses/ carpets/peaches)
+2	−H +Me	+br[23]	2–	6a	– 1c	ˈitneen gineeh gudaad (two new pounds)
+2	−H +Me	+O	2–	6a	– 3a	ˈitneen gineeh mɑSri (two Egyptian pounds)
+2	+H	+br/su/O	1–	3/4/5c	– 1/2/3c	ˈitneen mu9allimiin/sittaat/ 9asaakir Tuwɑɑl/ʃɑTriin/ mɑSriyyiin (two tall/clever/ Egyptian teachers/women/ soldiers)

II RELEVANT FEATURES (semantic, syntactic, morphological)			III FORM OF SYNTAGM (selected from I)			
Numerative	Nominal	Adjectival	A	B	C	Examples
+2	[+Co ±H]	+br/su/O	1–	a *wi* a[24] –	1/2/3c	sikkiina wi ʃooka/rɑɑgil wi sitt kubɑɑr/wisxiin/mɑSriyyiin (a large/dirty/Egyptian knife and fork/man and woman)[25]
+3–10	[−H −C −Me]	+br/su	3a–	1/2c –	1/2b(c)	talat biyuut/sagagiid kibiira (kubɑɑr)/kuwayyisa (kuwayyisiin) (three large/nice houses/carpets)
+3–10	[−H +C]	+br/su	3a–	7c –	1/2c(b)	talat xoxaat kubɑɑr (kibiira)/Sɑbħiin (Sɑbħɑ) (three large/fresh peaches)
+3–10	[−H ±C]	+O	3a–	1/2/7c –	3a	talat biyuut/sagagiid/xoxaat Tulyaani (three Italian houses/carpets/peaches)
+3–10	[−H +Me]	+br[23]	3b–	6a –	1c	talaata gineeh gudaad (three new pounds)
+3–10	[−H +Me]	+O	3b–	6a –	3a	talaata gineeh mɑSri (three Egyptian pounds)
+3–10	+H	+br/su/O	3a–	3/4/5c –	1/2/3c	talat riggaala/sittaat/ˈawlaad Tuwɑɑl/kuwayyisiin/Tɑlɑyna (three tall/nice/Italian men/women/boys)
$+10^{+}$	[−a −H −Me]	+br/su	4–	1a –	1/2a(c)	9iʃriin beet gidiid (gudaad)/kuwayyis (kuwayyisiin) (twenty new/nice houses)
$+10^{+}$	[+a −H −Me ±C]	+br/su	4–	2/7a –	1/2b(c)	9iʃriin siggaada/xooxa kibiira (kubɑɑr)/kuwayyisa (kuwayyisiin) (twenty large/nice carpets/peaches)
$+10^{+}$	[−H −Me ±C ±a]	+O	4–	1/2/7a –	3a	9iʃriin beet/siggaada/xooxa Tulyaani (twenty Italian houses /carpets/peaches)
$+10^{+}$	[+H +F]	+br/su	4–	3a –	1/2c(b)	9iʃriin sitt kubɑɑr (kibiira)/kuwayyisiin (kuwayyisa) (twenty old/nice women)
$+10^{+}$	[+H +F]	+O	4–	3a –	3b	9iʃriin sitt mɑSriyya (twenty Egyptian women)
$+10^{+}$	[+H +M]	+br/su	4–	4/5a –	1/2c(a)	9iʃriin mu9allim gudaad (gidiid)/kuwayyisiin (kuwayyis) (twenty new/good teachers)
$+10^{+}$	[+H +M]	+O	4–	4/5a –	3a	9iʃriin mu9allim mɑSri (twenty Egyptian teachers)

Notes

1 This is a shortened and to some extent rewritten form of a paper that appeared in *Archivum Linguisticum*, Vol IV (New Series) under the heading 'Aspects of gender revisited, with special reference to Sindhi and Cairene Arabic'. Space does not permit the inclusion of the Sindhi material in the present volume.

2 'Some universals of grammar', in *Universals of Language*, ed Joseph H. Greenberg (Cambridge, Mass, MIT Press (2nd edn), 1966), *p* 113.

3 John Lyons, *Introduction to Theoretical Linguistics* (Cambridge University Press, 1968), *p* 288.

4 *ibid*, *p* 287 – 'From the semantic point of view, gender distinctions in the noun are usually redundant'.

5 H. A. Gleason, *An Introduction to Descriptive Linguistics* (revised edn) (Holt, Rinehart & Winston, 1961), *p* 227.

6 Frank Palmer, *Grammar* (Penguin, 1971), *p* 105.

7 Palmer, *loc cit*; 'in languages where there is a fairly fixed order of words, and where that order indicates the grammatical relations between the words, concord and government would appear to be unnecessary luxuries (or difficulties)'. *Cf* also (*p* 106): 'these categories become redundant and are often lost, as gender has been lost in English'. Roger Fowler writes to similar purpose in his *Introduction to Transformational Syntax* (Routledge & Kegan Paul, 1971), *p* 87: 'Inflecting Latin adjectives for gender and number is functional because it associates an adjective and the noun it modifies, an association not evident in the unpredictable word-order: it serves no function in French because which adjectives go with which nouns can be inferred from word-order'. Such views are, of course, longstanding and are often traceable to western Classical traditions, more specifically to comparison between 'synthetic' aspects of Latin and 'analytic' equivalents in English.

8 *Cf*, for example, W. S. Allen, 'A study in the analysis of Hindi sentence structure', *Acta Linguistica* 6/2–3 (1950–51), *pp* 68–86; also J. Burton-Page, 'The syntax of participial forms in Hindi', *Bulletin of the School of Oriental and African Studies* 19/1 (1957), *pp* 94–104, and the same author's 'Compound and conjunct verbs in Hindi', *BSOAS* 19/3 (1957), *pp* 469–78; also my 'Aspects of gender revisited', *Archivum Linguisticum* (New Series), Vol IV, *pp* 29–35.

9 Willem L. Graff, *Language and Languages* (Appleton, 1932), *p* 195.

10 Georges Simenon, *Marie Qui Louche* (Presses de la Cité, 1951), *p* 111.

11 Gleason, *Introduction*, *p* 227.

12 *ibid*, *p* 229.

13 See above *pp* 118–9.

14 For elision as in the case of 'wis(i)xa', see above *pp* 82–3.

15 In an interesting and informative article entitled 'Concord in spoken Egyptian Arabic', *Archivum Linguisticum* (New Series), Vol III (1972), *pp* 7–17, Dr Hilary Wise considers gender as a noun-inherent feature and also proposes that a feature [±Product] should be recognized, apparently – if I have understood correctly – to account for such facts as those we are considering. This seems unsatisfactory, firstly because it affords no recognition to an inescapable and simplifying distinction between 'Origin' and 'Non-Origin' and, secondly, because the proposal manifests a tendency to ascribe to the noun an undue number of features that belong elsewhere among the many and varied distinctions that have to be recognized in the noun phrase. Moreover, the Arabic noun and adjective are less obviously differentiated than in languages nearer

home, and even if, for the sake of argument, one is prepared to accept in the case of, say, '9agami' (Persian, a Persian [man]) or any similar form, that an associated noun has been transformationally deleted, nevertheless we still have to recognize the difference of syntactic behaviour we have noted (and there are many others) between the 'Origin' and 'Non-Origin' classes. The facts that members of the 'Origin' class are specially marked suffixally and that they lack comparative forms corresponding to *eg* ''akbɑr' (<'kibiir' (big [one])) elsewhere are further indications of the analytical utility of an 'Origin' class.

16 It is just conceivable that this morphological difference is ultimately traceable to a semantic distinction but this is problematical and not relevant to our present purpose.

17 The lengthening of the vowel of '–ha' in the example, like much else that is noticeable in the transcription, lies outside the scope of the paper and belongs to the (morpho)phonology of the language.

18 This is one reason why it is misleading to equate the familiar Indo-European languages with those of the Semitic family in respect of gender.

19 In a more precise sense than the verb in *eg* its iterative aspect (*cf* 'break' versus 'smash', 'cut' versus 'chop', etc, distinctions corresponding to regular morphological alternation in Arabic).

20 Though perhaps not strictly germane to the themes of this paper, the difference of behaviour that is observable between duals referring to parts of the body occurring in pairs ('inalienable' possession) and others ('alienable') is worthy of passing notice. *Cf* 'rigleen' ([two] legs), 'beteen' (two houses) but 'rigleeha' (her [two] legs) versus ''ilbeteen bitu9ha' (her two houses) (*lit* 'the two houses belonging to her'). In the 'alienable' case, the particle 'bituu9' (belonging to) is essential; the inclusion of the article ''il' relates to an area of definite–indefinite differentiation that does not concern us. 'Pairs' of this kind do not require special recognition in the analysis of concordial distinctions within the noun phrase.

21 My examples unfortunately do not include a 'mensurative' phrase but I would expect '9iʃriin gineeh gudaad/mɑSri' (twenty new/Egyptian pounds).
Other more general omissions include compound adjectives of colour and the ordinal adjectivals. Neither is necessary or prejudicial to the position adopted in this paper and to consider them would involve much that need not detain us here.

22 Hilary Wise, *op cit.*

23 No example of +su is available.

24 This is, of course, something of an over-simplification, since the co-ordination of nominal subclasses is subject to certain selectional constraints.

25 Further research is necessary to elucidate the apparent inconsistency between *eg* 'siggadteen Tulyaani' and 'sikkiina wi ʃooka mɑSriyyiin'.

Six

'Covert matters best disclosed'

One may possibly agree that a general theory must characterize the concept of transformations from deep structure, but, having regard to deep structural possibilities of choice (? presuppositions), one finds it difficult to see how the theory can escape the implications of the fact that man's 'innate specification' for language means little apart from the uses to which it is put. Speech is typically in the form of dialogue and a semantic theory needs to accept as a reasonable task among others the recognition of regular role relationships between interlocutors affecting phonological, lexical, and syntactic form. Examples are provided below from a number of languages, for the most part within the unifying function of personal address and reference.

For de Saussure and others following him in both Europe and America, language was 'social' in only a very limited sense, that by which individual idiosyncrasies and imperfections of speech are to be ignored and the uniformity of data assumed in response not only to the needs of an analyst but also to the 'collective will' of a community. This is not the place to speak of either 'ideal speaker-hearers' or the implied control of 'sujets (*sic*) parlants' by academies and other embodiments of 'collective consciousness', nor of 'social facts' and of 'langue' (or its descendant 'competence') as one of them. Firth's conception of *semantics* differed from and extended beyond that of de Saussure, Bloomfield, and Chomsky, to mention but three distinguished linguistic innovators. He did not regard words or sentences as self-evident units of language, nor words as semantic units *par excellence*, lexical encapsulations of dictionary definitions. The latter were too often uninformative, if not frankly misleading, nor were they recognizably of a 'structural' linguistic kind but were couched rather 'in shifted terms'. Meaning was not *given* for Firth; it was waiting to be discovered and stated, and as we have seen, the business of descriptive linguistics was to make statements of meaning. In reacting to such views, we should remember not only that Firth was deeply influenced by Malinowski and the latter's ethnographic view and experience of language but also that, as far as Firth was concerned, it was an indispensable part of the formation of a scholar in linguistics to work for some years with informants, native speakers of this or that language, at home and in the field. Some may think it a pity that, for whatever reason, this training has of late years tended to go by default.

Of theories that have been proposed in recent times, one cannot but much admire the elegance of the Chomskyan transformational-generative and certain of its variants as well as the lucidity of the language in which it is often expressed, yet at the end of the day one is left uncertain of the adequacy of its observational scope and consequent explanatory power, and unconvinced of the justification it provides for its claims to account, even in its own terms, for the linguistic 'competence' of the idealized speaker-hearer. Moreover, on the performance front, linguists who for long have been subjecting their texts and observed facts of natural languages to close, detailed, subjective-objective analysis on the home ground of linguistics, so to speak, have often been conscious of editing out speakers' hesitations, false starts, and the like, but they have tried to ensure that editing takes place in deference to norms governing the linguistic behaviour of collocutors. Again, current references to 'the place of semantics in a grammar' seem to imply an unwarrantable belief that there is general agreement on what is meant by 'semantics'. Firth, as we have said, was anxious to find ways of handling, even imperfectly, the rich diversity of contemporary speech in the face-to-face encounters of interlocutors. He saw the simplistic division of meaning into denotation versus connotation (or whatever other terms happen to be used to mark what is essentially the same dichotomy) as positively Procrustean in its application to conversation(al language) and totally incognizant, for example, of obviously relevant biographical relationships between speakers. Hence his considerable insistence on the need for awareness of role and status relations as well as of the functions (agreement, disagreement, encouragement, condemnation, blessing, cursing, boasting, appealing, praising, blaming, persuading are among his own examples) that inform speech so pervasively. Speech, after all, was to help people deal with other people and the world around them, at once a mode of behaviour and way of getting others to behave. Experience indicates that linguistic research on particular languages can only be conducted successfully if language is seen as meaningfully organized formally and functionally at one and the same time. Nor is this quite the same thing as looking for *correlations* between forms of language and the extra-linguistic circumstances of their use.[1] For Firth, the use of language for maintaining patterns of living was one of its most important characteristics. Sentences could be 'grammatical' in the transformational-generative sense but if they lacked what he called 'the implication of utterance' by which 'renewal of connection' was established with life as *homo linguisticus* typically conducts it, then they were invalid, a house of cards. The text was more important than the rule, though the latter was crucial to necessarily rigorous statement, and texts were to be validated by reference to typical categories of participants in generalized contexts of situation, with the verbal action of participants receiving pride of place but their non-verbal action also demanding notice. Any linguistic statement was to be evaluated situationally, at least socio-culturally as well as formally. Whether or not we can at present recognize a set of situational norms was not strictly relevant – the important thing was that the linguistic choices in whose terms meaningful distinctions are recognizable are made simultaneously in terms of linguistic and socio-cultural differences, all within a framework of language uses or functions. Sentential propositions, 'complete thoughts', lexical conceptualization and the like were insensitive to the analytical requirements of on-going patterns of speech and the need for a syntagmatic emphasis in linguistic analysis was also clear. To the extent that his rare exemplifications of the 'context of situation' were rather ritualistic pieces of language, Firth tended in practice to weaken his own case, but this was his habit and we can be quite sure that he was strongly opposed to any stultifying kind of behaviourism. He knew, for instance, from long experience that Indians and Pakistanis use language for what seem substantially the same purposes as Englishmen – to curse, congratulate, compliment, cajole, and so forth – but they do so in such linguistically different ways that, in order to understand the linguistic choices made, long and painstaking research, with the socio-cultural dimension consciously included, is unavoidable. The context of situation was to provide 'bridges' between mutually exotic languages-cum-cultures, bridges of a more crossable kind than purely 'formal' and/or 'substantive' universals. One was to put texts into their contexts of situation and explain their functions within them, bringing speakers into mutual relationship with themselves and others and with environmental features abstracted as far as seemed relevant from the totality of goings-on. We did not have linguistic form on the one hand and meaning on the other. The object of study was unitary.

It cannot be said that the typical grammarian's and lexicographer's view of meaning offered or offers much encouragement to Firth's semantic ambitions. Moreover, recent suggestions that there is a set of universal semantic features on which each language draws before combining them in characteristic ways, would be sure to include such concepts as time and space relations, completeness and incompleteness, cause and effect, conditionality, arithmetical number, etc, and may represent a kind of compromise between extreme forms of either Whorfian relativity or an absolute 'world out there', but the categories of experience involved – like those of colour sensation and anthropological kin relations much favoured by semanticists – are remote from those of Firth's functionalism and indeed from everyday experience of speech. The colour 'red' is one thing, the lexical item *red* quite another and how far it is to be properly translated by *eg* '*laal*', '*ˡaħmar*', '*rouge*', etc around the world is to be investigated. It is, moreover, far from a simple question of colour denotation that is involved in consideration of, say, *red wine*, *red hair*, *red cow*, *red cheeks*, and so on. At the grammatical level, too, similar reactions are occasioned by, let us say, case-grammar as expounded to date. Fillmore argues well and convincingly that the sentence functions 'subject' and 'object' are surface structure phenomena in transformational terms and puts forward sound proposals for the recognition of grammatical case as playing an important part in language organization.[2] In spite of the undoubted interest of such work and its implications not only for sentence structure generally but also for such further categories as 'complement' and 'adjunct', it is nevertheless still underpinned by the kind of exclusively referential semantics that Firth tried to see beyond. Fillmore speaks elsewhere of the 'apt' use of language and actually employs the terms 'role' and 'situation', but does so in a limited denotational manner, to the exclusion for instance of the biographical 'identity' of interlocutors that Firth rightly saw as important in the interlocking of language form and role relationship in conversational exchange.[3] The very use of the terms, however, suggests that perhaps we may hope for some future extension of the notion of competence genuinely to encompass knowledge of language use.

But it is time that, in accordance with the professed object of this book, some illustrations were provided of the kind of meaning in language that linguists have so far largely tended to ignore and which is nevertheless part of the speaker's native knowledge of his language. We shall not attempt to explore such questions as the interrelationship of, say, speech *function* (*eg* language on the field of play) with *concept* (*eg* cricket) with *group* (*eg* cricket team) with *setting* (*eg* cricket match) but shall simply give examples of language forms that have commonly cropped up in languages of the writer's experience and which, though seemingly large enough fish, have slipped distressingly easily through the mesh of an exclusively denotational net and which the rag-bag of 'metaphor' quite fails to catch. In deference to the special interest that Firth clearly entertained in the consequences for language of differences of role and status between speakers, primary attention has been paid to the single theme of personal address and reference. To the extent that kindred interlocutors may be involved, it will be seen from the examples of living speech adduced below how different is a Firthian approach to language from that typically adopted by the anthropologist and (general) semanticist; we shall be concerned with forms of address used between kin and including kin terms themselves, not with an idealized, quasi-mathematical system of kin relations. The term 'sibling', for example, *qua* linguistic form cannot be on our agenda. The demonstration of this difference of approach is the sole concern, so that, however desirable, careful experiments with suitably selected groups of informants have not been devised with a view to such proper purposes as the elimination of idiosyncrasies, the spanning of receptive as well as productive aspects of usage, and the deepening of our knowledge of reciprocity of use.

Perhaps there are parallels between the English 'House of Windsor' or 'House of David' and the (Libyan) Tripolitanian Arab's talk of 'ħooʃi' (<ħooʃ 'house' + -i 'my') = 'my wife' and even the Hindi/Urdu speaker's reference to his wife in 'meeree (*my*) ghar (*house*) mẽe (*in*) see (*from*) aa (*come*) rahii (*-ing*) haĩ (*are*)' = 'my wife is coming', although we may wonder in passing what the word-bound semanticist is going to make of the last sentence. In Zuara Berber, too, 'əlɡilət' = 'family' elsewhere than in the environment of + '–iw' (my) but 'əlɡiltiw' = 'my wife', while the morphologically related form 'ləɡyal' (elsewhere = 'children') in association with '–iw' = 'my family' [*sc* inner family of wife and children]. But if a close friend asks after your wife, he must use the form 'ləɡyal' [morphologically plural] = 'wife' and this is accompanied by plural verbal forms, *eg* 'mamak (*how*) llan (*are*) ləɡyal (*the wife*)?' – and it has to be a *close* friend to ask the question at all! With reference to his wife, a man may use the singular or plural third person pronominal forms 'nəttat' or 'nətnin' and, if asked who he means, will reply 'ləɡyal'. Such forms-cum-meanings are appropriate to exchanges with interlocutors not members of one's family. Let us consider in informal manner something of the modes of reference to one's wife or husband within the extended family in Zuara, to a young man 'fəRħat' (F), let us say, and his wife 'Nafisa' (N), both perhaps living with F's parents.

If F asks his mother about N, he uses 3rd pers *plural masculine* verbal forms in *eg* 'mani llan?' (Where is *she*?) (*lit* 'Where are they [masc]?') or 'mani flənn?' (Where has *she* gone?) or 'matta hadigən ɣadi?' (What is *she* going to do there?). Similarly, when newly married, and certainly in the presence of his parents, F uses the plural imperative to N, *eg* 'wəllɡət əlkanun dsirdət əlɡalət' (Light the brazier and clean the tea-things). F cannot talk about N to his father at all – the preceding sentence 'mani flənn?', for example, addressed by F to his father is an enquiry after more than one previously mentioned person, *ie* 'Where have *they* gone?' and the sentence can only be disambiguated by reference to the relationship obtaining between interlocutors. F may use a 3rd pers sing fem in reference to N when talking to *eg* his sister, as 'mani təfla?' (Where has she gone?), but not to either of his parents. He cannot use 'əlɡiltiw' or N's name to anyone within the family; both these forms are appropriate only to the circumstance of F addressing N in private.

It is not only the biographical identity of the person addressed that is important but also that of the speaker. Thus, for example, any female relative can ask after N directly by name, *ie* 'mamak təlla nafisa?' (How is Nafisa?), and with accompanying singular forms. They would be precluded, however, from saying to F 'mamak təlla əlɡiltik?'. As to N's usage, she cannot say of F to her father-in-law either 'mamak yəlla [sing]?' or 'mamak llan [pl]?', but to her mother-in-law she is free to use either the singular in, say, 'mani yəlla?' (Where is he?) or her husband's name in 'mani fəRħat?', since there is no ceremony between women. She will *never*, however, be able to use F's name to her father-in-law. A man's modes of reference to his wife – to the English-speaker apparently circumlocutory but embodying cultural values beyond our present scope – are paralleled by a third person's reference to F when addressing N, and once again, possibilities of choice differ in proportion to the sex of the speaker. In this case, a man addressing N may use F's name in *eg* 'matta (*What* (*is*)) əlħal (*the condition*) nfəRħat (*of F*)?' (How is F?), but unlike a female counterpart, he could not use the word 'argaz' (man, husband) as in 'matta əlħal nmərgazim?' (How is your husband?). The opportunities that remain for systematic research and formulation are immense; for the linguist to scorn them might invite comparison with the ostrich. In examining, let us say, differences between the Berber vocative particles a and i (*cf* 'a(*O*) məmmi (*my son*) wəttɑggedʃ (*do not be afraid*)' versus 'wəttɑggedʃ i məmmi'), we find that the use of 'i' is tied to such varied conditions as (i) post-verbal position, (ii) the class of nouns of relationship, (iii) women's speech, (iv) the speech function of affectionate address. Any (syntactico-)semantic theory that fails to account for all four at one and the same time is frankly inadequate.

An adequate theory must also account for the extremely widespread (?Islamic) practice of the older generation affectionately addressing the younger with the term that is properly reciprocated to them by the younger. Thus, Berber 'yəmma' (elsewhere (*my*) *mother*) is regularly used by a mother to her child, *eg* 'əssusəm (*listen*) i yəmma əssusəm' (listen, my child); similarly, 'i ɡəmti' (O my aunt) is regularly used by an aunt to her nephew or niece. Notwithstanding the fact that 'i' is almost invariably a mark of female speech, older male parents use 'i baba' (elsewhere = '(my) father') to a son, although a younger father would almost certainly not do so nowadays. 'i baba' may also be used by a paternal uncle, whose responsibility it would be to care for his nephew in the event of the death of the latter's father; 'i xali' is the corresponding address form from a maternal uncle. Thus, 'a' + 'baba', 'yəmma', 'ɡəmti' belong to the addressive usage of son/daughter or nephew/niece to appropriate older relative, while the forms 'i baba', 'i yəmma', 'i ɡəmti' are received in reverse. These 'i'-forms and also the reciprocal or bi-polar use of a kin term (*eg* 'baba' by father to son) are always marks of affection and never used with *eg* brusque orders. At the same time, the limits of the extended family are partly determinable by such linguistic means. Thus, 'lalla', for example, is any older woman from either side of the inner family, who – addressed 'a lalla' by a child – is precluded from reciprocal usage and would therefore never address the child as *'i lalla' but rather in the form 'i məmmi' (son) or 'i yəlli' (daughter).

Strikingly similar linguistic behaviour is to be found throughout the Arab world. Consider, for instance, the meaningful distinctions involved in the differential use of forms of address among Jordanian kinsfolk in the region of Irbid.[4] Consanguinal terms of address are divisible on a basis of (i) male versus female reference, (ii) male versus female use. Forms containing an accented suffix '–óo' refer to males only and are only used by males with reference to males; corresponding female usage (same referents) is as shown:

	Male use	*Female use*
brother	xɑyyóo	xuuy *or* ya xuuy
(maternal) uncle	xɑɑlóo	xáali *or* ya xáali[5]
(paternal) uncle	ɡɑmmóo	ɡámmi *or* ya ɡámmi
grandfather	jiddóo (*or* siidóo)	jíddi *or* ya jíddi

Contrariwise, a diminutive affix (variously '–ee–' and '–ay–') is used by females only and – with the single exception of 'bnayyi' (my son) – with reference to females. Thus,

	Male use	*Female use*
mɑɑmɑ (mother)	y ɑmmɑ	meemti
ˈuxt (sister)	ya (ˈu)xti	xɑyti

bint (daughter)	ya binti	bnayti
ˡibin (son)	ya (ˡi)bni	bnayyi
9amme ((paternal) aunt)	ya 9amti	9meemti
xaale ((maternal) aunt)	ya xaalti	xweelti

It will be seen, therefore, that the sex of both addresser and addressee are significant variables in the choice of kinship terms of address. Noteworthy, too, in passing are the facts of the exclusion of the vocative particle 'ya' from association with 'óo'-suffixed forms and of the associability of 'ya' with the diminutive forms only when the addressee is unrelated and unknown to the speaker, further indication if such is needed of the direct relevance of the biographies of interlocutors to linguistic analysis.

In addition to biographical distinctions, differences of speech function are directly involved in regular variations of linguistic form. For example, the inclusion or exclusion of 'ya' as between 'xuuy' and 'ya xuuy' would relate to the degree of *persuasiveness* involved, exclusion involving a stronger entreaty for help. Similarly, questions of formality/informality are inextricably bound up with linguistic choices made; the use of '–óo' and '–ee/ay–' forms outside the family context is dictated by a functionally varying *intimacy*. Therefore, in considering terms of address, regard has to be paid not only to such grammaticalities as, say, number, imperative, etc but also to speech function as well as to such interlocutors' attributes as age, sex, status, etc.

Again, as in Zuara, and indeed as elsewhere in the Arab world, the use of 'reciprocal' address forms is common in Irbid. If a boy addresses his father's second wife in the quasi-teknonymous manner of 'ya mɑrt (*woman, wife*) ɑbuuy (*of my father*)', she may return this form of address to him in place of 'ya bin (*son*) joozi (*of my husband*)'. Usage is generally governed by the degree of affection involved. Again, a vocative 'ya (ˡu)xti' may variously be:

(i) mutually exchanged between two genealogically related sisters
(ii) mutually exchanged between brother and sister (*ie* the brother may receive 'ya (ˡu)xti' from his sister)
(iii) received by a male child as a form of endearment from an older unrelated female
(iv) given by an adult to a female stranger as a mark of 'polite formality'

How, then, can one avoid the requirement of something like the 'context of situation'? Far from being able to rely on the usual crude 'definition' of 'ˡuxt' as 'sister', all we can say in general about 'ya

(ˈu)xti' is that a female person must be involved in the exchange. Translation, of course, is only possible *ex post facto*, having regard to the kind of considerations we have outlined. Firth's context of situation did not after all envisage a Skinnerian type of behaviourism and to dismiss it as linguistically uninteresting is at best unreflecting.

In Hindi, too, kinship terms are freely used in addressing friends, acquaintances, and even strangers, yet how differently from Arabic. Nevertheless, in both languages, a wife is reluctant to mention her husband's name and may indulge in the most intricate circumlocution in order to avoid doing so in the belief that she would otherwise place him at some kind of disadvantage. Even in direct address she is likely to use a form of teknonymy, by which kin are addressed in terms of their relationship to a third related person rather than in accordance with the direct relationship between addresser and addressee (*eg* 'O Mohan's father'). For rather different reasons, husbands do not 'name' their wives, while among Hindus, I am told, a daughter-in-law cannot utter the name of either parent-in-law, although the constraint is not mutual. It is said, too, that the personal names of gurus (spiritual guides) are forbidden, while parents do not as a rule address their eldest son by name. Such matters, like all human institutions, are naturally subject to change, the cultivation of which is currently frenetic, yet it would be quite naive to think that distinctions of the kind we are talking of are about to disappear, whatever modifications may or may not be applied to, say, Indian social systems. We are more likely to turn up interesting universals of human linguistic use if we concentrate on such semantic areas as address and reference, looking at language for what it indicates of social distinctions of inferiority/parity/superiority/etc as well as age/class/sex/religion/nationality/etc, not to mention degrees of affection/intimacy/conformity or not/etc and such psychological 'bonuses' as 'inferiority complex', etc. In the process of linguistic analysis, whether we admit it or not, whether we are conscious of the fact or not, we cannot help but take cognizance of such distinctions in considering the use of, say, kin terms, if they are what happens to interest us at a given time. Again, inside or outside the family, in languages like Urdu, Hindi, and many others, the grammatical category of number should be thought of as relating far less to an arithmetical distinction between '1' and '1+' than to personal interrelationships of status; a cultured Urdu speaker introducing his friend to a third person will certainly say something like 'yeh (*this*) meer– (*my*[self-deprecatory form of first person pronoun]) –ee ['plural' suffix, marking respect] dost (*friend*) haĩ (*are* [again plural of respect])'. To anyone saying 'But this is not semantics', one's answer might be 'Well, maybe, but it is highly, indeed deeply, meaningful, and in any case what *is* semantics and, *a fortiori*, universal semantics?'.

Address, reference, and appellation of the kind we have seen something of within the family is equally interesting outside. Not long ago I met a Malay lady whom I had previously known as Miss Hamid Don and was surprised when asking as to her married name to be told it was Mrs Hamid Don. Why do Americans talk of 'the given name'? Is it to avoid obliging Muslims to enter their *Christian* names on forms? Marghanita Laski reminded us in a newspaper article some years ago that, although French village folk may address you as 'Monsieur/Madame X', you should not at once include 'Y' in reply or you may sound as patronizing and insulting as by the use of a false Cockney accent back to a Cockney addressing you. How should non-communists, she asked, only partly in fun, address people in Russia? What is the linguistic behaviour appropriate to this or that group in matters of greeting and leave-taking? It is desperately easy to offend even the most tolerant, and offence can last a lifetime – sometimes in dangerously high places. One can find oneself as a Britisher strangely *dépaysé* in the United States. Many Americans want to move on to first names right away, to which the average cis-Atlantic person is at first not at all sure how to respond. Facts of personal reference, written as well as spoken, can also be extremely interesting in America. To consider very cursorily something of the journalistic register, the issue for 5th July, 1968, of *The News Gazette* of Champaign/Urbana, Illinois (where the Summer Institute of the Linguistic Society of America was held in that year) contained an article referring to the death of a small girl in a swimming pool accident. The child was seven years old but was spoken of as *Miss Smith* in a manner quite impossible in British English. In the same obituary article, the dead girl was stated to *be survived by* her mother, grandmother, brothers, and sisters (all of whom were named), also *survived by* six uncles (all named), and to *leave* eight aunts (again all named), a manner of reporting which I found regularly followed, however strange to my eyes and conceivably to those of Americans from other parts of the country. In the same issue the headline *Miss Jones Succumbs*, somewhat irreverently interpretable by the British reader, referred in fact to the lady's demise in hospital at an advanced age and clearly shows French influence (*succumb* < Fr succomber). So perhaps, too, on the women's pages, among the announcements of betrothals, marriages, and subsequent events, things are more reminiscent of the earlier 'fiançailles' of France or more generally of continental European practice than of anything known in Britain. Here I found myself among the *brides-elect* (is there a singular form?) and reading such headlines as *Foltz*

Vows Read June 8 (is it the bride who is called Foltz, or her husband-to-be?), *Sharon Sickler Married* (can this be read aloud, and, if so, how variously?), *Miss Jeanette Bach Bride – Marries*[6] *Paul Christensen, June 29*, and *Harry Alsops* (to me an unaccustomed plural in the presence of the first name) *Are Visiting His Relatives*. It has been suggested to me that the great mobility of Americans may partly account for a style of reporting that aims at keeping scattered relatives, who still receive the newspaper, informed of family developments at home, but I am in no position to judge the validity of the suggestion, though it is plausible enough. At all events, it seems clear again that forms of language involve more to interest the linguist than mere sentence structure.

Firth's approach was inductive from the grass roots up, so to speak. You did not start with grammatical analysis; you secured your texts first, having regard in part to the effective daily functioning of language users in various types of situation. Language was activity that we were to try to classify somehow, notwithstanding its bewildering complexity. His context of situation was intended to help reduce some of the complexity and at the same time to sharpen us up as observers, as much of so-called 'indexical features' – as that, for example, by which a Catholic in England of a certain educational background can be recognized as such by his or her stressing of *re-* in *refectory* – as of more generalized features of lexicon, grammar, and phonology by which we proclaim the many aspects of ourselves, grouped and subgrouped with others and more or less conscious of the cross-classificatory options open to us. The decision as to whether *a perfect gift of chattels* was *constituted* by showing them to the *donee* and *speaking words of gift* can only be made by someone playing his part as lawyer, and so can the utterance, whether spoken or written. Of course, such language registers or varieties have much in common. If this were not so, the notion of 'a language' would be inconceivable, but as Robins has put it, for Firth 'the whole of language use, including the selection of the appropriate vocabulary items, is a vastly complex amalgam of specific language uses, and a general explication of meaning can only come about as the end product of indeterminately numerous detailed studies.'[7] In the same place, Robins also observes pertinently that 'reference', which Firth has been accused of ignoring, was or could be subsumed under 'relevant objects' in the categorial grid he proposed for the context of situation.[8] Not that Firth himself would probably have wished to stress the fact.

In contrast with Firth, I do not myself think that the association between 'collocation' and either 'function' or 'register' is any closer or less close than between the latter and individual lexical items. Collocations belong as much to the language that is shared by registers and functions as to those features that particularly characterize them. This is not to say, of course, that there are not key collocations for a given function, say, but simply that collocation is essentially a formal, not a functional concept. We should expect to find in an account of the language of personal address and reference in Hindi, for example, the particular item 'mātā' (mother),[9] but by no means all the collocations of which 'mātā' apparently forms part in association with *eg* 'tulsi' (a plant), 'gau' (cow), 'durgā' (a goddess), 'gangā' (the Ganges) 'shitalā' (smallpox), 'dharti' (land), 'vidyā' (learning), 'sandhyā' (evening), 'gitā' (book), etc. I am insufficiently aware of the facts of Hindi lexico-grammatical organization to say whether in fact this is idiom and that collocation, too insensitive to Hindu cultural values to say that in any given case we are concerned with, say, religious value, taboo, euphemism, or what else may be. I am, however, quite sure that for the linguist to say 'mātā' = 'mother' and to leave it at that should be unthinkable. One needs to develop a thoroughgoing inquisitiveness about language as on-going behaviour, about appropriateness of choices of language, which in both production and response frequently relate to conventional regularities, more or less subtle and as often as not socio-cultural in kind. A satisfactory theory must account for such constraints as well as those of a formal grammatical kind. At present our hypothetical constructs are apparently too often premature, resting on empirically inadequate foundations. The validity of a linguistic analysis must partly be judged on the validity of its non-linguistic premisses, and however stringent a linguistic theory, it will fail if due consideration is not given to the influences of the extra-linguistic and on-going conditions of language use.

In conclusion, with regard both to what has gone before and to what is now to follow on the subject of buying and selling in Cyrenaica, it is perhaps not untimely to recall that more than one American friend has said to me in the past how he or she has been struck by the number of times the British say 'thank you' in the course of buying and selling something in a shop. The implication is that one only thanks someone 'for good cause', not for instance when passing one's money over the counter. Yet neither the shopkeeper nor his customer is evincing any measure of subservience, say, in behaving in the way they do; they are just 'lubricating' the transactional process at appropriate developmental points. If misunderstanding arises between people speaking what to all intents and purposes is the same language, how much greater are the chances of misapprehension when mutually foreign languages are concerned!

Notes

1 The following paper on the language of buying and selling in Cyrenaica is no doubt criticizable for this reason among others.

2 C. J. Fillmore, 'Towards a modern theory of case', in revised form in *Modern Studies in English*, eds D. A. Reibel and S. A. Schane (Prentice-Hall, 1969). Fillmore speaks of the *same* semantically relevant relation obtaining between *the door* and *open* in, *eg*, *the door will open* and *the janitor will open the door*, and again between *this key* and *open* in, *eg*, *the janitor will open the door with this key* and *this key will open the door*. Such examples lead him to question the validity, except at a superficial level, of postulated functions like 'subject of intransitive verb' (*the door* in *the door opened*), 'object of transitive verb' (*the door* in *the janitor will open the door*), 'object of preposition' (*this key* in . . . *with this key*), etc. Instead, he proposes to name the functions of nominals in such sentences as 'agentive' (*the janitor*), 'instrumental' (*this key*), and 'objective' (*the door*), none of these functions to be identified with surface structure relations like subject and object. The syntax of a verb like *open* is then to be described by saying that it requires an objective and tolerates an instrumental and/or an agentive. If only the objective occurs, then the objective noun is subject; if instrumental also occurs, either the objective or instrumental noun may be subject (*ie*, *this key will open the door*, as well as *the door will open with this key*); if agentive occurs, then the instrumental noun cannot be the subject but, if it occurs, it appears in a prepositional phrase after the objective (*the janitor will open the door with this key*).

3 See C. J. Fillmore, 'Types of lexical information', in *Semantics*, eds D. D. Steinberg and L. A. Jakobovits (Cambridge University Press, 1971/2), *p* 376.

4 I am much indebted to Dr Mohamed Elanani for the Jordanian facts to which reference is made.

5 The difference of vowel quality in the first syllables of these and other forms also partly reflects the difference beween female and male speech. 'Backness' and 'emphasis' in Arabic are often male features.

6 An interesting use of the present tense (*cf* the date of the paper), which belongs to the language of newspaper headlines. Verbal tenses and voices in the latter are not as those elsewhere, partly no doubt because space is 'of the essence'. *Cf* H. Straumann's example *Motorist Refused Licence*; the form *Refused* could probably be interpreted as past tense only in 'reported speech', *eg Motorist Refused Licence, Claims Solicitor*, which is in fact ambiguous.

7 R. H. Robins, 'Malinowski, Firth, and the "Context of Situation"', in *Social Anthropology and Language*, ed E. Ardener (Tavistock, 1971), *p* 33 *ff*.

8 See for example, J. R. Firth, 'Personality and language in society', *The Sociological Review*, 42/2 (1950), reprinted in J. R. Firth, *Papers in Linguistics 1934–1951* (Oxford University Press, 1957), *p* 177 *ff*, especially *p* 182.

9 The examples and their transcription have been taken from the monograph 'Terms of kinship, modes of address and reference in Hindi' by R. R. Mehrotra (Banaras Hindu University, 1970).

Seven

The language of buying and selling in Cyrenaica: a situational statement

The subject-matter of the following paper is fairly self-evident from the title. The concept of 'collocation' has been used rather more loosely here than in, say, 'Linguistic "goings-on"' above, and 'correlation' is spoken of between texts and extra-linguistic circumstances of use in a way that in the preceding essay was said to be undesirable. It has nevertheless been felt useful to include the paper as an early illustration of Firthianism, no doubt much improvable today but written and published while Firth still occupied his chair at SOAS, and as an attempt to come to terms with the on-going nature of speech and the circumstances surrounding it. Although the writer does not agree with the somewhat extreme view of Firth himself that all texts demand explication partly in situational terms, it nonetheless seems clear that any systematic activity requires systematic use of accompanying language. Arabic below is seen as part of the activity of buying and selling, not as 'corresponding to' such activity. It is also clear yet again that linguistic dependencies and constraints are by no means subject to a requirement of either a juxtapositional or earlier-to-later consecutiveness in time. The research on which the paper is based was, of course, carried out some time before the discovery of oil in Libya, which for all one knows may have profoundly affected the forms of activity and accompanying language described below; the linguistic principles involved, however, must remain unaffected.

During a period of seven months spent in Cyrenaica in 1949 with the special purpose of investigating the Bedouin Arabic of the Jebel, I selected for particular attention the language of buying and selling. Accompanied by my research assistant,[1] I visited markets of all types, from the general and animal markets in Benghasi to the cereal and animal markets in Barce and the general (weekly) markets in such

Jebel villages as D'Annunzio (ilbayyáɑÐɑh) and Gubba, where open-air shops and the market combine. In addition, I accompanied my assistant on shopping expeditions and also spent a good deal of time sitting in shops of the covered market in Benghasi. Unfortunately, no suitable tape-recorder was available at the time and it was necessary to rely on on-the-spot observations, which were compared after each research session. With the exception of the first of the three texts which conclude this paper, the Arabic forms given are based on the Bedouin usage and pronunciation of my assistant.

The business of language, we are variously told, is to express thoughts and emotions, to convey information, to influence behaviour in others, to act as a tool in co-operative action, and so on. Where particular languages are concerned, preliminary classification is suggested by such current designations as, say, legal English, the language of advertising, greetings and salutations, etc. But assertions as to the nature of language in general and designations of restricted languages do not as a rule envisage the concept of *context of situation*, 'a group of related categories at a different level from grammatical categories but rather of the same abstract nature'.[2] The concept of context of situation is part of a theoretical approach which eschews both excessive subjectivism and the dualism by which forms of language are rigidly separated from such purposes of language as those above and many others. By adhering to the principle that meaning must be sought in use, we are able at the situational level to make a systematic classification of material on the basis of correlations between texts and their environments.

It is impossible to give an exhaustive list but correlation with some or all of the following appears possible for many texts:

1 the spatio-temporal situation of persons in the context (hereafter called 'participants'), *eg* on a bus, in the morning, passing in the street, etc;
2 the activities of participants, *eg* buying a suit of clothes, eating, giving a lecture, etc;
3 speech functions, *eg* boasting, cursing, flattering, blaming, etc;
4 biographies of interlocutors, *eg* specific trade or profession, geographical and class origins, educational standard, interrelationship, etc.

It is not suggested that other categories of correlation may not be found necessary, nor that every text will permit statement to be made under *all* of the categories 1–4 above. Much depends, too, on what is meant by, *eg* 'activities' – such terms are only definable by the use made of them. Subdivision of categories will often be required and, indeed, is exemplified in the preliminary scheme above: bus-conducting is doubtless as much an activity as buying a train-ticket and, contrariwise, we can as legitimately speak of the language of train-ticket purchasers as of that of bus-conductors. The setting-up of generalized biographical 'personalities' is essentially a matter of subdividing: in highly ritualized activities such as buying a train-ticket in England we all behave in many respects similarly from a linguistic point of view, but even if here differences are less marked than, say, in the manner of men's boasting and cursing, nevertheless differences there are, and in order to account for them the category of personality is often usefully employed.

Some, like Malinowski,[3] have stressed the pragmatic nature of language, and looked upon verbal behaviour as part of the job in hand. The pragmatic view has been a fruitful one in modern linguistics but it should not be too narrowly interpreted. On the face of it, the research worker in the field might expect to be able to select, say, harvesting, boatbuilding, mining, etc, with a view to restricted language study. In practice, however, he all too often finds native participants either silent in the performance of their tasks or talkative mainly on topics without any apparent connection with the job they are doing. Such Bedouin couplets as 'ya zárɡ injál(l), jáɑk ilmánjal' (Be lush (?), O crops, the sickle comes to you) and 'Ðámmɑw ɣúmrik, jállɑw hámmik' (They have gathered your [fem sing] sheaf, they have driven away your care) – used respectively by the reaper and the man who follows him gathering the harvest into sacks – belong to Cyrenaican 'magic', in Malinowski's sense, but there is very little other linguistic material to record. On the other hand, some activities, of which buying and selling is an example, are conducted with a great deal of talk. It will be seen, therefore, that statement for linguistics is likely to be of two main kinds:

1 a large number of relatively short texts correlating with a variety of contexts of situation, and
2 a limited number of situations[4] for which the verbal material is considerable.

This paper is of the second type.

In order to make a satisfactory statement, the linguist constantly has to select some features and suppress others of both the text and its environment. When doing so, however, he should not lose sight of the text *as a whole*. Arabic 'Subáɑħ ilxáyr' (Good morning), taken *in vacuo*, may be said to belong to the language of greetings, and differs in many respects from, say, 'yɑftuħállɑ', which is only used as the refusal of a bid in buying and selling. But, as a rule, greetings form part of a complex pattern of activity which is peculiar to buying and selling; therefore, 'Subάαħ ilxáyr' – as far as it contributes to the pattern – may be considered, like 'yαftuħάllα', as belonging to buying and selling, provided that texts of adequate extent are given in support. 'Subάαħ ilxáyr' in buying and selling and 'Subάαħ ilxáyr' elsewhere differ for the linguist rather as a line of a given length differs for the mathematician according to whether he is considering it as a side of a rectangle or the radius of a circle. It will be necessary to return to and develop this theme at other points in the paper.

There is need to distinguish between the language with which an activity is *conducted* and that with which it is *explained* or *discussed*. Situations involving the second category may well include the research worker himself but, even if he does not intend to submit a language of explanation to situational analysis, there are many excellent reasons, chiefly methodological, why he should devote careful study to it. Before reasons are stated, consider the following two specimens of such language, given to me by bystanders in the cereals section of the Benghasi 'fúndug' (general market) and in the animal market (súug issá9y) of the same town. I should explain, with reference to the first passage that I had spent many days in the '*fundug*' without observing anything said to, by or about the women who were always present sieving and cleaning cereals. These women are an integral part of the scene, and it is essential to know something of the role they play and the artefacts they handle.

1 itjíi init tíejir 9índαk ɣάllαh ɣαlíiθih.[5] tibbi itħúTT iθnáyn θilíeθ Subάαya yɣάrublan ilɣάllαh lάk bayʃ yħíid ílwuSαx. uSSubάαya ynάĐĐfan filɣάllαh; yɣάrublan bilɣurbíel wySάffan wyjálwlan búTTubαg. yínufxαn bilfám wyjálwlan bayʃ yħíid iʃʃi9íir fαwg milgάmuħ w bayʃ itkúun ilɣάllαh nuĐíifih. ilɣάllαh iθθigíilih túg9ud wittíbn yTíir. 9agάαb iʃʃi9íir wittíbn y9αTúuh luSSubάαya bilíeʃ.

(Suppose) you come along as a merchant with some cereals – mixed wheat and barley. You'll want to put two or three women on to sieving these cereals of yours, to get rid of the dirt. The women clean the cereals by passing (them) through a sieve, and by purifying and separating (them) by means of the reed-platter. They blow with the mouth and juggle (the platter) so that the barley will settle separately on top of the wheat, and the cereals will be clean. The heavy cereals remain (on the platter) and the chaff blows away. The barley and chaff left over are given to the women for nothing.

2 *Note*. The 'kifíil' or 'Đάαmin' is one who testifies that the vendor's goods are not stolen property. I have no transaction re-

corded in which a participant acted in this role, and, therefore, have no attested examples of such potential material as '9áddi jiib kifíil' [buyer to seller or to auctioneer[6]] (Go and bring a guarantor), or 'háak iliflúus, ní9irfak' (Here, *you* take the money, I know *you*) [buyer to guarantor, threatening him that if anything is wrong, then the guarantor will be held responsible]. The following explanation was given to me of the part the 'kifíil' is called upon to play:

ilbayyíe9 líezim ykuun 9índih wrúgah. kan ma 9índiʃ lazim ilħíejih itkuun maSrúugah. fíih illi yíʃru bilwrúgah ilgidíimih w fíih illi yríidu wrúgah jidíidih. ilbayyíe9 kan ma 9índiʃ wrúgah bílkil, ilbaladíyyih ma it9aTíiʃ wrúgah nayn yjíi kifíil. húu illi yfíerim filwrúgah imta9 ilbaladíyyih; ygúul lilmamuuríin 'Sáaħib urrízig haÐa um9arúuf'. ásm ilkifíil yħuTTúuh filwrúgah wybáhhtu issíimih ħatta húm wysajjlúuha filwrúgah.

The seller should have a certificate. If he hasn't, then the goods may well have been stolen. Some will buy on the strength of an old certificate, others will want a new one. If the seller hasn't got any paper at all, the municipal authorities won't issue one without a guarantor. He's the man who signs the municipality's certificate, telling the officials that the owner of the property is known (to him). The guarantor's name is entered on the declaration, and (then) they too (*sc* the officials as well as the purchaser) inspect the brand, which is (also) registered.

The above two texts belong, not to the language of buying and selling, but to the language of explanation of buying and selling. The importance of such a language – from the point of view of both methodology and subsequent statement – is considerable. It enables the linguist to talk to native speakers about the activities which interest him in order to relate the text to the cultural matrix, *ie* to bring into relation objects, activities, and the several *dramatis personae*, and to determine the relevance of his recorded material to the statement he proposes to make.

Personalities and persons in buying and selling situations

Activity in a market-place is extremely complex, and that which goes forward in any one section is a 'play within a play'. The actors, moreover, are not of equal importance, nor are their lines all to be allotted to buying and selling language. One man has goods for sale, another wishes to buy; both seek the most advantageous price. These are the essential conditions, and no text or part of a text is here considered as belonging to buying and selling unless it can be uttered by seller (bayyíe� 9 *or* bíeyi9) to buyer (ʃarráay *or* ʃíeri) or *vice versa* in the course of transaction. The context of situation is abstract, not a piece of reality, and although, in the instance, more than two people are generally present, nevertheless the seller and the buyer are the only relevant *personalities* in buying and selling situations. An exception to this is provided by the auction, an important category of buying and selling. For the auction situation, *three* personalities are recognized – the auctioneer (dallíel), the buyer, and the owner (Sáaħib urrízig *or* Sáaħib ilmíel), the last-named playing a minor linguistic role.

Buyer, seller, etc, are, of course, generalizations. In the instance, a given buyer may be Bedouin or townsman, wholesaler (tíejir bijjímlih) or retailer (tíejir bilgaTTáa9i *or* tíejir buTTáruf), one who buys in small quantities and then sells at his own pitch in the same or another market (SamSáar), or someone who is not a businessman at all but buys for his own use (kassíeb). Similarly, one personality in the abstract frequently corresponds to many people in fact; one buyer, for example, to many potential purchasers of an article which is being bid for, one seller to a group of Bedouins.

There may, of course, be other relevant *persons* – as distinct from *personalities* – but in the statement here envisaged, their status is similar to that of relevant objects since their participation is non-verbal. Such are the 'kifíil' and the women sifters mentioned above; the bystander in general; the bystander who helps the buyer and seller to reach agreement ('wuSíiT' (mediator)); the member of the poorer classes who sweeps up the remains of the cereal-heaps and is given them for his pains ('kanníes' (sweeper)); the municipal official in his office who registers transactions and collects taxes (mamúur); the guard on the gate who checks that the tax-certificate is in accord with the goods being taken out ('wáridyih' (guard)); and that essential figure of the cereal-market, the man who measures the grain (kayyíel).[7] The following examples, though recorded in Cyrenaican markets, do not belong to buying and selling language in the terms of the present statement. Reference to them could only be made by considerable extension of the situational analysis.

1 'kayyíel' to bystander; sack of barley in everybody's way: 'kúrr hána!' (Pull (it) over here!)

2 'kayyíel' to seller; both of them standing with full measure (mayzúurah); buyer farther off with sack almost full of cereals purchased from others:
'ʃíilha líh!' (Carry it over for him!)

3 buyer to bystanders:
'9aTúuh urríiħ iʃway'. (Give him some air [*sc* don't crowd in so, let people see]!)

4 buyer to bystander, and reply:
A: (buyer) 'haluħmáar lilbáy9?' (Is this donkey for sale?)
B: 'láa, Sáaħbih gáal máwʃ lilbáy9'. (No, its owner said it wasn't.)

5 bystander to bystander in Barce:
'hána ámrag min bunɣáazi'. (It's quicker here than Benghasi.)

6 bystander to buyer; seller has signified agreement with price offered:
'mabrúuk, xúð uɣlímak!' (Congratulations, take your sheep (flock)!)

7 buyer to bystander, seeing small satchel full of cereals:
'wáyn Sáaħib iʃʃkáarah?' (Where's the owner of the satchel?)

8 bystander to buyer; latest bid was £5.95:
'úɣlig iʃʃlímih!' (Cover the gap!) [*sc* make it £6]

9 bystander to auctioneer; owner, informed by auctioneer of highest price obtainable, refused to sell:
'háði illi itdáwwur 9aláyha' (That's just what you were looking for) [*sc* How do you like it now that you are not going to get your percentage?]

10 buyer to 'kayyíel'; transaction completed:
'háak mayzuurtáyn!' (Take a couple of measures (for yourself)!)

11 buyer to 'kayyíel', proffering money:
'háak ħágg il9áyʃ!' (Here's the price of a meal!)

12 auctioneer to owner; transaction not yet started:
'tíbbi it9aTíini 9almíyyih 9áʃrah?' (Will you give me ten per cent?)

13 seller to 'kayyíel'; buyer not satisfied that cereals offered constitute a complete measure:
'ya kayyíel, it9íel kayyílilna halmayzúurah!' (Measurer, come and measure this out for us!)

14 mediator to bystander:
'9aTáw jiniiyáyn w 9iʃríin líekin na tuwaSSáTut ibjiniiyáyn w xamsíin'. (£2.20 was offered but I helped them strike a bargain at £2.50.)

15 bystander to buyer; buyer in process of feeling lamb's back: 'báhhit ilɡargúubah!' (Look at the ham!)

Technical and non-technical textual elements

Comparison with other situational categories enables us to abstract a *technical* language of buying and selling, of which an example – 'yaftuħálla' – has been quoted above, and of which others will be given below. Such elements or parts of texts constitute, so to speak, the key for the text; by their means, any instance of buying and selling can be ascribed without hesitation to that category. But there is much overlapping material between contexts of situation, some of which, although not in the technical subcategory, may also properly be allotted to buying and selling since there is mutual expectancy between the situation and such material. The verbal context is after all only part of the situational whole; limitations are put on the text by other features of the situation and *vice versa.* If we can argue from, say, 'yaftuħálla' to a buying and selling situation, we can equally argue back again from the situation to the language which is used during examination by the buyer of the object of sale. The following is an example of this language of investigation, taken from the cereals market:

Seller: 'kánnak itʃímm?' (Why are you smelling it?)
Buyer: 'báalak ʃiɡíir maTmúurah'. (Perhaps it's barley from an (underground) store [*sc* it may be damp].)[8]
Seller: 'láa, ʃiɡíir iʃwalíet'. (No, it was in sacks.)

Such an exchange may also belong to a situation in which, say, a father is involved with his son bringing home cereals from the market, but, with technical elements elsewhere in the text, it may with equal validity be allotted to buying and selling, although to a different subcategory from that to which 'yaftuħálla' belongs. Elements which correlate exclusively with features of buying and selling situations are termed *technical*: other elements, operative in other situations but customary in buying and selling, are termed *non-technical.* It may be noticed that two or more apparently non-technical elements may, in collocation, constitute a technical whole (see, for example, the auctioneer's description of the object of sale below).

Further classification of elements, technical and non-technical, may be made on the basis of personality. The technical 'áyʃ ɡaTáwk fi . . . ?' (What have you been offered for . . . ?) belongs exclusively to buyer-language and the non-technical 'kánnak itʃímm?' above to seller-language. With the seller intent on selling his wares and the buyer on getting them, if at all, at the best price, one would not expect, say, 'míɡza ubwáahi' ((They are) good goats) from the buyer, nor 'ɡayyíen halkábiʃ' (He's thin, this ram) from the seller.[9]

Object of sale

'yaftuħálla' is potential in any instance of buying and selling: 'kánnak itʃímm?' is not. The reason for this is the infinite range of possible objects of sale. If statement in this paper were confined to the buying and selling of one commodity – let us say, cereals – then doubtless not only the cereals themselves but a large number of other objects would have to be considered relevant.[10] But cereals are not considered here for themselves but rather as an example of an abstract and generalized *object of sale*. Similarly, 'kánnak itʃímm?' is an example of a generalized linguistic category correlating with what is termed below the *investigation* stage of the transaction. Instances of investigation language are, like instances of the object of sale, infinite in number. It is relevant to note, moreover, that investigation may be non-verbal or proceed simultaneously with bargaining.[11] For stages other than investigation, the text is more severely restricted but no more economic statement of relevant objects is possible. The seller's ritualistic conclusion 'táakul bílhana' (I hope you enjoy (eating) it) may correlate with the purchase of anything edible, just as his 'tumággal' is an invitation to try out anything for sale from a cart to a camel. In the present analysis, therefore, the principal relevant object is the object of sale considered as an abstraction.

Locale

Some qualification to the statement that the object of sale is the only relevant object might appear necessary in view of the fact that linguistic differences – even between technical elements – correlate with the difference between transactions in shops[12] and those in markets. But since most goods sold in shops may also be sold in markets, and since those which are not cannot be economically listed, the difference is better stated in terms of locale. Thus, for example, 'áyʃ ɡaTáwk fi...?' (What have you been offered for...?), the characteristic market enquiry as to the object of sale, can never correlate with the shop.

Categories of transaction

There are three major categories of transaction:

1 market auctions
2 market transactions exclusive of auctioning
3 shop transactions

Personality differences between (1) and (2) have already been described. Both (1) and (2) differ from (3) in respect of relevant *persons*; the mediator, for example, has no part to play in the shop. Let us now consider these categories in greater detail; it is convenient to deal with auctions first.

Auctions

Four stages may be recognized:

1 the auctioneer's opening
2 investigation, including description by the auctioneer, of the object of sale
3 bidding
4 conclusion

There is mutual expectancy between stages. The characteristics of each stage are as follows:

Stage 1 Proceedings are initiated by the auctioneer's '9alay bab allάαh, fatħ ilkiríim'. No one has yet bid (9alay bab allάαh) and a generous opening bid (fatħ ilkiríim) is called for. The effect produced is that interested buyers and onlookers will gather round the auctioneer and the object of sale, the owner usually placing himself in the background but within earshot. The spatial relations of participants does, however, differ as between open market auctions and those of a covered market as in Benghasi. In the latter situation, the merchants, *ie* the principal type of buyer and one of whom is usually the owner, remain in their shops while the auctioneer walks up and down in front of them crying his wares. This difference between the two types of auction does correspond to linguistic differences but the latter are few and it has not, therefore, been felt necessary to subdivide the auction category.[13]

The element '9alay bab allάαh', technical to buying and selling as a whole, is not, unlike 'fatħ ilkiríim', specific to the auction. The two elements are habitually collocated in this category of transaction.

Stage 2 With the auction opened, buyers inspect the object of sale, but verbal activity for this stage is less likely than for the investigation stage of other transaction categories. An example, however, is 'wαrríina sínnih' (Show us his age [*sc* by opening his mouth]), which was recorded at a camel-auction in Gubba. The auctioneer, too, may remain silent but often – especially when the object of sale is animal – he gives a short description which is, of course, invariably in the nature of a song of praise. The following is an example of an auctioneer's description of a cow; he has led the animal around for the buyers to see and to demonstrate that it is able to walk properly:

'ħallíebih, silíimit ili9yúub w híedyih. awwálilha wáldih.' (She's a good milker, free from defect(s) and placid. She's only calved once.)

Such a text is full of elements habitually collocated and correlating with the particular object of sale, but interest in this paper centres on the fact that the whole can only correlate with Stage 2 of an auction.

Stage 3 *Stage* is an abstract category and the numbering of stages does not necessarily imply sequence in time. Thus the auctioneer's 'mínu illi 9índih ɣaráÐ/rúɣbɑh?' (What am I bid?) may, in the instance, be uttered in the same breath as the opening '9alay bab ɑllɑ́ɑh, fatħ ilkiríim'; nevertheless, it is here considered as marking the opening of Stage 3, and has the effect of eliciting an opening bid.

The opening bid is stated in terms of money-reference, *eg* 'jiniiyáyn w sittíin' (£2.60). Subsequent bids may also be so framed, but it is common for bids to be raised by a fixed amount usually made known to buyers by the auctioneer.[14] If the latter practice is followed, then 'zíidha' (Raise it!) is the buyer's reaction to the statement of the last bid by the auctioneer, corresponding to the raising of a finger, catalogue, etc, at our own auctions. Silence or 'dállil' (Carry on [auctioning]!) is the buyer's reaction when he wishes to bid no further.

All bids are repeated by the auctioneer in terms of money-reference and in accordance with a characteristic pattern. The price, *eg* 'jiniiyáyn w sittíin', is called out at least twice, each time with rising intonation. This feature contributes, as will be seen, to the distinction drawn between Stages 3 and 4. Repetition of bids on this pattern belongs, like 'zíidha' and 'dállil' above, exclusively to the auction.

When the auctioneer sees that there is reluctance, even if momentary, towards further bidding, he uses the cry 'harɑ́ɑj, yɑ́rbɑħ, yáksab', the characteristic phonetic features of which in utterance are: the high monotone on which the two syllables of 'harɑ́ɑj' are pronounced; the very long second vowel of 'harɑ́ɑj'; the fall from mid on the prominent or accented syllable 'yɑr-' preceding the low level pitch of atonic '-bɑħ'; the utterance of 'yáksab' from the standpoint of tonicity and pitch, as an 'echo' to 'yɑ́rbɑħ'; the perceptible silences between the three words.

'harɑ́ɑj, yɑ́rbɑħ, yáksab' is the equivalent of English 'Going . . . going . . .' and is commonly followed by 'mínu illi 9índih izyíedih?' (What further offers am I made?), to which the response 'zíidha' may or may not be obtained. 'ɣaráÐ' and 'rúɣbɑh' are also possible for 'izyíedih' here, but, as we have seen, 'mínu illi 9índih ɣaráÐ/ rúɣbɑh?' is also characteristic of the opening stage: 'mínu illi 9índih izyíedih?', however, can only correlate with a slackening in bidding.

The buyer's 'áyʃ 9ɑTɑ́wk fi . . .' which opens the bargaining stage in non-auction market transactions (see below) may also correlate – in the auction – with the buyer's arrival on the scene when bidding is already in progress. It is a common element of texts for *covered* market auctions, in which the buyer, *sc* the merchant in his shop, is frequently unaware of the latest bid made.

Stage 4 The auctioneer perceives that no further bid is forthcoming and, with the proviso that the owner's agreement must be sought, proceeds to knock down the article to the last bidder with 'harɑ́ɑj' (usually repeated, but not followed by 'yɑ́rbɑħ, yáksab'), and an announcement of the final price. This announcement is made once only and on a falling intonation (*cf* Stage 3 above).

Subsequent activity differs between open and covered market auctions. For the former, the owner almost invariably stands nearby listening to proceedings; for the latter, he is probably nowhere near the auctioneer when he puts an end to bidding. In the covered market, therefore, the element 'mɑbrúuk' which may seal a bargain in any category of transaction, is uttered by the auctioneer with a rider that sale at the price offered is contingent upon the owner's agreement, which he then sets off to seek.[14] In the open market, however, the auctioneer, having announced the final price, turns to the owner, whose reaction is either 'mɑbrúuk (9aláyh)', if he agrees, or 'yɑftu-ħɑ́llɑ', if not. The meaning of 'yɑftuħɑ́llɑ', therefore, differs between auction and non-auction situations: in the former, it marks conclusion of the transaction; in the latter, it is a refusal during the bargaining stage.

Market (non-auction) and shop transactions

These categories share a common pattern of stages as follows:

1 salutation
2 enquiry as to the object of sale
3 investigation of the object of sale
4 bargaining
5 conclusion

It is convenient, therefore, to consider both categories together and to point out differences between them as we proceed.

Stage 1 Shop and market situations differ in that for the latter it is possible that in the instance no greetings are exchanged. This is on the whole more likely to be so when the buyer is a townsman. As a rule, however, both because of the importance attached in the society to the greeting of one's fellows and, more particularly, because of the possible attendant benefits in the transaction, proceedings are opened by the buyer with an appropriate salutation. The form of greeting varies considerably, and especially in accordance with the time of day. Market transactions are conducted very early in the morning and do not, therefore, expect such greetings as 'misáa ilxáyr' (Good evening), which, habitually, collocated with the answer 'alláah ymassíik bilxáyr', can only belong to the shop. For both categories we may, of course, expect:

B: 'Subáaħ ilxáyr' (Good morning)
S: 'alláah ySábbħak bilxáyr' *or* 'xáyr w márħabah' *or* 'xáyr w marħabtáyn'.

or again

B. 'issiláamu 9aláykam' (Good morning/afternoon/etc)
S: '9aláykam issilíem w rúħumt alláah.'

Stage 2 It may be that for some texts no elements can be allotted to this stage. For example, the customer in the shop, having waited for others to be served, may have found the article in which he is interested and, when his turn comes, may point to or touch it to the accompaniment of 'báyʃ haÐa?' (How much is this?), an element which marks the beginning of Stage 3. Similarly, in the market, the situation in which a seller is already engaged in bargaining precludes a newcomer from using the buyer-language which is ascribed below to the present stage.

Where elements of the text *are* allotted to this stage, difference must again be recognized between shop and market situations. With a view to economic statement taking in more of the material, it has been found useful to set up the personality categories of buyer and seller as higher orders of abstraction than shopkeeper, shop-customer, market-vendor and market-purchaser; nevertheless, these subcategories of personality are implicit to the analysis made in terms of locale (*ie* shop and market). The very common '9índak (ʃi)... lilbáy9?' (Have you a/any... (for sale)?) belongs exclusively to shop-customer's language. It is assumed that what is – or potentially is – on view in a shop is both for sale and the property of the shopkeeper: the following attested examples of Stage 2 language can only correlate with the different trading conditions – and greater confusion – of the market:

1 (buyer's enquiry as to availability for purchase)
B: 'halħáwli lilbáy9?' (Is this lamb for sale?)
S: 'láa, ilħáwli fi jímlih' (No, the lamb is included) [*sc* with other sheep present] *or* 'iini9am, máwʃ ilhín' (Yes, it doesn't belong with *them*.)

2 (buyer's enquiry as to ownership of goods)
B: 'hann9ajíet lák?' (Are these sheep yours?)
S: 'rízig ħalíel'[15] ([*lit* Worthy living]) *or* 'lálla kílli ʃíi'[15] (Everything is God's.)

both of which replies, in simpler terms, tell the buyer that the sheep indeed belong to his interlocutor.

As already stated, *stages* are abstractions made for the purpose of linguistic classification and statement and their numerical order does not necessarily correspond to a successive order in time. Thus 'halħáwli lilbáy9?' may be followed immediately by (B) 'áyʃ 9aTáwk fíih?' (What have you been offered for it?). The utterance of 'áyʃ 9aTáwk fíih?' may, in terms of time, precede or be simultaneous with examination of the lamb; nonetheless it is an element allotted in this statement to Stage 4 (bargaining).

Stage 3 We have already seen that this stage may be non-verbal and that, when verbal, the verbal context will correlate with the particular object of sale. No difference between shop and market is statable. Some further typical examples of elements belonging to this stage are:

1 (seller to buyer examining group of sheep individually)
(i) 'ma fíihinʃ ma itnággi' (There's nothing to choose between them.)
(ii) 'haðáyn in9ajíet xíirih' (These are fine sheep.)

2 (seller offering barley for sale)
S: 'ʃúufah' (Look at it [*sc* and feel it, if you like].)
B: 'inħúgg fíih' (I'm doing so.)

Stage 4 The buyer's 'áyʃ 9aTáwk fi . . .?' *or* 'áyʃ u9Tíi'[16] (What offers have you had for (. . . it/this one/etc)?) marks the opening of this stage in *market* transactions. The meaning of the word '9aTáwk', within the limits of the present statement, is that, collocated with 'ayʃ . . . fi . . .', it marks the opening of the bargaining stage of market transactions. We are not, for example, grammatically concerned with the verb '9aTáa, y9áTi' (to give), nor with analysis of '9aTáwk' as '9aTaw+k', nor with the grammatical designation of '9aTáw' as 3rd pers pl masc perfect tense, active voice, etc.

'áyʃ 9aTáwk fi . . . (*or* áyʃ u9Tíi)?' is habitually collocated with one of the following seller-elements:

1 '(ma zíel) 9alay bab alláah' ((It is still) at God's door), when no offer has yet been made;
2 'bíi9 wíʃri' (Buy and sell!), usually when offers have been made but the seller wants to hear the new buyer's offer;

3 ‘9iʃríin (gíriʃ)’ [17] (Twenty (piastres)), when the seller tells the buyer the latest offer he has had.

The form of extended collocation with following buyer-elements depends upon which of the three is used. Thus all three may be extended by (B) ‘in9aTíik kílmih wíħdih, wáaħad w 9iʃríin’ (I'll give you a firm offer of twenty-one), but (1) and (2) only by (B) ‘itxallíiha líi ib . . . ?’ (Will you let me have it for . . . ?) and (1) only by (B) ‘báyʃ itríidih?’ (What do you want for it?), (3) – and (3) only – may have the effect of the buyer's turning his back and moving away.

The above patterns are not those of the shop. Here the opening of Stage 4 may correspond to either buyer or seller utterance. In the first case, ‘báyʃ . . . (*eg* haÐa)?’ (How much . . . (is this)?) is the invariable formula; in the second, a number of possibilities are open to the seller, including the characteristic ‘(in)kan itríid [18] tíʃri, insáa9dak’ [19] (If you want to buy, I'll help you [*sc* I'm prepared to strike a bargain with you]). This opening, *ie* without stating a price, is then collocated with (B) ‘bayʃ . . .’

Market and shop transactions differ, too, in the participant who takes the initiative in naming a price. In the market, this may be either seller or buyer, and, indeed, it is more frequently the buyer; in the shop it is invariably the seller.

Market only: S: ‘bíi9 wíʃri.’ B: ‘itxallíiha líi ibjiníi w sab9íin?’

Market and shop: B: ‘báyʃ itríidih?’ S: ‘háði ibjiníi w sab9íin.’

This is, of course, a corollary of the fact that the seller's is only market-language.

When the seller in the market has stated a first price, the buyer, if interested, may reply with either a higher or a lower one. He cannot, however, do so indiscriminately. Thus either ‘jiníi w 9iʃríin’ (£1.20) or ‘jiníi w sab9íin’ (£1.70) as buyer-elements, may collocate with the seller's ‘jiníi w sittíin’ (£1.60). The lack of arithmetical symmetry in the figures given is not accidental, for the buyer is not free to use either reply and is in both cases anxious to secure the lowest possible price; in the first case, the seller has stated his highest price and in the second his lowest, and the difference in linguistic terms does not lie in the difference between the two buyer-elements but between the extended collocations of

1 S: ‘. . . jiníi w sittíin’. B: ‘. . . jiníi w 9iʃríin’ *and*
2 S: ‘. . . jiníi w sittíin’. B: ‘. . . jiníi w sab9íin’.

Thus (1) collocates with a preceding (B) ‘áyʃ 9aTáwk fi . . . ?’ but not with (B) ‘báyʃ . . . (haði)?’ and (2) with (B) ‘báyʃ . . . (haði)?’ but not with (B) ‘áyʃ 9aTáwk fi . . . ?’ *ie*

1 B: 'áyʃ 9aTáwk fíih?' (What have you been offered for it?)
S: 'jiníi w sittíin.' (£1.60)
B: '(in9aTíik kílmih wíħdih) jiníi w sab9íin' ((I'll give you a firm offer of) £1.70).

and

2 B: 'báyʃ haði?' (How much is this one?)
S: '(ib)jiníi w sittíin.' (£1.60)
B: '(in9aTíik) jiníi w 9iʃríin (xaláaS)' ((I'll give you) £1.20 (– my last word)).

Similarly, the characteristic buyer-elements 'win aħsánit' and 'úxxur kílmih ibkám?' prehend an earlier 'bayʃ . . .', and only 'bayʃ . . .', *ie*

B: 'báyʃ haði?'
S: '(ib)jiníi w sittíin.'
B: 'win aħsánit' (And if you are good to me [*sc* make me a reduction]) *or* 'úxxur kílmih ibkám?'[20] (What's the last price you'll take?)

It will be seen, therefore, that mutual expectancy between textual elements is cumulative, and looks both forward and back. Elements are not strung together in time; time, but not 'timing', is largely irrelevant to the statement.

Other technical and non-technical elements characteristic of Stage 4 are as follows; they are potential both to shop and market with the exception of those asterisked, which for reasons given below are limited to the market.

1 Seller-elements
(a) technical
(i) 'kílmih yíebsih' (*lit* A hard word) [*sc* I've given my price and I shall not alter it];
(ii) 'yaftuħálla' *or* 'yáftaħ rábbi'[21] (No) [when refusing a bid];
(iii) '(jiníi w sittíin) 9alay ɣáyrak'* (Someone else has already bid (£1.60));
(b) non-technical
(iv) 'xallíiha 9ánnak' (Leave it [*eg* sheep] alone) [*sc* if you won't offer a fair price, someone else will];
(v) 'yijjáð9an'*[22] (He can't be serious) ['rhetorical' appeal in ridicule of the price offered];

(vi) 'jáwha ilgguggáal'* (Sensible men are here [*lit* have come to it]). (Said on arrival of a new group of prospective buyers both to put the 'present' buyer in his place and to flatter the newcomers);
(vii) 'tuwaTTáyt' (You're too low [*sc* in your offer]).

2 Buyer-elements
(a) technical
(i) '(háyya, ya síidi) xallíina níʃru' ((Come on, old man) let us buy!)
(ii) 'ħíll ráasak w bíig' (Make up your mind to sell!)
(iii) 'báalak inbáagat' (*lit* Perhaps it [*eg* sheep] has been sold) [said after seller's refusal of buyer's offer, and tantamount to 'Perhaps you'll change your mind'];
(iv) 'ájgar mínni' (*lit* Don't maltreat me) [*sc* make me a reduction];
(v) 'bígtih ibkílmit urráajil?'* (Do you agree to what the man says?) [asking seller whether he accepts price suggested by mediator];
(b) non-technical
(vi) 'tigalláyt' (You're asking too much.)

The following examples are such that, abstracted from texts and considered as isolates, they may correlate with utterance by either seller or buyer. They are nonetheless typical of buying and selling.

1 'ágrab' (Bring (your price) nearer!)
2 'kiláamak ikwáyyis' (That's a good line of talk you have.)
3 'ílgarab máhumʃ káyfak gaafTíin' (People can't really be as mean as you.)
4 'xallíiha gíegdih báruÐha' (Let it stay where it is) [*sc* if that's your price, I'm not interested in buying/selling it.]

The asterisked examples above cannot operate in the shop situation. Difference of relevant persons expects difference of verbal context. Quite apart from 'name'-parts like that of the 'wuSíiT', the market is crowded with 'extras' as, in the instance, the numerous buyers make the rounds of the numerous sellers in search of the best bargain. However, the following extract is not marked as an exclusively market-text as opposed to shop until the very end, but such marks are bound to be present somewhere in any text of adequate length.

B: 'xuð fíiha jiníi w sittíin' ((Will you) take £1.60 for it?)
S: 'yaftuħálla' (Nothing doing.)
B: 'báalak inbáagat' (Perhaps you'll change your mind.)

S: 'wallάahi, igbíel il9áyn' (Heavens, you only have to look at it) [*sc* to see it's worth more than your offer.]
B: 'xallíiha gíe9dih bάruÐhα' (You can keep it.)
S: 'binnuSíib' (Take it or leave it) [*lit* it depends on fortune, *ie* whether the seller keeps it or sells it at the price he wants.]
B: 'ubɣάaytαk' (As you will.)
S: 'máalαk w míel haddúuwαh? jiníi w sittíin 9alay ɣáyrαk' (What are you making all this fuss for, anyway? Somebody else has already offered £1.60.)

Having reached the last seller-element, we are now able to complete the beginning of this exchange with, say,

B: 'haði áyʃ 9αTάwk fíiha?' (What have you been offered for this one?)
S: 'bíi9 wíʃri' (State your price.)
(B: 'xúð fíiha . . .')

and there can no longer be the slightest doubt about the correlation of the text with the market.

Stage 5 Conclusion of the transaction correlates variously with verbal and/or non-verbal activity on the part of the buyer and seller as follows:

1 non-verbal:
Buyer, refusing to bargain further, turns his back and moves off;
2 verbal:
either
Buyer accepts seller's price, usually with 'bíehi/Tάyyib/xαlάαS (niħna umwααfgíin)' (All right [we're agreed]) and, in the market, offers his hand to the seller;[23]
or
Seller accepts either in the form 'bíehi/Tάyyib/xαlάαS, 9αTάyt ilkílmih' (All right [you have given the word]) or, more usually, in that of 'mαbrúuk (inʃαllα)'[24] (Congratulations), which is habitually collocated with B: 'αllάαh ybαrik fíik' *or* B: 'mαbrúuk'.

It is interesting to note that once agreement has been reached, seller-language can be of a type excluded in the bargaining stage. Text III below provides an example, where the seller, having agreed to sell, points out defects in the object of sale.

I have one attested example of S: 'xαlάαS, inʃάllα ṭάrbαħ fíiha' (Done! May you find fortune with it!) marking the seller's acceptance, but the form 'tάrbαħ' – usually collocated with its cognate 'ríbiħ' elsewhere – belongs characteristically to an extension of the situation which involves payment, registration of market transactions (in animals) and a final exchange of good wishes. It is not necessary for this activity to follow a strict temporal sequence, nor indeed for all its parts to correspond to verbal exchange between buyer and seller. Examples are:

1 (Agreement has been reached on the sale of wheat at 19 piastres per measure; the buyer counts out the money into the seller's palm)
B: '. . . haðáyn tisi9Tάaʃ' ([And] that makes 19.)
S: 'Suwáɑ. táɑkul bílhana' (Correct. May you enjoy it!)

2
S (signifying agreement): 'mɑbruukáɑt inʃallɑ.'
B (handing over money): 'xúð, ya ʃíeyib. áj9alɑk tárbaħ' (Here you are, old-timer. May it [*sc* the money] bring you good luck.)

3 (payment made after registration and payment of tax in the market-office)
S: 'xɑláɑS, 9ɑTáyt ilkílmih.'
B: '9áddi gayyídhin ɣáɑdi' (Go and register them over there.)
S (on return from office): 'híet ijjiniiyáyn' (Hand over the £2.)
B (tendering money): 'xúð. íd9i birríbiħ' (Here you are. Wish me luck.)
S: 'ɑlláɑh yrábbħɑk' *or* 'ɑlláɑh yáj9alɑk tárbaħ' (Good luck to you) [*lit* May God make you prosper.]

It is often difficult to separate the situational and collocational levels of statement, for the situation 'determines' in large measure collocability in any given text. At first sight it appears that to say '*x* collocates with *y* in buying and selling situations' is just another way of saying 'buying and selling situations expect *x* in collocation with *y*'. There is nevertheless a difference of emphasis implicit in the two statements: the first emphasizes the collocation, the second the situation. The level of collocation is primarily concerned with interior relations in texts; that of the situation with exterior correlations for texts. Although (extended) collocation has necessarily been introduced into the present statement, nevertheless emphasis has been placed not so much on the collocation of element *x* with element *y* as on the correlation of *x* or *y* or $(x+y)$ with personalities and features of the situation.

In the enquiry stage of open-market transactions, a high degree of probability attaches to a buyer-element which may be stated as B: 'hal(*a*) l(*b*)?', where *a* and *b* are variables. If the object of sale is stated, let us say as cereals, then the 'spread' of possible *a*-elements is restricted to '(hal)gámuħ/ɣállɑh/9úrmɑh/ʃi9iir'.[25] For *b*, we may have '(l)ɑk/ilbay9/man', *ie*

halgɑ́muħ	lɑ́k?	(Is this wheat yours?)
ɣɑ́llɑh		(Are these cereals yours?)
9úrmɑh		(Is this heap yours?)
ʃi9íir		(Is this barley yours?)
	lilbáy9?	(Is this wh./cer./heap/bar. for sale?)
	ilmán?	(Whose is this wh./cer./heap/bar.?)

If from these possibilities selection is made, then response on the part of the seller is also restricted. Thus, B: 'halgɑ́muħ lilbáy9?' does not prehend 'rízig ħalíel' *or* 'lɑ́llɑ kílli ʃíi' but rather 'láa . . .' *or* 'íini9am . . .'; any of these four elements, however, may accompany 'halgɑ́muħ lɑ́k?'. In the terms of this article 'rízig ħalíel', for example, is looked upon as an extended collocation for 'halgɑ́muħ lɑ́k?' and *vice versa.* It is primarily to handle mutual expectancy between seller- and buyer-elements that (extended) collocation has been employed. Lexicographical or stylistic statement might envisage collecting the collocations of 'rízig' or 'ħalíel' and stating correlations for them with several situational categories. Here, however, attention is not focused on either form *qua* collocable nor on the whole *qua* collocation but rather on the whole as a seller-element *linked* to the buyer-element 'halgɑ́muħ lɑ́k?' To quote another example, both B: 'áyʃ 9ɑTɑ́wk fi . . .?' and S: 'ma zíel 9alay bab allɑ́ɑh' correlate exclusively with features of buying and selling situations, but statement is incomplete unless we add that S: 'ma zíel 9alay bab allɑ́ɑh' prehends B: 'áyʃ 9ɑTɑ́wk fi . . .?'

A text is a kind of snowball, and every lexical item and every collocation in it is part of its own context, in the wider sense of this term; moreover, the snowball rolls now this way, now that. To make progress in statement at all possible it is necessary for the linguist to select from his material and to focus attention on some elements to the exclusion of others. Not every part of a text lends itself to collocational statement, nor will it always be necessary to make statements about *every* (habitual) collocation in a text. For instance, 'xɑllíini injárrbih' (Let me try it/him) and 'uSSyirɑ́ɑn wilmáyz' (walking and galloping [horse]) are examples from Text III below of habitual collocations which are irrelevant to the present statement; they are not limited to buying and selling situations nor can such situations be said to expect them. Again 'ta9áal' (Bedouin 'it9íel') – see Text I below – collocates almost invariably with 'ya(a)'[26] in *any* situation involving one person calling another to him, but although the use of the individual elements 'ta9áal' and 'ya dalláal' and of the larger element 'ta9áal ya dalláal' (Over here, auctioneer!) is indeed relevant to covered market auctions, nonetheless, the collocation of 'ta9áal' with 'ya' – habitual though it is – is irrelevant.

TEXTS

The following three texts belong respectively to the auction, market and shop situations. The whole of the material is allotted to the categories of stage and personality which have been established. Technical elements are enclosed in square brackets; non-technical elements in round brackets; elements not ascribed to either category are unbracketed. Both technical and non-technical elements are further classified – and lettered in the texts – according to the following scheme:

(a) elements correlating with the particular situational category illustrated, *ie* auction/market/shop;
(b) elements correlating with more than one of the three categories;
(c) elements correlating with the object of sale;
(d) elements correlating with other features of the situation.

eg [ya dalláal[a]], (táajir walla barráani[a]) (see Text I).

Notes follow each text and the 'speeches' of the texts are numbered in order to facilitate subsequent reference.

TEXT I (Auction)

Auction of waistcoat in Benghasi covered market; merchants in their shops on both sides of the passage along which the auctioneer passes to and fro; shoppers in and around the shops or passing by; time of day am or pm.[27] The auction has been in progress for some time and no part of the text is ascribable to Stages 1 and 2.

Note. The most important differences between Benghasi and Bedouin pronunciation are indicated in the notes.

	Text	*Translation*	*Personality*	*Stage*
1	(ta9áal[d]),[28] [ya dalláal[a]]!	Here auctioneer!	B (1st merchant)	3
2	[kám[29] 9aTáwk f[b]] (ilfármilah[c])?[30]	What have you been offered for the waistcoat?		

(*Auctioneer goes over to merchant, who examines garment*)

3	(míyyah[31] w xam-síin (gírʃ)[b]).	150 piastres.	A	3
4	[zíidha[a]]!	Raise it!	B	3

(*Auctioneer resumes progress up and down market, calling the latest price*)

	Text	*Translation*	*Personality*	*Stage*
	(*In lower voice to merchants only*)			
5	(míyyah w sittíin, míyyah w sittíin[b]). [izzyáadah[a]][32] (9áʃrɑh[b]) [wuTTyáaħ[a]] (9iʃríin[b]).	160, 160. 10-piastre raise(s) and 20-piastre discount.[33]	A	3
6	[zíidha hazzyáadah[a]]!	Raise it (that amount)	B (2nd merchant)[34]	3
7	(míyyah w sab9íin, míyyah w sab9íin[b]).	170, 170.	A	3
	(*The price reaches 190 piastres*)			
8	[harɑ́ɑj, harɑ́ɑj], (míyyah w tis9íin[b]), [yɑ́rbɑħ, yáksab[a]] . . .	Going at 190 . . . going . . . going . . .	A	3
9	[zíidha[a]]!	Raise it!	B (3rd merchant)	3
10	(miitáyn, miitáyn[b]).	200, 200.	A	3
	(*To merchants only*)			
11	[izzyáadah wɑ́ɑħad wuTTyáaħ itnéen[a]].[35]	Raise one, discount two.		
12	[zíidha[a]]!	Raise it!	B (*not* merchant)	3
13	(miitáyn w 9áʃrɑh, miitáyn w 9áʃrɑh[b]). [harɑ́ɑj, harɑ́ɑj, nibbi inbíi9, nibbi nírmi, haÐɑ ħáddi, la lɑ́wm 9alay iddalláal[a]].	210, 210. Going . . . going . . . I'm about to sell, I'm going to part with (it), this is my limit, let no one blame the auctioneer.	A	
	(*Auctioneer moves closer to merchant he knows to be interested in the object of sale*)			
14	[mánu[36] illi yzíid fíik[a]]? (táajir wɑllɑ bɑrrɑ́ɑni[a])?	Who's raising you? A merchant or an outsider?	B (merchant)	3

	Text	*Translation*	*Personality*	*Stage*
15	wallɑ́ɑhi, barrɑ́ɑni . . . (labbáas[c]). 9índɑk wallɑ 9índah? [37] [ma 9áʃ [38] fiih ħádd yzíid[a]].	An outsider . . . he wants to wear it himself. Do you want it or shall he have it? There's no one (else) bidding.	A	3
16	báahi, madáam (labbáas[c]), 9ɑTíiha líh. ma 9áʃ (9indi ɣɑrɑ́Ð[a]).	All right. Since he wants it for himself, give it to him. I don't want to bid further.	B	3

(*Auctioneer moves away from merchant and halts close to purchaser*)

	Text	*Translation*	*Personality*	*Stage*
17	[harɑ́ɑj, harɑ́ɑj, miitáyn w 9áʃrɑh[a]]. (*to the purchaser*)	Going . . . going . . . sold at 210.	A	4
18	[míyyah w tis9íin mɑgbúuÐ[a]]. (mɑbrúuk 9aláyk[b]), [kan áaba [39] ybíi9 Sɑ́ɑħib ilmáal[d]].	190 to pay (*lit* paid). Congratulations to you, if the owner (of the property) agrees to sell.		
19	(mɑbrúuk[b]). 9áddi ʃáawurɑh fíisa9. rɑ́ɑni nibbi in9áddi – mistí9jil.	Thank you. Go and ask him quickly. I'm in a hurry and want to be off.	B (purchaser)	4
20	ħɑ́ɑÐur. ana [40] máaʃi.	All right. I'll go right away.	A	

Notes to Text I

Speech

1 (ta9áal), correlating with the spatial disposition of buyer and auctioneer, belongs only to the *covered* market auction.

1 It is the collocation of [ya] (grammatically the vocative particle) with [dallaal] which marks the element as technical to the auction. Elsewhere the same man – as a different personality – is addressed otherwise, while in situations in which the auctioneer does not

participate, 'dallaal' is usually collocated with 'il' (grammatically the definite article).

2 [kám (*or* áyʃ) 9ɑTɑ́wk f–] belongs to the auction and shop situations.

3 (míyyah w xɑmsíin) is not expected *qua* (míyyah w xɑmsíin) but rather as an example of words and collocations of money-reference. In this respect it differs from such a non-technical element as (mɑbrúuk[b]) and cognate forms, which is expected *qua* 'mɑbrúuk'. Both elements belong to all three situations.

5– *Repetition* of (míyyah w sittíin) and subsequent similar elements
6–7 is technical to the auction.

Not only is there mutual expectancy between the buyer's [zíidha] and the auctioneer's statement of price, but expectancy between two price statements, preceding and following [zíidha], is mutual and specific.

The collocation [izzyáadah . . . wuTTyáaħ . . .], habitually extended to include words of money reference, is technical to the auction. (9áʃrɑh) and (9iʃríin) are variables belonging to the general category of money-words; nevertheless, there is a precise relationship between them in this collocation, and this relationship is technical to the auction. *Cf* [izzyáadah wɑ́ɑħad wuTTyáaħ itnéen] below.

8 The technical element here is the whole collocation [harɑ́ɑj, harɑ́ɑj . . . yɑ́rbɑh, yáksab], to which extended collocation with words of money-reference is not essential.

11 *Cf* [izzyáadah] (9áʃrɑh) [wuTTyáaħ] (9iʃríin) earlier. This use of [wɑ́ɑħad] and [itnéen] in the sense of ten and twenty piastres respectively is technical to the auction.

13 It is possible that [nibbi inbíi9 . . . 9alay iddalláal] is peculiar to Benghasi.

14 Individually [mánu illi . . . fíik] and [yzíid] are widely distributed in collocations which correlate with a variety of situations. When they themselves are collocated, however, correlation is exclusively with the auction.

15 Similar remarks to those in the preceding note may be made for [. . . yzíid] and [ma 9áʃ fih ħádd . . .].

16 'ma 9áʃ (9indi ɣɑrɑ́Ɖ)' is not technical to the auction, unlike the auctioneer's [mínu illi 9índih ɣɑrɑ́Ɖ?] 'What am I offered?', which elsewhere, like [mánu illi yzíid fíik?] and [ma 9áʃ fih ħádd yzíid] in the present text, must be abstracted as a whole rather than in the parts [mínu illi] and [9índih ɣɑrɑ́Ɖ].

17– [harɑ́ɑj (,harɑ́ɑj)] is not collocated at this point with [yɑ́rbɑħ,
18 yáksab]. It is habitually collocated here with words of money-reference, which are not repeated. For this reason [miitáyn w

9áʃrah], a variable element, has been considered as one with [haráaj, haráaj] in the text. Similar remarks apply to the following [míyyah w tis9íin] collocated with the technical [magbúuÐ]. [kan áaba . . . ilmáal] is classified as a d-element, since it can only correlate with the *covered* market auction, in which the spatial disposition of owner and auctioneer differs from that obtaining in the open market.

TEXT II (Market)

Bedouin participants in an open-air market; the object of sale, greatly prized by the Bedouin, is a horse.[41]

	Text	Translation	Personality	Stage
1	(issiláamu 9aláykam).	Good morning.	B	1
2	(9aláykam issilíem w rúħumt alláah[b]).	Good morning.	S	
3	(ilmán hall[a]áʃgar[c])?	Whose is this roan?	B	2
4	(lálla kílli ʃíi[a]).	Mine (*lit* everything is God's).	S	2
5	[áyʃ u9Tíi]?	What has been offered?	B	4
6	[ma zíel 9alay bab alláah[a]].	Nothing as yet.	S	
7	[áyʃ sínnih[ac]]?	How old is he?	B	3
8	(rubáa9[c]).	Four.[42]	S	3
9	[ilmán búuh[ac]]?	Whose is his sire?	B	3
10	(búuh uħSáan[c]) 9áyt xalíifih.	(It's) A horse belonging to the Khalifa section.	S	3
11	[áyʃ bura(a)ríimih[ac]]?	What are his whorls?[43]	B	3
12	walláahi, (iluħSáan giddáamak[c]) w (tumággul[a]) ah!	Well, the horse is (there) in front of you. Try him for yourself!	S	3
13	[áyʃ ybáyyi9 fíik líh[a]]?	What's making you sell him?	B	3
14	walláahi, xámis mil-(xáyl[c]) 9índi w ma urríid indíir ʃi (umráaħ[c]).	Well, I've (already) five horses and I don't want to	S	3

	Text	Translation	Personality	Stage
		make a stud (of them).		
15	[aymítta jíbtih lilfúndug[a]]?	When did you bring him to the market?	B	3
16	tawwa ɣáyr jíit giddam jáyytak.	I came just before you did.	S	3
17	[ayʃ Tábgah[ac]]?	What's his temperament like?	B	3
18	(Tábgah bíehi, walla gúmrah ma taggábna, imdárrib galay kílli ʃáyy[a]). itgúullih xúʃʃ finnáar yxúʃʃ fíiha.	Excellent. Believe me, he's never given us any trouble. He's thoroughly trained – tell him to go through fire, and he will.	S	3
19	(yáak jarráay[bc]).	I hope he's fast.	B	3
20	(jarráay[c]). walláahi (ma yalħa-gánnih xáyl[bc]) w [ilbáyg wíʃʃra bittú-jurbah[a]]. xúðih w (járrbih giddam rakkáabt ilxáyl[cd] w ílli yguulúuha míeʃyih galáyy[a]).	He (certainly) is. Take it from me no horse can catch him, and (, anyway,) you can try him out before buying (*lit* buying and selling is by trial). Take him and put him through his paces before the experts (*lit* horsemen) (here) and whatever they say, I'll accept.	S	3
21	ma gílit ʃi gáyb. haÐa xabár kíllih bíehi. kiða (jíibih lílfuÐa[a]). xallíini injárrbih f(uSSyiráan wilmáyz[c]).	Well said! That's very fair (*lit* this talk is all of it good). Bring him to the maidan,	B	3

	Text	*Translation*	*Personality*	*Stage*
		then, and let me try him out walking and galloping.		
22	árja (inʃíddlɑk ɡaláyh ilɡíddih[c]). hɑ́w, rɑ ilɡíddih [máyʃ filbáyɡ[bc]].	Wait until I saddle him for you. The saddle's not for sale, though, mind you.	S	3
23	láa, ma urríidhaaʃ, ɡíndi ɡíddih uTrɑbilsíyyih.	No, I don't want it. I've a Tripolitanian one.	B	3
	(*The horse is saddled*)			
24	dúunɑk xúðih w láa (itmáyyz[c]) ih ʃíi fi ɑ́ruÐ fíiha ħáyT ilɡayníet (wíħdih min iħθíyyih ilwɑrrɑniyyíet Tɑ́ɑyrih[c]).	Here you are, then, take him, but don't gallop him on stony ground, because one of his back shoes is off.	S	3
	(*As he mounts*) bismillíeh urruħmɑ́ɑn urruħíim.	(In the name of God the All-merciful)	B	3
	(*The buyer tries out the horse, returns and dismounts*)			
25	(jáyyid[c]). ɑllɑ́ɑh ybarik ɡaláyh.	He is fast, and a fine horse (*lit* God bless him).	B	3
	[báyʃ itríidih? úxxur sɑ́wm[b]].	What do you want for him? (Your) final price.		4
26	wɑllɑ́ɑhi, [ma urríidʃ inzíid ɡaláyk[b]. xúðih bayʃ bíɡit[b]] xúuh ɡáamin ɑ́wwɑl.	Well now, I don't want to overcharge you – take him for what I sold his brother at last year.	S	4
27	báyʃ bíɡtih?	How much was that?	B	4

	Text	Translation	Personality	Stage
28	bíϑtih b(ɑrbiϑíin jiníi[b], fi hassúug ϑalay yád(d) mɑmúur ilbaladíyyih[a]).	Forty pounds, in this (very) market, in the presence of the municipal officer.	S	4
29	[w in aћsánit].	Make me a reduction.	B	4
30	[iliћsínih itzíid, ma túnguS ʃíi[b]].	No, the price is a fair one.	S	
31	(bíehi[b]), ya síidi. [ásћabih ʃɑ́wr ilmɑmúur bayʃ níkitbu ilkuuʃíenih[d]].	All right, my friend. Lead him over to the office (*lit* official) so that we can fill in the form.	B	5

Notes to Text II

1–2 Again, both buyer- and seller-element are considered as one collocation correlating with the market and shop.

5–6 [áyʃ uϑTíi] and [ϑalay bab allɑ́ɑh] may, individually, belong to the auction, but, when collocated, belong exclusively to the market. The collocation of [ϑalay bab ɑllɑ́ɑh] with [ma zíel] is also technical to the market.

7–19 It is not the individual elements [áyʃ sínnih ?, ilmán búuh ?, áyʃ burɑríimih ?, etc] but rather their aggregate collocation that identifies both the market situation and the particular object of sale.

18 Typical seller-element, correlating also with an animal object of sale. Without (wɑllɑ ϑúmrɑh taϑϑábna), the element could equally belong to the auction; with it, correlation is only with the market.

19 Correlation is with the market and auction situations.

20 (ma yalћɑgɑ́nnih xáyl) may also belong to an auctioneer's initial description.

21 The available open space is not a relevant feature of the auction and shop situations.

22 [. . . máyʃ filbáyϑ] correlates with either the market or the auction.

25 By stating himself pleased, the buyer places himself at a disadvantage for bargaining. It is to be expected therefore that Stage 4 in this example will be short.

[báyʃ . . . sɑ́wm ?] correlates with either the market or the shop.

26 Both technical elements correlate with the market and the shop. Unlike 'yzíid' (grammatically 3rd pers sing) (see Text I), 'inzíid' (1st pers sing) does not belong to the auction.

28 (fi . . . ilbaladíyyih) correlates with a valuable object of sale. That it is not stolen is guaranteed by (9alay . . . ilbaladíyyih).

29–30 See speeches 5–6 of Text III (and Note thereto).

TEXT III

The customer wishes to buy a bed; not finding what he wants in one shop, he finally strikes a bargain in another.[44]

	Text	*Translation*	*Personality*	*Stage*
1	(Subáaħ ilxáyr).	Good morning.	B	1
2	(alláah ySábbħak bilxáyr[b]).	Good morning.	S (1st shopkeeper)	
	(*Customer walks over to a bed on view in the shop*)			
3	[báyʃ haÐa[a]], ya ħíej?	How much is this, Hāj?	B	4
4	(ibxámsih jiníi[b]).	£5.	S	4
5	[w in aħsánit[b]].	Make me a reduction.	B	4
6	[iliħsínih itzíid, ma túnguSʃ[b]].	The price is a fair one (*lit* fair dealing would increase, not decrease (the price)).	S	
7	(báalak it9aTíih líi bárbu9ah jiníi[b]).	Perhaps you'll let me have it for £4.	B	4
8	walláahi, (ma yxallúSniiʃ[a]) lajil xáaTur niħna injíibu fíddibaʃ háÐa min uTráablis wilmáʃy wijjáyy (ykallífna muSa(a)ríif wáajdih[a]).	Good Lord, it wouldn't pay me, since we bring these goods from Tripoli and the return trip costs us a great deal.	S	4
9	ya ħíej, [bíθθiman háÐa ma ħádd yji yíʃri mínnak ʃáyy[b]].	Nobody's going to come and buy anything from	B	4

	Text	*Translation*	*Personality*	*Stage*
		you at that (sort of) price, Hāj.		
	(*Customer proceeds to another shop*)			
10	[9índak ʃi[b]] (siríir[c]) [lilbáy9[b]] ?	Have you a bed to sell?	B	2
11	9índi wáaħad, (ɣayr ɣáali iʃway[a]).	I've got one, but it's rather expensive.	S (2nd shopkeeper)	2
12	(kiða xallíini inʃúufah[d]).	Let me have a look at it, then.	B	2
13	(tufáÐÐal[a]).	Certainly.	S	2
	[in kan tibbíih[b]] ilrúuħak [insa(a)9dúuk[b]].	If you want it for yourself, I (*lit* we) will make you a reduction (*lit* help you).		4
14	[báyʃ haÐa[a]] ?	How much is it (*lit* this)?	B	4
15	haÐa b(árbu9ah jiníi[b]).	£4.	S	4
16	[úxxur kílmih ibkám[a]] ?	What's your last price (*lit* word)?	B	4
17	walláahi, (lukan wáaħad mawʃ ínit, ingúullih ibxámsih[b]).	Believe me, if it were anyone but you I'd ask him five.	S	4
18	[na in9aTíik kílmih wíħdih[b]], (θilíeθih jiníi w núSS[b]).	I'll make you a firm offer (*lit* give you one word) of £3½.	B	4
19	[yaftuħálla[b]], ya siidi. (xallíih gíe9id fi muTráaħah[b]).	Impossible. Let it stay where it is (*lit* in its place).	S	4
	(*Customer moves to go*)			
20	ásma9. injíik bi9ad uÐÐúhur, [nadfá9lak θilíeθih jiníi w sab9íin[b]] w náaxðih.	Listen. I'll come (to you) this afternoon, pay you £3.70 and take it.	B	4
	(*Customer crosses threshold of shop on his way out*)			
21	(ma zíel tibbíilih[45] tirkíib[c]).	It still wants some repairs.	S	5

Notes to Text III

Speech

1–2 The whole collocation of the buyer- and seller-element is considered as one, and correlates with the shop and market situations only of those we are considering.

3 [bayʃ], alone or collocated with words grammatically definable as noun or pronoun, is technical to the shop. As the use of 'ya ħíej' here indicates, the customer and both shopkeepers were, in fact, known to each other; I can, however, detect no element of the text correlating with this fact (but see speech 17).

5–6 Again the buyer- and the seller-element together constitute one (habitual) collocation, which correlates with the shop and market situations only. The whole, in turn, is habitually collocated with preceding words and collocations of money-reference.

7 'báalɑk . . . b . . .' correlates with the shop and market only.

8 Characteristic shopkeeper 'gambits'. Notice the equally characteristic use of '–na' (grammatically 1st person *plural* pronominal suffix) with singular reference in (ykallífna), *cf* [insa(a)9dúuk] in speech 13.

9 Shop and market only.

10 [9índɑk ʃi . . . lilbáy9 ?] is, of course, abstracted en bloc.

12 Correlating with the fact that the object of sale is not on view.

13 It is realized that 'tufɑ́ÐÐɑl' correlates with a great variety of situations. Nevertheless on the very many occasions I visited shops, I do not think an instance of 'tufɑ́ÐÐɑl' was ever missing. There would be some justification for abstracting the 'protestation' 'wɑllɑ́ɑhi' similarly.
[in kan tíbbi (*or* itríid) . . . insáa9dɑk] belongs to the shop and market, but [in(sa(a)9d)úu(k)] – grammatically 1st person plural – belongs to the shop only.

14 Following words of money-reference are to be expected, since the seller has already used his [in kan tíbbi . . . insa(a)9dúuk], which elsewhere is possible as a reply to [báyʃ haÐɑ ?].

16 In shop and market situations only. Collocates invariably with preceding words of money-reference.

17 Again, shop and market only. This element correlates to some extent with the prior acquaintance of customer and shopkeeper. It is not used unless the shopkeeper has seen the customer at least once before.

18 [na . . . wíħdih] also belongs to the shop and market only, and is habitually collocated with following words of money-reference.

19 [yɑftuħɑ́llɑ] operates in all three situations but can only be an

owner-element in the auction. Collocation is habitually with preceding words of money-reference.
(xɑlli . . . muTrɑ́ɑħɑh) belongs to the shop and market.
20 It is the whole collocation of [nadfá9lɑk] with words of money-reference that is technical to the shop and market.

Notes

1 Mr (later Lt-Col) Idris Abdalla of the Ḥāsa tribe, who are centred on his birthplace, the Jebel village of Cyrene. Idris Abdalla subsequently served his country as Assistant Secretary of State for Defence and as its ambassador overseas. I am much indebted to him for what knowledge I gained of his language, and deeply appreciative also of the forbearance he showed in response to the constant questioning which must have sorely tried his patience.
2 J. R. Firth, *Papers in Linguistics 1934–1951, p* 182.
3 See B. Malinowski, *Coral Gardens and their Magic* (Allen & Unwin, 1935; Indiana University Press, 1965), Vol ɪɪ, Ch 1, and his Supplement 1 to *The Meaning of Meaning* (1923) by C. K. Ogden and I. A. Richards.
4 'Situation/s' is used here and elsewhere as an abbreviation for 'context/s of situation'. The term is not used for *instances* of contexts of situation.
5 For the purpose of reading connected texts, note that '–h' of the ending '–ih/–ɑh' is only pronounced before pause, and that word-initial 'i–' and 'u–' are elided when the preceding word ends in a vowel.
6 These terms are explained below.
7 The 'kayyíel', who is licensed by the municipality, is paid, normally by the buyer, either in cash or in kind. In a large market such as the Benghasi 'fúndug' he is usually in partnership with other measurers, with whom he shares his takings. Sometimes – in Barce, for example – he is given any cereals left over, which, mixed as they are with dust, he sells as animal fodder.
8 Cereals not for immediate sale or consumption are often stored in a 'mɑTmúurɑh' or 'kief' (cave). The 'mɑTmúurɑh' is smaller than the 'kief' and, indeed, may be part of it. Both may take the form of holes dug in the ground.
9 These examples are, in fact, among my recorded material.
10 For example, the heap of cereals (9úrmɑh), the large sack of wool or hair (uɣrɑ́ɑrɑh), the smaller sack of hemp or flax (iʃwɑ́ɑl), the sieve (ɣurbíel), the reed-platter (Tubɑ́g), the measuring canisters of the kayyíel (mayzúurah, núSS mayzúurɑh, wɑ́ggɑh, etc), and so on.
11 *Cf* Seller (to buyer feeling sheep): 'ismíen, umɣáyr ʃáddid 9ázmɑk!' (They're fat. Just pluck up your courage [*sc* and give me what I am asking]).
12 Shops may be either permanent buildings or open-air 'shops' in the village markets where the shopkeeper (fɑrrɑ́ɑʃ) spreads his wares (tájrɑh *or* ubÐɑ́ɑ9ɑh) on the ground.
13 Such differences are illustrated in Text I below.
14 *Cf* Text I.
15 Characteristically Bedouin.
16 Grammatically, 3rd pers sing masc perf *passive*. Other possible forms are '9úTyat [3rd pers sing fem]', 'u9Túu [3rd pers pl masc]', and '9úTyan [3rd pers pl fem]'; the particular form used correlates with the particular object of sale.
17 Or any appropriate example of words and collocations of money reference, *eg* 'jiniiyáyn' (£2), 'θilíeθih jiníi w rúbu9' (£3¼), 'miitáyn w xɑ́msih' (205 [piastres]), etc.

18 Or 'tíbbi'. 'itríid' is characteristically Bedouin and 'tíbbi' townee, but both may be heard from Bedouins in the market or shop.
19 Or 'insa(a)9dúuk', a grammatically plural form which is associated particularly with the shop.
20 These two elements are not necessarily replies to the first stated price but may be used at any time during bargaining.
21 *lit* 'May God open (*sc* your mind to reason).'
22 *lit* 'He behaves like (an irresponsible) youth.'
23 Hands are slapped together rather than shaken. The action was described to me as 'yúxuTbu iidáyhum 9aláyha' (they slap hands on it).
24 *lit* 'It will be blessed (I hope)'. The form of mɑbrúuk will vary with the object of sale; for example, if sheep are sold, 'mɑbruukɑ́ɑt' is to be expected.
25 The list is not beyond all doubt exhaustive.
26 Grammatically, the vocative particle.
27 Unlike the open market, which is restricted to the (early) morning.
28 Bedouin 'it9íel'. The diphthong 'ie' is not a feature of Benghasi speech.
29 Bedouin 'ayʃ'.
30 Bedouin 'fɑ́rmulɑh'.
31 Bedouin 'míyyih'.
32 Bedouin 'izzyíedih'.
33 The discount is allowed to the final purchaser. It is not announced publicly, so that the buyer (usually a merchant) may sell for at least the price announced. The discount is also allowed to any buyer known genuinely to require the article for his own use.
34 One personality in the abstract situation may, of course, correspond to more than one man in the instance.
35 With half-close front spread vowel in the final syllable; *cf* Bedouin 'iθnáyn'.
36 Bedouin 'mínu'.
37 Bedouin '9índih'.
38 Bedouin '9atʃ'.
39 I have only ever seen the commoner negative form transcribed as 'ma baaʃ'. The evidence of the affirmative form does not seem to have been available to other workers in the field, and must assuredly lead to reconsideration of the negative form from the historical and comparative standpoint; *cf*, for example, Ester Panetta, *L'Arabo Parlato a Bengasi*, *p* 239. Other examples from Benghasi of the use of 'áaba' are: '(in) kan áaba yjíi, injíibih im9áay' (if he wants to come, I'll bring him with me), and 'lukan áaba yjíi, rɑh jáay (or jáa), lakin m(a a)abáaʃ' (if he'd wanted to come, he would have done, but he didn't want to). 'yíbbi' may be used for 'áaba' in both these attested examples.
40 Bedouin 'na'.
41 Lengthy investigation is therefore to be expected.
42 As far as the age of a horse is concerned, there might seem to be more than one series of numerative forms in use among the Bedouin. My assistant, a man with considerable experience of horses, gave me the following in ascending order of age: 'ħɑ́wli/iθnúwi/iθlúuθi/rubɑ́ɑ9/xɑmɑ́ɑs/sidíes'. Later in the Jebel, I was given: 'ħɑ́wli/rubɑ́ɑ9/θiníi/xɑmɑ́ɑs/sidíes', a horse of more than 5/6 years being termed '9al(ay) lɑ́wwɑl gɑ́ruħ' or, simply, 'gíeriħ'; but 'rubɑ́ɑ9' seems oddly used – preceding 'θiníi' – for a two-year old.

Remarks made at Cyrene by a Bedouin shepherd discussing the nomenclature of sheep may be relevant. These were: 'ilħɑwlíyyih híi illi 9úmurha sánih, wib9adáyn missánih w fɑ́wg la9ínid, gúul, θilíeθ isníin, yingɑlílha rubɑ́ɑ9yih, w miθθilíeθ isníin w fɑ́wg yingɑlílha (in9ájih) isdísih' (The ḥawliyya is the one [up to] a year old; then from above one year up to, say, three years, it is called *rubā'ya*, and from three years on, *isdisa*.)

Some of these forms – 'rubáɑ9' and 'ħáwli' are examples – commute in different systems and therefore differ in meaning according to the animal involved. 'rubáɑ9' appears in a 3-term system of size- (not age-) words for goats: 'jady (small)/rubáɑ9 (medium)/tays (large)'. Compare 'ħáwli' and 'θiníi' in a size-system for (male) sheep: 'ħáwli/θiníi/kábiʃ'. Again, 'rubáɑ9-yih' occurs as the appropriate form for a (medium-sized) she-goat, but the form is not recognized for horses; in contrast, the 'masculine' form 'rubáɑ9' is not recognized for sheep. The subject is clearly not without linguistic interest, but, unfortunately, I was unable to follow it further.

43 Considerable importance is attached by the Bedouin to the presence, disposition, and shape of whorls in the horse's hair. There are two major categories: 'burɑ(ɑ)ríim istu(u)báɑr' (good-luck whorls) and 'burɑ(ɑ)ríim ʃikál' (bad-luck whorls); 'uħSáɑn wbúrɑh' is a horse with the former type, and 'uħSáɑn áʃkal' one with the latter.

44 The following text was recorded at a time when my assistant was furnishing his flat in Benghasi. The two shopkeepers were not, of course, Bedouin, but the material is nonetheless possible for Bedouin Arabic. The transcription conforms to Bedouin usage.

45 Bedouin 'itríidlih'. 'tíbbi/itríid' is here an invariable form.

APPENDIX: Brief comparative bibliographical indications

The question of whether or not to include a bibliography has not been easy to answer. Nothing is gained by putting one in because it is 'the done thing', and the uncomfortable truth is that in the important field of grammar, for instance, Firth for all practical purposes wrote nothing. It is not only that he devoted most of his energies to phonology but also that the recognizably Firthian notions of the present book are such that permeate the whole of Firth's writings without being easily detachable from them. It may well also be true that one gained more from conversation and discussion with him. It certainly cannot be said that those who are Firthian among British linguists have established any clearly agreed approach to grammar, for instance. There is, however, more of Firth's influence than might at first appear in F. R. Palmer's *Linguistic Study of the English Verb* (Longmans, 1965), although the book in which it is to my mind most marked is H. Straumann's *Newspaper Headlines* (Allen and Unwin, 1935). In general, however, one can only suggest perusal of the two collected volumes of Firth's writings – *Papers in Linguistics 1934–1951* (Oxford University Press, 1957) and *Selected Papers of J. R. Firth 1952–59*, ed F. R. Palmer (Longmans, 1968). Such perusal might then be supplemented by the collection of articles on Firthian phonology entitled *Prosodic Analysis*, ed F. R. Palmer (Oxford University Press, 1970), by the relevant sections of R. H. Robins's *General Linguistics: an Introductory Survey* (Longmans, 1964; 2nd edn 1971) and by the same author's 'Malinowski, Firth, and the "context of situation"' in the miscellany *Social Anthropology and Language*, ed E. Ardener (Tavistock, 1971). The article by Olasope O. Oyelaran in *Linguistic Studies Presented to André Martinet*, Vol I, ed A. Juilland (*Word*, 23/1-2-3, 1967), *pp* 428–458, presents a useful introductory exposé, well reasoned and in short compass, of aspects of Firthian theory, and can be read in conjunction with the editorial introduction to the aforementioned *Selected Papers of J. R. Firth 1952–59, pp* 1–11.

Neo-Firthianism, on the other hand – nowadays increasingly labelled 'systemics' – has been developed in fairly agreed fashion and requires to be included not only for the contrasts with Firthianism it presented at least in its earlier form but also for the purpose of familiarizing some readers with British divisions in the subject. Among the titles from earlier neo-Firthianism and in subsequent lists, some books or parts of books have been asterisked variously for ease of comprehension and/or for characterizing a particular 'school'. An undergraduate student, say, should be thoroughly acquainted with them towards the end of his second year; for the most part they may also serve the mature student as an introduction to the several proposals concerned as to how we can look at and talk about language. Here, then, firstly, are some 'early' neo-Firthian suggestions:

M. A. K. Halliday, 'Categories of the theory of grammar', *Word* 17 (1961), *pp* 241–92

*M. A. K. Halliday, A. McIntosh and P. Strevens, *The Linguistic Sciences and Language Teaching* (Longmans, 1964), *pp* 21–55

R. M. W. Dixon, *What IS Language?* (Longmans, 1965), *pp* 91–7

*J. Ellis, 'On contextual meaning', in *In Memory of J. R. Firth*, eds C. E. Bazell *et al.* (Longmans, 1966), *pp* 79–95

G. N. Leech, *English in Advertising* (Longmans, 1966), *pp* 8–22 and *pp* 67–101

*G. N. Leech, *A Linguistic Guide to English Poetry* (Longmans, 1969), early chapters on general linguistic aspects

For the purpose of 'up-dating' neo-Firthianism, the following are suggested:

M. A. K. Halliday, 'Lexis as a linguistic level', in *In Memory of J. R. Firth*, eds C. E. Bazell *et al* (Longmans, 1966), *pp* 148–62

*M. A. K. Halliday, 'Notes on transitivity and theme in English', *Journal of Linguistics* 3/1–2 (1967) and 4/2 (1968)

*M. A. K. Halliday, 'Language structure and language function', in *New Horizons in Linguistics*. ed J. Lyons (Penguin, 1970), *pp* 140–65.

*R. D. Huddleston, *The Sentence in Written English* (Cambridge University Press, 1971)

R. A. Hudson, *English Complex Sentences: an Introduction to Systemic Grammar* (Amsterdam: North Holland, 1971)

J. McH. Sinclair, *A Course in Spoken English: Grammar* (Oxford University Press, 1972)

*M. A. K. Halliday, *Explorations in the Functions of Language* (Edward Arnold, 1973)

One of the more recent American developments is that associated with what is termed 'variation' and the theoretical need to think in terms of variable rather than 'watertight' rules of, say, grammar or phonology. The work of scholars like William Labov in, for example, his *Sociolinguistic Patterns* (University of Pennsylvania Press, 1972) and Charles-James N. Bailey in, for instance, *Variation and Linguistic Theory* (Washington, DC: Center for Applied Linguistics, 1973) has numerous points of contact with Firthianism. So, too, has much else in the interdisciplinary area labelled *sociolinguistics*. Whether or not sociolinguistics should properly be regarded as *inter*disciplinary or as unequivocally intra-linguistics, so to speak, the student should certainly endeavour to gain some insight into its scope and relevance by scanning such miscellanies (usually compendious) as the following:

Language and Culture in Society, ed Dell Hymes (New York: Harper and Row, 1964)
Advances in the Sociology of Language (2 vols), ed Joshua A. Fishman (The Hague: Mouton, 1971)
Language in Social Groups (Essays by John J. Gumperz), ed Anwar S. Dil (Stanford University Press, 1971)
Sociolinguistics, eds J. B. Pride and Janet Holmes (Penguin, 1972)
Language and Social Context, ed P. P. Giglioli (Penguin, 1972)
Directions in Sociolinguistics, eds John J. Gumperz and Dell Hymes (New York: Holt, Rinehart and Winston, 1972)

It also seems reasonable to include for purposes of comparison a few titles that are sufficiently representative of sundry other 'schools' of linguistics in America whose tenets and emphases, not to mention terminological usage, are – with minor qualification in the case of 'tagmemics' – in noticeable contrast with those of Firthianism. It may, however, be the case that Firthianism and, say, transformationalism share more in their approaches to phonological and lexicogrammatical study than at first sight appears. Needless to say, choice of titles has been invidious and one's own favourites are often missing. The order of presentation is roughly chronological between and within 'schools', the transformational point of departure being taken as the year in which Chomsky's *Syntactic Structures* appeared, although transition from the earlier Bloomfieldian 'structuralism' was also heralded in Z. S. Harris's paper 'Co-occurrence and transformation in linguistic structure' (*Language* 33/3, 1957). The final chapter entitled 'Linguistics in the present century' of R. H. Robins's *Short History of Linguistics* (Longmans, 1967) provides a useful 'overview' of the modern period up to 1967. These are times, however, of accelerated change and the 1960s and early 70s have been especially dominated by rapid developments in transformational linguistics. It would be wrong now, for instance, to regard all titles under the subsequent heading 'Transformational' as belonging to one homogeneous approach; an important division is between 'autonomous syntax' represented by Chomsky, on the one hand, and the 'generative semantics' of, say, McCawley and Lakoff, on the other. In fact, notwithstanding an apparently shared transformationalism in modes of expression, a generative semanticist's point of departure from what has been termed 'natural logic' implies so fundamentally different an orientation from those holding to Chomsky's point of view that perhaps separate classification should have been made below. Fillmorean 'case grammar', too, should perhaps have been entered independently. At all events, the evolutionary factor alone, not to mention the hot 'debates' in the influential United States between 'formal' linguists and 'socio'-linguists *inter alios*, between the protagonists of theories of competence versus theories of performance, and so on, would make it extremely difficult to furnish a fully representative bibliography matching the exactly contemporary 'state of the game'. Such a bibliography would in any case not be well suited to the nature of this book.

'Bloomfieldian'

*L. Bloomfield, *Language* (New York: Holt, 1933; London: Allen and Unwin, 1967), especially Chapters 2, 9–12, 16

*B. Bloch and G. L. Trager, *An Outline of Linguistic Analysis* (Waverly Press, 1942)

*C. C. Fries, *The Structure of English* (New York: Harcourt Brace, 1952; London: Longmans, 1957)

Z. S. Harris, *Structural Linguistics* (formerly entitled *Methods in Structural Linguistics*) (Chicago: University of Chicago Press, 1951)

*H. A. Gleason, *An Introduction to Descriptive Linguistics* (New York: Holt, Rinehart and Winston, 1955; revised edition 1961)

*C. F. Hockett, 'Two models of grammatical description', *Word* 10 (1954), *pp* 210–34; reprinted in *Readings in Linguistics I*, ed M. Joos (Washington, DC, 1957), *pp* 386–99

*C. F. Hockett, *A Manual of Phonology* (Indiana University, 1955)

C. F. Hockett, *A Course in Modern Linguistics* (New York: Macmillan, 1958)

C. F. Hockett, *The State of the Art* (The Hague: Mouton, 1968)

'Tagmemic'

K. L. Pike, *Language in Relation to a Unified Theory of the Structure of Human Behavior* (originally printed in 3 parts during the period 1954–60 by the Summer Institute of Linguistics, now in one volume. The Hague: Mouton, 1967)

R. E. Longacre, *Grammar Discovery Procedures* (The Hague: Mouton, 1964)

*B. Elson and Velma Pickett, *An Introduction to Morphology and Syntax* (Santa Ana: Summer Institute of Linguistics, 1964)

*W. A. Cook, *Introduction to Tagmemic Analysis* (New York: Holt, Rinehart and Winston, 1969)

'Stratificational'

S. M. Lamb, *Outline of Stratificational Grammar* (Washington, DC: Georgetown University Press, 1966)

*D. G. Lockwood, *Introduction to Stratificational Linguistics* (New York: Harcourt Brace Jovanovich, 1972)

'Transformational'

N. Chomsky, *Syntactic Structures* (The Hague: Mouton, 1957)

N. Chomsky, *Current Issues in Linguistic Theory* (The Hague: Mouton, 1965)

*N. Chomsky, *Aspects of the Theory of Syntax* (Cambridge, Mass: MIT Press, 1965)

N. Chomsky, *Language and Mind* (enlarged edition) (New York: Harcourt Brace Jovanovich, 1968, 1972)

eds J. A. Fodor and J. J. Katz, *The Structure of Language: Readings in the Philosophy of Language* (Englewood Cliffs, NJ: Prentice-Hall, 1964)

P. M. Postal, *Aspects of Phonological Theory* (New York: Harper and Row, 1968)

N. Chomsky and M. Halle, *The Sound Pattern of English* (New York: Harper and Row, 1968)

*John Lyons, *Chomsky* (London: Fontana/Collins Modern Masters series, 1970)

*R. A. Jacobs and P. S. Rosenbaum, *English Transformational Grammar* (Waltham, Mass: Blaisdell, 1968)

C. J. Fillmore, 'The case for case', in *Universals in Linguistic Theory*, eds E. Bach and R. Harms (New York: Holt, Rinehart and Winston, 1968), *pp* 1–89

*C. J. Fillmore, 'Towards a modern theory of case', in *Modern Studies in English*, eds D. A. Reibel and S. A. Schane (Englewood Cliffs, NJ: Prentice-Hall, 1969), *pp* 361–75

D. T. Langendoen, *The Study of Syntax* (New York: Holt, Rinehart and Winston, 1969)

Marina K. Burt, *From Deep to Surface Structure* (New York: Harper and Row, 1971)

J. D. McCawley, 'Prelexical syntax', in *Monograph Series on Languages and Linguistics*, No 24 (Washington, DC: Georgetown University Press, 1971), *pp* 19–33

G. Lakoff, 'On generative semantics', in *Semantics*, eds D. D. Steinberg and L. A. Jakobovits (Cambridge University Press, 1971), *pp* 232–96

*J. T. Grinder and Suzette H. Elgin, *Guide to Transformational Grammar* (New York: Holt, Rinehart and Winston, 1973)

Index

Page references below are to terms used in the book with or without gloss or specific illustration. Well worn grammatical and phonetic terminology is in general omitted. Names of authors and languages to which reference has been made are also included. Matter in the Appendix is excluded and notes are referred to only when names or terms or important aspects thereof would otherwise go unnoticed. Where no basic conceptual difference is involved, morphologically related forms appearing in the book have not been entered separately and the 'minimal' form has usually been given pride of place over bracketed relata (*eg* aspect (aspectual)); similarly, 'positive' and 'negative' forms are listed under the former (*eg* omissible (inomissible), productive (non-productive); *exception* discontinuous (continuous)). [*Also* . . .] refers to 'alternatives' which, unfortunately, have been used as 'stylistic variants' or otherwise interchangeably between different papers. A bracketed [*See* . . .] is sometimes used to refer the reader to closely related concepts and terms.

UNIVERSITY LIBRARY
NOTTINGHAM